'LESSER BREEDS'

'LESSER BREEDS'

Racial Attitudes in Popular British Culture, 1890–1940

Michael Diamond

Anthem Press

Anthem Press
An imprint of Wimbledon Publishing Company
www.anthempress.com

This edition first published in UK and USA 2006
by ANTHEM PRESS
75-76 Blackfriars Road, London SE1 8HA, UK
or PO Box 9779, London SW19 7ZG, UK
and
244 Madison Ave. #116, New York, NY 10016, USA

British Library Cataloguing in Publication Data
A catalogue record for this book is available from the British Library.

Library of Congress Cataloging in Publication Data
Diamond, Michael.
Lesser breeds : racial attitudes in popular British fiction, 1890–1940
p. cm. – (Anthem nineteenth century studies)
Includes bibliographical references and index.
ISBN 1-84331-216-6 (pbk. : alk. paper)
1. English fiction–20th century–History and criticism. 2. Great Britain–Social
conditions–20th century. 3. Ethnic relations in literature. 4. Ethnic groups
in literature. 5. Religion in literature. 6. Race in literature.
I. Title. II. Series.
PR888.R34D53 2006
820.9'3552–dc22 2006012202

1 3 5 7 9 10 8 6 4 2

ISBN 1 84331 216 6 (Pbk)

Printed in EU

To Bell with my love

CONTENTS

INTRODUCTION   1

CHAPTER 1   *The Yellow Peril and the Background to Villainy*   11

CHAPTER 2   *Chinese Villains and Masterminds*   35

CHAPTER 3   *Gordon and Arab Nationalism*   61

CHAPTER 4   *French North Africa and the Lure of the Desert*   75

CHAPTER 5   *The Sheikh and His Imitators*   87

CHAPTER 6   *Ghettoes and Stereotypes*   109

CHAPTER 7   *Jewish "Pride of Race"*   133

CHAPTER 8   *The Jews and Some Famous Authors*   143

CHAPTER 9   *Jews on Jews*   153

CHAPTER 10   *Coping with Africa*   167

CHAPTER 11   *Blacks in the Carribean and at Home*   189

AFTERWORD   209

NOTES   211

INDEX   225

INTRODUCTION

"Before the war Derek Vane had been what is generally described as a
typical Englishman. That is to say, he regarded his own country...
whenever he thought about it at all... as being the supreme country
in the world".[1]

In the half century from 1890 with which this book deals, racial
differences were thought to divide human beings irrevocably. There
was little understanding of how far the population of Britain was the
result of interbreeding, and the words "race" and "racial" were often
used where we would talk now in terms of nationality. Most British
people implicitly or explicitly believed in a racial hierarchy graded
by colour, with the whites at the head, and another among the whites
with the British at the head of that. White Canadians, Australians
and New Zealanders counted as British who happened to live
overseas. "Pride of race" was a surprisingly common expression.
Although it sometimes applied to the Jews and others, it usually
referred to the English, who were often confused with the British.
This last point did not seem to matter, as the Scots were less prickly
then.

It was even possible to write in 1906, that "the different races
persist with a uniformity truly marvellous... Though individuals of
one may have and very frequently do have for individuals of another
very deep and true feelings, it is nevertheless a fact broadly speaking
that race hates race".[2] This was an extreme view, even a century ago,
but the illusion of racial purity was rarely challenged, in popular
fiction at any rate. The English were Anglo-Saxon as could be seen
from their appearance. A hero could be described as "a tall strongly
built, fair-haired, blue-eyed Saxon, with the clean lines, the smooth
skin, the muscular grace of his race"; a heroine as having "many of the
so called English attributes – the corn-gold hair and the sea-shell

colouring which one sees up and down the little ocean-girt island; her eyes, too, were sea-blue, as the eyes of a true islander so often are".[3] This particular heroine has only "many" of the English attributes as she is half French, and is described as being "of mixed race".

These attributes were matters of pride. A hero whose "fair, almost golden hair, close-cut moustache, and easy athletic bearing stamped him as an Englishman" "felt a sudden pleasure in the fact that he was a healthy, hard-working, self-controlled Englishman, and not one of the dissipated, immoral foreigners whom he supposed she had known. Though not particularly insular, he found himself indulging in a pleasurable pride that he was not a sallow-faced Italian".[4] The quotation is from a novel of 1920, but W S Gilbert had satirised its like over forty years earlier – "For he might have been a Roosian, /A French or Turk or Proosian, /Or perhaps Italian!"[5] Not only moral qualities but social attitudes, too, were ascribed to race. A novelist wrote in 1913, that "by heredity he had the strongest feelings as to who were fit for Englishmen to associate with in foreign countries". Nowadays such feelings are ascribed to social conditioning. It might just be possible to suggest today that "cotton and the growing of it interests all native-born Egyptians; it's in their blood, like wool is in Australians'", but "in their blood" would not be taken so literally.[6]

Race was supposed, by and large, to determine personal qualities. This led to unjustified generalisations, according to which, if a Jew was mean and ruthless in his business dealings, it followed that the others were. On the other hand, if there was no way round the fact that a Jew was generous and merciful, it did not follow that the others were, because existing prejudices decreed that he must be an exception. As Brian Street has put it, "a particular 'character' could be attributed to a whole people on the strength of casual personal observations". Primitive man was assumed to spend his whole life in fear of spirits, and in being exploited by self-serving priest and kings. These assumptions might contain a lot of truth, but lacked a sense of proportion.[7]

There are so many novels which illustrate the racial attitudes of their day that strict selection has been necessary, even though this book deals with the treatment of only four groups – Chinese, Arabs, Jews and Blacks.* In making the selection, preference has been given to popular fiction, as, by definition, it cannot challenge conventional thinking. If it did, it would not be popular. Particular attention has been given to

---

* The word is used in its contemporary sense. At the time, any dark-skinned people were often described as 'blacks'.

works, which were greatly read in the day, but are now forgotten. They are full of incidents, conversations and authorial comments, which provide the historian with information, hard to find elsewhere, about how people thought at the time. For the original readers, by contrast, most of the interest was in the plots, but they are less relevant to the theme of this book, and no attempt has been made to recount them in full.

On the other hand, many direct quotations are included, a lot of them offensive today. They are necessary to illustrate the mind-set of previous generations. Words that they used so casually and which are unacceptable now indicate just how different that mind-set was. "Chink" and "nigger", have dropped from use, like "native" or "dago", precisely because they were used so contemptuously in the past.* This book is written in a quite different spirit, and readers are asked not to shoot the messenger.

Attention has hitherto been given only to the racial attitudes of a few popular authors who are still read today, at least by a small cult readership. Sapper and his followers have probably received the most attention.[8] They are part of the story, but old ground has mostly been avoided here. Richard Usborne has remarked that in the works of Sapper, Dornford Yates and John Buchan, Americans "don't quite count as foreigners".[9] This is true, but they were far from the only novelists to assume, wrongly, that the United States and Britain were Anglo-Saxon countries. In P C Wren's *Beau Ideal* of 1928, an American says of himself and his English friend, "As became good Anglo-Saxons, we were ashamed to express our feelings, and were for the most part gruffly inarticulate where these were concerned".[10] In Wren's series of novels about Anglo-Saxons serving in the French Foreign Legion, the ideals of British and Americans are so similar that it does not matter much when the American characters take over the later volumes. Even the American ambassador to Britain wrote shortly before the First World War, "They think in terms of races here, and we are of their race, and we shall become the strongest and happiest branch of it".[11] In fact innumerable gallant British heroes of fiction have an American collaborator, an early example being the young American in *Dracula* (1897) who takes a leading part in the hunt for the demon Count. This was not only about American sales. Americans were seen as cousins and natural partners. Even when the rich racial mix of Britain and the United States is acknowledged for once, as it was in a now obscure novel of 1924, the superiority of

---

* "Negro" was used by those who did not wish to be offensive by using "nigger", until it too was discredited.

the two countries is no less stoutly maintained. The hero "had always recognised that the English were a mixed race; but this cross-breeding he had felt had produced a prize breed, a lord of the earth". This seems to be the author's view, which is developed further when another character remarks, "It is curious, isn't it, that the two great races of the world, the two outstanding peoples, are the British hotchpotch and the American hotchpotch? The purest races, such as the German and the French, can't begin to compete with us mongrels".[12]

Another illusion was that Americans in general had an unstinting admiration for the British. In a novel of 1909, an American girl, "when she was a child had heard American women saying that the ideal Englishman was the ideal man; that nowhere could you find the fine flower of manhood as you found it in the British Isles". The girl's father for once is anti-British because of his Irish descent. Throughout the book he plots to get the British out of Egypt, but even he declares at the end: "That my daughter is alive, unoutraged, uninjured, I owe to the courtesy of my enemies, the enemies of my race. I still wish the English out of Ireland, but I can wish the Egyptians no better luck than that the English should stay here for ever".[13] A rare and grudging acknowledgement that the United States was changing appeared in *The Bookman* in 1919: "Our propagandists in the United States tell us that the pro-British people there are at pains to impress upon us that we must not talk of the Americans as Anglo-Saxons. They wish to be regarded as a new race with special qualities of their own... The fact remains that whatever the biological stock, it has been brought up on Anglo-Saxon models: its language and institutions are Anglo-Saxon; it is impossible to get away from the fact that America is set in Anglo-Saxon moulds".[14]

* * *

"Now and then a white-helmeted negro constable would stroll by, symbolising at once the long arm of Britain and her understanding of the black races".[15]

The link between a feeling of racial superiority and colonialism is well known. Now that few people believe in the concept of racial superiority, those who used it to justify colonial rule seem like hypocrites, but many were perfectly sincere. The characteristics of the British – or English – as portrayed in fiction, equip them above all to fight and to rule other races, even though they may not be particularly intelligent or sensitive. "One thing at least had been clearly hinted to the whole of Europe: that if those

English could not write music, they could work; if they could not make pretty things, they certainly could fight".[16] The same point was made nearly forty years later, but perhaps because, most unusually, the writer was black, he made it humorously. A white Englishman says, "If we were a nation of artists, musicians and writers, the British Empire would not exist... It is those among us who have no imagination and commercial minds who have founded that incredible Institution. The virtues of the Empire builders are courage and snobbery. I'm right and you're wrong, damn you – pride and suet pudding".[17]

Out in the Empire, the British, being heavily outnumbered by the peoples they ruled, felt threatened by them. Most refused to treat even the most sophisticated "natives" as social equals, and opposed the more liberal policies of Westminster governments, when they existed. Many novelists based their books on their colonial experience, and popular fiction was a means by which colonial attitudes became influential in the mother country. After all, everybody could agree that the English abroad had to stick together. The embittered hero of one novel is anxious to forget all women, but nevertheless answers a young woman's cry for help in the desert. "The fact that she was English was the sole reason for the action that had so surprised himself. Race loyalty had, in an extreme moment proved stronger than his determination". When she turns out to be Irish, his "grave face relaxed. 'It's the same thing', he said indifferently. She negatived his assertion with a scornful wave of the hand".[18]

The British were supposed to be bad at describing their own qualities, which were instinctive. One of P C Wren's heroes comforts and forgives a Ramon Gonzales who has betrayed him, saying "he acted according to his lights – I to mine". When asked what exactly his lights are, he can only stutter. "Oh – I don't know – Home... Family... One's women folk. School... Upbringing... Traditions... One unconsciously imbibes ideas of doing the decent thing... I've been extraordinarily lucky in life... Poor old Ramon wasn't".[19] Poor old Ramon is a "dago".

These British qualities were visible for all to see. "There was something eminently clean and wholesome about these colonels and captains. There was not a bad face among them. Evidences of subtle intellect were wanting", but each was marked by "firmness, decision, executive power – and, above all, that fine suggestion of it being impossible for any of them to do an ungentlemanly thing that does really seem to be the perpetual stamp and sign of Englishmen in the two Services".[20] One could multiply such quotations. Here is just one more from another popular but equally forgotten author. British diplomats are riding in Morocco: "There was a suggestion of reliability in the stolid, assured manner in which they gripped their horses; a note of dominant authority and infallible justice, in their stiff bearing and set features... all of which stamped them unmistakably as sons of the race which stands high in every corner of the earth, and that by force of plain sincerity".[21] With the rise of American power Americans were granted similar virtues. Arthur Conan Doyle has a British colonel tell an American, "we and you have among our best men a higher conception of moral sense and public duty than is to be found in any other people". He adds that the Americans will be drawn into assuming world power, just as the British were.[22] These are the sentiments of Kipling's *The White Man's Burden*.

Kipling, it is often said, indignantly, was a racist. Of course he was. So were nearly all his contemporaries. This does not mean that everyone thought the same. Opinions differed, for example on how to rate other racial groups, how much responsibility came with Britain's place in the sun, how to react to British people who fell short of the standards expected of them and to foreigners who exceeded expectations. Popular fiction is revealing about all these questions. Only English fiction has been chosen, because it is fitting that we should explore all aspects of our own cultural past. But it is important to remember that until quite recently racism was universal. Britain was not more racist than other countries. On the contrary, although Britain has by no means been free of antisemitism, there has never been a strong intellectual tradition of seeking to make it respectable, as in France, let alone gas chambers as in Germany, or pogroms as in Russia. If Sax Rohmer's depiction of the fiendish Chinese, Dr Fu Manchu is racist, it is no more so than the attitudes of the Chinese themselves. On the other hand, if attitudes to black people were no worse than in many other Western countries, they were certainly no better, and form the most painful part of the record.

Of course racism is wicked not only when it leads to mass murder. It causes unfair discrimination, cruelty, unkindness, waste of talent and loss of self-esteem among its victims. The question therefore arises whether the writers and readers of the fiction of our period were wicked too. No large-scale energetic effort was made to fight racism until the nineteen-sixties, so to assert that they were, is to write off most inhabitants of the British Isles until then. The issue is surely more complicated. Few people wanted to harm members of other racial groups. For the most part readers of light fiction were guilty of not questioning the assumptions of society, reflected in their favourite authors. They were themselves protected from the bad consequences of these assumptions, and so scarcely noticed them.

They were narrow-minded, but they were surely not evil, even if some of the consequences of their beliefs were. Some even thought that because the British were best, they should do most to help other peoples. This is no worse than patronising. One of P C Wren's characters exemplifies the confusion of a man who knows that Britons are superior, but perhaps not *all* of them. "But bless me after all, aren't bad Englishman as bad as everybody else?… Yes, but somehow it's a different kind of badness… I don't know".[23]

Perhaps the most pernicious attitude of all was the horror of inter-racial marriage and inter-racial sex. It was an attitude which received official support from the Lord Chamberlain, who operated the censorship of the stage. If inter-racial sexual attraction was shown to be disastrous, the play would be licensed for performance. If the relationship was allowed to work, the play would be banned.[24] In fiction, the censor was, effectively, public opinion. In novel after novel, the English protagonist falls in love with somebody who is taboo through being from a different racial group. If there is to be a happy ending, it has to be shown that the original racial classification was a mistake. To achieve this, characters are discovered to have a misleading skin colour for some reason, or, unknown to everybody, to have been adopted as a child. They may look and behave entirely as though they are white and English, but the revelation that they are not creates tremendous problems. Nobody seems to see that if they look and behave the same, the rest does not matter. Blood was considered more important than looks and behaviour. It was believed that it would out in the end. This was why it was essential at all costs to avoid having children of "mixed blood". To be a "half-caste", to use the term then common, was an abomination, because such a child was sure to inherit all the worst and none of the best qualities of each parent. In any case, even those who did not subscribe to this last very common supposition accepted that mixed race children should not be brought into the world, because society would give them such a hard time. For all its faults, society knows better now.

The Chinese

Why they were feared as a threat to Western Civilisation; how this fear inspired so many bestsellers; how respect for China's own ancient civilisation dignified the Chinese villains of the popular novel and the stage.

CHAPTER 1

The Yellow Peril and the Background to Villainy

"The general history of our dealings with China has been that we have forced ourselves undesired upon them and into their country. I believe we are too apt to forget this".[1]

"'You cannot impeach a whole nation'; this was said by one who cannot have known the Chinese. Their duplicity remains a byword".[2]

It is astonishing to what extent the Chinese fired the imagination of the British public during the half century up to about 1940. Events in China itself were intensely dramatic during that period, and, although the Chinese population of Britain was tiny, it inspired an interest out of all proportion to its size. It may seem strange that the Chinese should inspire fear because a long historical period was not yet over when China, politically and economically, was at her weakest, and Britain was immensely strong. In May 1898, the Prime Minister, Lord Salisbury, made a speech in which he contrasted "great countries of enormous power, growing in power every year" with countries which decade after decade "are weaker, poorer, and less provided with leading men or institutions in which they can trust... there is no firm ground on which any hope of reform or restoration could be based".[3] China's inclusion in the latter category was taken for granted. Yet only two months later *The Spectator* used a phrase that was to remain a cliche for many years. In defiance of the state of international relations as they then stood, the magazine put forward the possibility of "a Japanese military caste controlling China and organising a native army and navy". It described such a Sino–Japanese danger as "the Yellow Peril".

When *The Spectator* article was published, there were already stirrings in China of the revolt against everything Western, which became known as the Boxer Rebellion. When the rebellion exploded two years later, fear of the Boxers was expanded to fear of the Chinese as a whole. After all, the whole population shared the Boxers' aim of expelling all Europeans from China; it was easy to believe that they shared their murderous methods. The political and military weakness of China was all very well, but a huge population was apparently driven by intense hatred of the West. They seemed a terrible threat without Japanese leadership. In fact fear of a Sino–Japanese alliance did not disappear from fiction, even after the Japanese had helped to suppress the Boxer Rebellion, and even after Britain had concluded a formal alliance with Japan.

The Rebellion seared into the British imagination. Even before the height of the crisis, Westerners were being killed in China and the popular press of 1900 was full of alarming headlines, like

"Missionaries Abandoned. Britain Still Inactive.... Mutilated and Disembowelled Bodies of Missionaries".[4] The murder of the German minister in Peking led the *Daily Mail* to declare that "the Peking mob is notoriously the cruellest and the most bloodthirsty in the world".[5] In an article on "Chinese Massacres of the Past", the paper pointed out that "the pages of modern Chinese history are stained with blood – the blood of helpless and defenceless men and women". Particularly in the past forty years, "there has been a constant succession of brutal murders – murders usually brought about by the passionate hatred of the yellow man for the white".[6]

The climax came when the Boxers closed in on the European legations in Peking. Reports were hard to come by and unreliable. By the time news reached Britain that an international relief column had at last lifted the siege, *The Times* had wrongly printed the obituary of its own correspondent. The *Daily Mail* even reported that the legations had fallen, the massacre recalling those of the Indian Mutiny. "China stands confessed before the world a murderer among nations. Her... dragon's teeth are ensanguined with the lives of the innocent women and children". A lesson must be given to "the fiendish race which has thus satisfied its lust for blood and its hatred of the foreigner". The story was all the more dramatic because the besieged band of Westerners was reported to have made a last stand in the British legation "They fell, fighting bravely, we may be sure, to the last, under the good old flag which, when all is said and done, is the white man's flag in every quarter of the globe".[7]

The murders of Westerners in China over the preceding few years made the *Daily Mail* report all the more believable, and the Boxers were certainly out for blood. What stuck in the public mind was not that the legations had been relieved, but that a hate-filled band of Chinese had surrounded innocent Westerners – men, women and children – and threatened them with death. French, Germans, Russians and Americans as well as British had been the potential martyrs. For many years the public retained a vivid picture of the whole of Western civilization in danger from the Yellow Peril. This image had not lost its force when Sax Rohmer introduced Dr Fu Manchu into fiction as "the titanic genius whose victory meant the victory of the yellow race over the white" and the leader of a secret society "which sought to upset the balance of the world – to place Europe and America beneath the sceptre of Cathay".[8] Rohmer's biographers, his widow and a close friend, attributed the origins of the Fu Manchu vogue partly to the fact that "the Boxer Rebellion had started off rumours of a Yellow Peril which had not yet died down".[9]

In one of his early onslaughts on Western civilisation, Fu Manchu threatens Parson Dan, the fighting missionary, who "with a garrison of a hundred cripples and a German doctor held the hospital at Nan-Yang against two hundred Boxers".

As early as 1898, when Lord Salisbury had made his notorious speech, M P Shiel had published his novel *The Yellow Danger*, and the publicity for the book even referred to *The Spectator* article of that same year. The villainous ruler of China, half Chinese and half Japanese, leads his yellow hordes against Europe. His cunning plan is based on the rivalry between the Western powers for territorial concessions in China. He offers more and bigger concessions to France, Germany and Russia, leaving Britain out in the cold. As he has foreseen, British objections lead to a European war. Only after the West has begun to destroy itself, are huge Chinese armies under Japanese generals flung against Europe. They capture Paris to make it the new capital of a Chinese dominated world; the Oriental master-mind is borne in triumph to Notre Dame, which is now filled with Chinese idols. Fortunately the gallant British sailor, who has already saved his country from its European enemies, eventually defeats the yellow men.

The interest of the book lies not in its preposterous plot but in its vivid evocation of the "Yellow Peril". The villain invites Marquis Ito, a Japanese statesman who really existed, to look into the future and see "the white man and the yellow man in their death-grip, contending for the earth". He argues that the white man's technological supe-riority is rapidly carrying him further and further ahead; the yellow man must strike while his superior numbers can still prevail. The hero is tortured by the Chinese; as a result he "shrank from hearing that there existed anything good, or human, or redeeming in the Chinese character". An instinct tells him that he would need "to go on believing this bad race to be *wholly* bad, *wholly* of hell; and that it was in order that he might so believe it, that the Chinese iron had been ordained to enter into his soul".[10]

Outside the realms of fiction, conciliatory voices pointed out that China had no history of external aggression. In 1912, a grand spectacle was staged at the Crystal Palace, portraying the history of the Manchu dynasty, and ending with its overthrow the previous year. A three-penny brochure sold to the audience declared that although "there would be much to fear should China decide to use her enormous power aggressively", the Chinese "have fought much among them-selves, but they have never gone forth to subjugate other nations". The writer declared that one day China would be a world power, and offered the Chinese people "the good wishes of all who love freedom and progress".[11] The show seems to have been a mixture of good will towards the Chinese and exploitation of their picturesque qualities. Part of the Great Wall and the terrace at the Imperial Palace were among the buildings shown in replica, and there was a miniature Chinatown, although *The Times* expressed disappointment that only one of the sixty "natives" wore a pigtail. The organisers rather compromised themselves to modern eyes by boasting that some of the costumes "were obtained during the looting of Peking" which followed the suppression of the Boxer Rebellion.[12]

The Crystal Palace event showed a more benign attitude than anything in popular literature. It is true that the works of Ernest Bramah view the Chinese affectionately, but for the Chinese of a remote past. Their elaborate pseudo-Oriental style scarcely endeared them to a large readership. It is hard to take two hundred pages in which, for example, "do come home with me" becomes "Precede me, therefore, to my mean and uninviting hovel, while I gain more honour than I can reasonably bear by following closely in your elegant footsteps". Hilaire Belloc praised the first of these books, published in 1900, but twenty years later he was referring to the sale of only a few thousand copies, and reduced to comparing the publication of such a literary gem to "the reading of Keats to a football crowd".

The football crowd preferred works like Percy F Westerman's *When East Meets West, A Story of the Yellow Peril*, which dates from the same year as the first Fu Manchu book. As in Shiel's *The Yellow Danger*, the attack from the East comes after the European nations have fought each other almost to a standstill. Westerman's account of Britain and Germany locked in mortal combat gains added interest though having been written and set in the last year before the First World War. In this fictional version of history, Britain defeats Germany in a great naval battle but huge losses to her fleet reduce her to a second class naval power. In accurately predicting these events, an eccentric but brilliant British scientist evokes the Boxer Rebellion whose "savage excesses" will reappear from beneath China's "thin yet deceiving veneer of Western civilization" and combine with "all the cruelties practised by the Samurai in days gone by". "The Chinese nation as a whole was pretty certain to relapse into acts of cruelty that would put the Middle Ages of European history into the shade".

Admittedly, Chinese grievances are not ignored. "When it suited the white man, the yellow man was kicked from pillar to post", for example in the immigration policies of Australia, New Zealand and South Africa. "China recalled the many times that European armies had invaded her capital and her largest cities, looting without regard to her religious and personal susceptibilities. It was merely revenge – revenge on a gigantic scale". The Chinese overran the south of France and provided a huge occupation force for southern Germany, but European civilization was saved through the biological weapons invented by the brilliant British scientist. Having maintained all along that they are the only hope, he waves aside references to the Geneva Convention – "as if the Geneva Convention will be read by a numberless swarm of Mongols, whose sole business is to slay… all the terrible means of destruction that science could suggest were in future to be employed against a foe to whom humanity was unknown".[13] The argument has a modern ring.

China's dominant political figure of the period, the Dowager Empress, Tzu Hsi, was easy to demonise. Seen as a cross between Catherine the Great and Lucretia Borgia, she was described as "the most remarkable woman sovereign and most unbridled female despot the world has known".[14] Now an old woman, beautiful but ruthless, she had risen from the ranks of the Imperial harem to become the true ruler of China dominating three successive Emperors, her rivals having died mysteriously, poisoned, it was believed, on her orders. During the Boxer Rebellion, she was thought to be siding with the Boxers while treacherously professing friendship for the West. On her death, eight years later, *The Times* said that the dominating passions of her life were "the lust for power and for gain" and that "she was never deflected from her course by pity, right or justice".[15] *The Fortnightly Review* reflected the opinion that she had indulged in "the passions of a Messalina and the cruelty of a Bluebeard".[16] It was said that "many romances have been written about this remarkable woman, but none is as extraordinary as the truth".[17] Nevertheless writers of fiction did their best. In one short story she forbids the Chinese community in New York to help a man who has incurred her displeasure. Even there "the name of the old lady who sat on the throne of Pekin had the power to terrify them; they well knew that she had means of striking at them across thousands of miles of sea".[18] Another story points out that "in an age when the women of the Western world were clamouring for opportunities to play a greater part in life", she had proved it possible "for a woman, born in the most conservative society of the globe, to achieve the supreme direction of five hundred million of human beings, and to make sport of the statesmen of Europe and America".[19] Louise Gerard is influenced by this point in her novel *It Happened in Peking*. She describes in sympathetic terms the Empress's uncertainty about whether to support the

Boxers, and is full of admiration for her: "call her bad, if such if your mental equipment, call her tigerish – which she often was – call her inconsistent (a good enough synonym for woman); call her minx, arrogant, but dare not say that she was not a stupendous woman, stupendously, marvellously gifted".[20] Gerard's admiration for the Empress is also bound up with her disapproval of the West's treatment of China. It does not excuse the Boxers' ferocity, but it explains it. However, as far as popular literature was concerned, the Empress's most important qualities were that she was powerful, ruthless and Chinese. Among characters owing her their inspiration was *The Daughter of Fu Manchu*, who takes over her father's international secret society, and makes rings round her opponents.

The most famous Chinese man of the period, the only one known in Britain, who also influenced novelists and dramatists – Li Hung Chang, was the archetypal mandarin, rich, clever, powerful and of venerable age. A biography published in 1903, two years after his death at the age of seventy-eight, claimed that writing his life was "writing the history of the nineteenth century in China".[21] His British links went back to 1863 when he worked with General Gordon to put down the Taiping rebellion. This episode inspired Gordon's nickname "Chinese Gordon", and was the first in the Gordon legend, although it was eventually overshadowed by his death at Khartoum.

Li, whose association with Gordon added to his appeal, was the top-ranking interviewee for influential Westerners visiting China. At times his reputation stood higher in the West than at home. During his triumphant European tour in 1896, he was being reviled in China for having negotiated the humiliating peace treaty with Japan. However, this did not prevent a writer to *The Times* protesting that "the almost royal receptions" accorded him in Moscow and Berlin "furnish a curious example of the fascination which Chang appears to exercise over the minds of European statesmen".[22] The crowds were equally enthusiastic in London. On the Bank Holiday Monday "the spectacle of a Viceroy of China with his suite being driven in such sumptuous equipages was throughly appreciated". They rode through the West End in Lord Lonsdale's magnificent carriages, each drawn by four chestnut horses, complete with postilions and outriders. Li wore the high-ranking mandarin's yellow jacket so beloved by the writers of popular fiction when describing high-ranking Chinese. He was applauded when he laid wreaths on Gordon's statue in Trafalgar Square and his tomb in St Paul's.

Li Hung Chang helped to inspire the creation of many rich and powerful fictional mandarins. *The Splendid Paupers* offers a good example. It was written by the campaigning journalist W T Stead for the 1894 Christmas number of his monthly magazine *The Review of Reviews*. That year the landed aristocracy had been hit by death duties for the first time, and the story envisaged the Duke of Devonshire being reduced to selling Chatsworth to the mandarin. The latter, who hates Europeans, clears the tenants off his estate, and builds a "Great Wall of China" to keep out intruders. He engineers a cholera epidemic to kill off the local population, and, to ensure that it is not replaced, sets off underground explosions which are taken for earthquakes. He takes over hostile newspapers, and establishes his power over the House of Lords by buying up the debts of the aristocracy. When a clergyman attempts to interrupt his triumphal entry intoChatsworth, he is decapitated by a bodyguard, who escapes punishment for his crime. Henceforth, the only white to enter the Chatsworth estate will be the mandarin's secretary.

Another Chinese country landowner appeared nearly a quarter of a century later in an anonymous magazine short story, which turns the plot of *The Splendid Paupers* upside down. He is an ideal landlord, beloved by his tenants, one of whom says that there is "not a better white man walkin' about on top of this 'ere earth". The greatest possible compliment to a yellow, brown or black man was to describe him as white. The story was set and written during the First World War, when the rich Chinese gives all the game on his estate to feed the local people. His popularity is maintained in spite of a press campaign against him, which argues that aliens should be banned from owning property. He detests all things German, and is supposedly instrumental in bringing China into the War on the side of the Allies.[23] The brief war-time alliance between Britain and China accounts for this unusually favourable treatment.

In fact, even *The Splendid Paupers* is not quite as anti-Chinese as it seems. The imposing figure of the mandarin was chosen as the most likely foreign stereotype to wreak havoc on the British aristocracy. Admittedly the stereotype contained a vein of cruelty, but the mandarin's behaviour is part of a satire on the new death duties, in which ludicrously extreme consequences are ascribed to them. With China already on the brink of defeat in her disastrous war with Japan, it is remarkable that the story foresees her vast, undeveloped resources making her a great power again one day. It is even predicted that millionaires of the future are more likely to be Chinese than American.

* * *

"Drugs, gambling and appeals to every human passion have their place in Limehouse. It is the distribution centre for opium and cocaine".[24]

"Beyond the low-ceilinged gaming rooms, hidden doorways lead to dark yards and hovels full of strange and often hideous histories".[25]

The portrayal of fictional Chinese was influenced by the popular image of the Chinese communities in Britain as well as by events in China. To an extent the two interacted. If the Chinese were dangerous in China, could those in Britain not be? The tiny Chinese population was scattered around several ports, but it was the Limehouse Chinatown near the London docks that fired the public imagination. The Liverpool community was larger, but still had only a few hundred residents in 1911, although census returns did not record the population of seamen, which varied with the number of ships in dock. There was an influx of Chinese into Limehouse during and after the First World War, but the population soon declined, until in the 1930s "Chinatown" almost disappeared. In 1931, the *Evening News* reported that only at night could you persuade yourself that the place was sinister, and that every Chinese "was a Fu Manchu". Three years later the *East London Observer* said that "Limehouse myths – which for generations have provided writers of thrillers with material for plots" had been exploded by the revelation that only about a hundred Chinese remained in Limehouse.[26]

These "myths" centred on opium smoking, vice and crime. The irony of the revulsion from opium hardly needs stressing in view of Britain's imposition of the drug on China during the nineteenth century. It was regarded as particularly pernicious to whites. An opium den features in the first chapter of Dickens's *The Mystery of Edwin Drood*, and, in the 1890s, the white widow of a Chinese claimed that Dickens had visited her husband's East End establishment and used it in his novel.[27] Later fiction writers tended to assume that every Chinese smoked opium. Even the masterful Dr Fu Manchu indulged, although "he used opium as he used men for his own purposes; but no man and no drug was his master".[28] The many descriptions of opium "dens" in fiction and the press did not differ markedly from Dickens's. *The Times* reported from Limehouse in 1913 on the "gentle way in which they play with the precious paste, twirling it so deftly in the flame of the little lamp and smearing it with loving tenderness in the bowl of the thick-stemmed pipe". The paper deplored the physical effects of opium, but pointed out what fiction writers tended to forget – that "all the 'dens' in these two streets together will not furnish from

one week's end to another any such spectacle of 'degradation' or
rowdyism as may be seen nightly in any public house".

If opium-smoking really was a speciality of the Chinese, they were
much less addicted to vice and crime than a reading of popular fiction
would suppose. A writer in 1900 protested that "the Chinaman in
Limehouse is a most peaceable, inoffensive, harmless character. He is
on good terms with his neighbours, most of whom speak well of
him… Limehouse is rightly proud of the honour done it by his being
where he is".[29] Twenty years later "in view of the emphasis recently
given to the darker side of Limehouse", a journalist protested that
"the best Chinese opinion is as strongly opposed to the drug traffic
carried on by some of the Chinese inhabitants of Limehouse as are
British people".[30] However, as vice is more interesting than virtue,
such remarks were not greatly heeded.

There were occasional violent outbursts of anti-Chinese racism. In
1906 the *Sunday Chronicle* launched a violent attack on the Liverpool
Chinese, alleging the seduction of poor English girls, some in their
early teens. It was alleged that "nearly all" Chinese laundries, shops,
boarding houses and restaurants were blinds for the "gambling,
opium smoking and indescribable vice which is carried on in the back
rooms and below and above stairs". The writer proclaimed that if he
had a child he would never let him or her go near a Chinese shop and
he conjured up the nightmare of mass Chinese immigration into
Britain.[31]

The spectre of interracial sex was the main theme of the Liverpool
campaign. According to the *Liverpool Courier*, "it is with a shock that
one sees such names as Mary Chung and Norman Sing. It is at once
sorrowful and sickening to observe apparently decent British women
succumbing to the attractions of the yellow man". Their children,
especially the boys, were "far more distinguished by the vices of their
parents than their virtues". Chinese women rarely came to Britain, so
it was true that Chinese men tended to mate with whites. However,
according to the Chief Constable of Liverpool, "the Chinamen have
no difficulty in getting English women to marry them, to cohabit
with them, or to act the prostitute with them, and in all these relations
they treat their women well, they are sober, they do not beat their
wives, and they pay liberally for prostitutes".[32] The well-informed
agreed that the Chinese made good husbands; not to be beaten was a
big plus point for working class women.

Alarm at the prospect of sex between white and yellow became
hysterical after the First World War. "White Girls Hypnotised by
Yellow Men" screamed the *Evening News*. It was the duty "of every

Englishman and Englishwoman to know the truth about the degradation of young white girls". However, it was widely admitted that much of the fault lay with the white women. "Englishwomen are selling themselves to Chinamen; they are seeking out Asiatics in streets where before the war no white woman ever walked... Their moral sense has gone. They behave as though hypnotised by the Celestials".[33] A magistrate at the Thames police court enraged Chinatown by saying that "to the ordinary decent Briton there is something repulsive about inter-marriage or its equivalent". He later explained that his remarks had been directed mainly against the white women. They could hardly expect the men to show them more respect than they showed for themselves.[34]

One writer asked, "whether marriage should be permitted between a white girl and an alien with a totally different standard of living and civilisation, except under the strictest safeguards".[35] The reply was indignant: "Some of our men, steady and hard-working people, have married white women and have been very happy and contented with them. Do you see a Chinaman in the police court charged with assaulting his wife? No. Do you see Chinese charged with bigamy? No. Have English wives run away from their Chinese husbands? No".[36]

The writers of popular fiction were not reassured. The young "Eurasian" woman tended to be a glamorous but sinister figure. In Sax Rohmer's *The Yellow Claw*, "this girl of demoniacal beauty" has "a devilish and evil grace" and "her beauty was magnificently evil".[37] In one of Rohmer's early Fu Manchu novels a beautiful "half-caste" is described as "wickedly handsome" – "I use the word *wickedly* with deliberation; for the pallidly dusky, oval face, with the full red lips, between which rested a large yellow cigarette, and the half-closed almond-shaped eyes, possessed a beauty which might have appealed to an artist of one of the modern perverted schools, but which filled me less with admiration than with horror".[38]

Somerset Maugham, the most popular dramatist of his day, was less melodramatic in *East of Suez*, but he still made it clear that a Eurasian woman was bad news. The play, first produced in 1922, is set among members of the British community in Peking. In the opening scene, they discuss a man who will never get a good job as he has a Eurasian wife – "The English are not an unkindly race. If they've got a down on half-castes there are probably good reasons for it... Somehow or other they seem to inherit all the bad qualities of the two races from which they spring and none of the good ones". In fact the play is the story of Daisy, Harry's half Chinese wife. She is beautiful and charming, but governed by her senses, and only too eager to resume an affair with Harry's best friend, George, after her marriage. She has disguised her lurid past from Harry, including her time as mistress of a rich Chinese. This man wants her back, and tries to have Harry murdered. He tells Daisy that she is a Chinese woman, and will be better off with him. He despises the West, which, he says, can only lord it over China because it has invented the machine gun. Daisy does revert to her Chinese background. Her passion for George is such that she is ready to be his mistress: "I'll live like a Chinese woman. I'll be your slave and your plaything. I want to get away from all these Europeans". George, however, is too honourable to betray his best friend, and he shoots himself. When Daisy, in Chinese costume and her face painted in Chinese fashion, confronts her husband, he sinks to his knees in despair as the curtain falls. The Eurasian woman has proved true to type – as immoral as she is attractive. Harry's marriage to her has ruined him, as the cynics anticipated. The rich Chinese and Daisy's mother are both unpleasant characters. Maugham, the master of pleasing West End audience, has confirmed their worst prejudices at every point.[39]

The British at home did not treat the Chinese badly for the most part. They seldom met them. By far the most hostile group were merchant seamen. Employers in the shipping industry liked to take on Chinese because they accepted low pay, rarely put in claims for industrial injury, and could be used to break strikes. In a bitter seamen's strike during the summer heatwave of 1911 every Chinese laundry in Cardiff was stoned or burnt out in what were described as "scenes without parallel in the history of the city". Unable to find any Chinese seamen on whom to vent their anger, the mob victimised the more vulnerable laundrymen. One newspaper reported that "the demonstrators were not ordinary working men, and certainly not the seamen strikers". Racism in the streets was accompanied by the occasional virulent letter to the press. One denounced the Chinese for "their filthy habits and treacherous nature as a menace to morality and peace" – A gun is your best friend with a Chinese crew. Five years later, during a desperate period of the First World War the *East London Observer* deplored the people trying to "ginger up" agitation against the employment of Asiatics whose "tradition of the sea and its service are much older than our own". Nevertheless, "British merchant seamen facing torpedos and mines" were not satisfied with cheap praise while shipowners were raking in fortunes by employing cheap Asiatic labour.[40] Then the *Daily Telegraph* declared that "there has been a good deal of talk in the East End about the 'yellow peril'", because the number of Chinese sailors in the merchant navy, and on shore near the West India Dock road was increasing.[41] A new Merchant Shipping Act, barring foreign sailors from British vessels if they could not understand English, did not apply to British dependencies, so suspiciously many Chinese sailors claimed to have come from Hong Kong or Singapore. Sometimes a Chinese who spoke English would sign on, and be replaced, before the ship sailed, by a friend who knew that the authorities could not tell one man from another.[42] There were more problems when British sailors back from the war found that the housing near the docks had been taken by Chinese.

These issues contributed to the atmosphere in which popular fiction was written, but novelists were more interested in opium and gambling, which were generally thought to be Chinese weaknesses, and Limehouse was considered a centre of crime and vice. Dr Fu Manchu's hideaways in various books extend all along the Thames from the East End to Windsor, and he is to be found in Limehouse less often than might be imagined. However, in the second novel in the series "We were heading for that strange settlement off the West India Dock Road, which, bordered by Limehouse Causeway and Pennyfields, and, narrowly confined within four streets, composes an unique Chinatown, a miniature of that at Liverpool and the greater one at San Francisco". In the same book the narrator has a nightmare vision – "I saw the tide of Limehouse reach, the Thames lapping about the green-coated timbers of a dock pier: and rising – falling – sometimes disclosing to the pallid light a rigid hand, sometimes a horribly bloated face".[43]

Rohmer took Limehouse drug trafficking as his central theme in *The Yellow Claw* and *Dope*, two novels in which Fu Manchu does not appear. He took the precaution of asserting that "*Dope* was not inspired by, nor is it distantly concerned with, any *cause célèbre*, recent or remote", but the book was quite obviously based on a sensational case which had immediately preceded its publication, and which greatly strengthened the link in the public mind between Chinatown and vice.

Billie Carleton had emerged from the chorus at the Empire music hall to become a rising star of the West End's lighter entertainment. In November 1918 she returned home from the Albert Hall, where she had attended the Victory Ball celebrating the defeat of Germany, and was found dead in bed the next day. She had died of an overdose of cocaine rather than opium, but she had been an opium smoker, and the cocaine had come from Limehouse. The cross headings in the report of the normally staid *Times* were sensational: "Orgies in De

Veulle's Flat", "Opium Lamp and Scales", "I knew Billie Carleton", "The Den of Ten Ping You". The Scottish wife of a Limehouse Chinese had visited the West End to prepare the opium and administer it to Billie Carleton and her friends. This inspired more sensational headlines from *The Times*: "An Opium Circle. Chinaman's Wife Sent to Prison. High Priestess of Unholy Rites". The prosecuting counsel described the story as "disgraceful to modern civilisation". Carleton had been staying for two weeks in the flat of De Veulle, a dress designer and former actor, and the excitement was prolonged beyond the inquest when he was charged with manslaughter and conspiring with Ada Lo Ping You to supply the drugs. He was acquitted, but moralists were further outraged when it emerged that in his youth he had "made curious friendships with older men".

In *Dope*, the entertainer Rita Dresden was clearly based on Billie Carleton. Witness the dialogue: "'Cocaine is her drug', 'One of them. She had tried them all, poor silly girl'". The financial backer of the drugs syndicate, himself an addict, who introduces Rita to drugs, and then, out of love for her, tries to wean her off them, is a highly respectable figure. He embodies the fear that addiction was threatening a class not previously at risk. Drugs and visits to Limehouse were certainly chic in West End circles at this period, and Rohmer satirises the craze in the silly socialite Mollie Gretna: "Oh, I shall be in a perfectly delicious panic when I find myself amongst funny Chinamen and things! I think there is something so magnificently wicked looking about a pigtail – and the very name of Limehouse thrills me to the soul". She envies the Scottish wife of the Chinese drug trafficker – "I have read that Chinamen tie their wives to beams in the roof and lash them with leather thongs. I could die for a man who lashed me with leather thongs. Englishmen are so ridiculously gentle to women!" Mollie was wrong about Chinese husbands, and about pigtails, which had become a rarity in Limehouse since they fell foul of the 1911 revolution in China.

The Chinese villain in *Dope* is a bigger fish than the police are used to. For them every second Chinaman in the Limehouse Causeway was a small importer of drugs, and they "failed to conceive the idea of a wealthy syndicate conducted by an educated Chinaman". He is "a wonderfully clever man" and escapes to China with his ill-gotten gains. Rohmer thinks it understandable that "the Chinaman, and not unjustly, regards the police as ever ready to accuse him and ever unwilling to defend him… (he) may therefore be robbed, beaten and even murdered by his white neighbours with impunity. But when the police seek information from Chinatown, Chinatown takes its revenge – and is silent".[44] After the early nineteen-twenties, Rohmer deals very little with Limehouse. The exception is *The Trail of Fu Manchu*, set in the great fog of 1934, the year the book was published, and the setting was necessarily described as "the ever-dwindling area of Chinatown".[45]

* * *

"I remembered Limehouse as it was – a pool of Eastern filth and metropolitan squalor, a place where unhappy Lascars, discharged from ships they were only too glad to leave, were at once the prey of rascally lodging-house keepers, mostly English, who fleeced them over the fan-tan tables and then slung them to the dark alleys of the docks. A wicked place; yes, but colourful".[46]

Ever since the publication in 1916 of his popular success *Limehouse Nights*, Thomas Burke was even more closely associated with the area than Sax Rohmer. Both men had got to know Limehouse as journalists. Rohmer had worked on a story about a Chinese master criminal, whom he never managed to meet but who inspired his best known character. He was quoted as saying that he knew nothing about the Chinese but he did know something about Chinatown.[47] Burke also claimed to know nothing about the Chinese. "All I knew of Limehouse and the district was what I had automatically observed without aim or purpose during my unguided wanderings in remote London".[48] Some of the stories in *Limehouse Nights* offended the lending libraries, which banned the book, despite the protests of Arnold Bennett. On the other hand, Burke was highly praised by H G Wells, and various critics compared him to Kipling, Gorki and Maeterlinck. As late as 1944, his publishers were boasting that his short stories, from *Limehouse Nights* onwards, were world famous, and that they depicted the "comedy, tragedy, romance, poverty and sometimes crude realism of a colourful, cosmopolitan population".[49]

Perhaps the most frequent mode was crude realism, laced with melodrama, but Burke's tales unlike most stories of the period, depict white and yellow people interacting with one another, not necessarily in criminal situations. In one story a fine lady goes slumming in Chinatown having heard that it "offered splendid material for studies in squalor, as well as an atmosphere of the awful and romantic. Her first glances did not encourage her with this idea; for these streets and people are only awful and romantic to those who have awful and romantic minds".[50] Nevertheless, Burke did not neglect the romance of the exotic. In a later collection he describes a Chinese festival: "In

the West India Dock Road, the return of the cemetery procession
dressed the evening mist with lanterns. Through the blue night, the
white and scarlet globes of Eastern Carnival mingled with the golden
clouds of fried-fish bars, and young blood stirred to the dance of
drums and gongs, and the fiery colour and the old songs".[51] Chinese
cemeteries and funerals had long fascinated journalists. Back in 1900
the *Daily Express,* expressing admiration for how well Chinese kept
their graves, reported that "when John Chinaman dies in this country
there are strange and mysterious rites performed at the funeral".[52]

Burke is impartial in his descriptions of Limehouse folk, and
sometimes the Chinese come off better than the native British. In
The Chink and the Child, the Chinese protagonist is a tragic figure. He
rescues a 12-year-old illegitimate girl from maltreatment by her
drunken violent white father. "His love was a pure and holy thing".
The father, a pugilist called "Battling Brown" is indignant when the
child is taken from him. "Battling did not like men who were not
born in the same great country as himself. Particularly he disliked yellow men.... Yeller! It was his supreme condemnation".[53] This racist
thug murders the girl, which leads to the Chinese killing him and
then himself. The story found a world audience when D W Griffiths
turned it into a film as *Broken Blossoms*. A white man also comes off
badly in another of these tales in which he thinks he has fathered a
child by a pregnant white girl. However, she has been so free with her
favours, that three Chinese have the same expectation. When one of
them turns out to be unmistakably the father, only the white man
reacts with bad grace, although he had not really wanted the child.

Burke's treatment of sexual relationships between Chinese men
and white women rarely involves the marriages which were usually so
successful. He concentrates on the lusts and casual affairs which the
newspaper moralists found particularly alarming. The white girl in
one story is too poor to give her mother a good funeral. She deserts
her Muslim protector who does not have the money she needs, and
makes an arrangement with a rich Chinese, "a loathly creature, old and
fat and steamy.... What he did to her in the blackness of that cur-
tained room of his had best not be imagined.... She came away with
bruised limbs and body, and with torn hair, and a face paled to death".
She also came away determined to kill him, and did. In another of
these tales, the girl "with the loveliest hair, east of Aldgate Pump" is
sacked by her Chinese employer, for pilfering. When he physically
pushes her out of his shop, she is furious at being manhandled by "the
loathly-yellow hands of a Chinky". She decides to show "the nasty,
dirty, slimy, crawling, leery old reptile" that he cannot get away

with catching a decent girl with "his beastly, filthy, stinking, yellow old fingers".[54] She exacts her revenge by setting fire to the shop when he is in it, using fire extinguisher bottles which, as only the two of them know, he has filled with kerosene to carry out an insurance scam.

Sometimes it is the Chinese who vows vengeance. One is besotted with a girl who spurns him because she is in love with a violent white criminal. She is known to be a police informant. When the law arrives to arrest the criminal, he turns on her, thinking that she has betrayed him, but the Chinese has taken a double revenge. In another tale of vengeance, the conductor of a music hall band makes advances to the female half of a trapeze act, the male half being her lover. "'Here – steady on, Chinky!' she cried, using the name which she knew would sting him to the soul".[55] As well as the more literary "Celestial", "Chink" and "Chinky" were used routinely in popular literature without necessarily causing great offence. This man reacts so strongly because he is only half Chinese. He deliberately gives the wrong musical cue to the male trapeze artiste, who falls to his death as a result.

Burke's tales cover an area of Limehouse beyond the few streets of Chinatown, and in some stories the Chinese do not appear. In others they live cheek by jowl with the whites. It is a harsh environment, if scarcely harsher than the entirely white working class world of the East End depicted by Arthur Morrison only a few years earlier. The philosophy of the whites is usually "A Chink… may be all right, but he's still a Chink; just as an Englishman may be all wrong, but is still an Englishman".[56] However, Burke was also aware that white people were attracted to the colour, which the Chinese brought into the grey world of London. In a late story a society audience of five hundred is persuaded to pay a guinea a head to hear the wisdom of a Chinese sage. They have fallen for a scam organised by a white Limehouse boy, and the sage is probably not Chinese either.[57]

Burke's greatest success was in depicting the Chinese as individuals rather than the usual stereotypes. In one of a series of articles directed against drugs and "dance dens", a *Daily Express* reporter described the dramatic entry of a Chinaman who "was not the 'Chink' of popular fiction, a cringing yellow man hiding his clasped hands in the wide sleeves of his embroidered gown". However, he cannot resist mentioning, a few lines later that the "fixed Oriental smile which seems devoid of warmth and humanity, was so typical of the novelist's idea of dopedom that he seemed like a vision conjured up by the surroundings". Like other papers, the *Daily Express* was much exercised at this time – 1922 – by a glamorous Chinese restaurateur, known as "Brilliant Chang", who was supposed to be highly involved with drugs. A couple of years later, after he had moved from the West End to Limehouse, he was imprisoned for drug offences and deported. According to a detective witness, he "carried on the traffic with real Oriental craft and cunning", and the Recorder of London told him "it is you and men like you who are corrupting the womanhood of this country". On rather weak evidence the newspapers accused Chang of sadistic treatment of women, to whom he was supposed to be enormously attractive, and of being the centre of a vast drugs network. In so doing they gave credence to the wildest fantasies of popular fiction.[58]

* * *

"I am Chu Chin Chow from China,
Of Shanghai, China
No Celestial blood is finer
In Shanghai, China".[59]

Show business was always ready to exploit the glamour of a usually fake Orient. Even Somerset Maugham began *East of Suez* with a scene entirely made up of mime and spectacle. He also included a marriage procession for its picturesque quality, which he left out of his Collected Plays because, as he admitted, it had nothing to do with the story.[60] Thomas Burke refers to "a Chinese juggler, who blasphemed his assistants in the language of Kennington Gate, and was registered on the voting list at Camberwell as Rob M'Andrew".[61] He reads like a poor man's version of the most famous "Oriental" performer of this period, Chung Ling Soo, a conjuror who used lavish costumes and props, like the gorgeous palanquin, which bore him on stage. In a famous routine, he played a victim of the Boxer Rebellion who thwarts the rebels by catching the bullets they fire at him. On 23 March 1918 the trick failed and Chung Ling Soo died of his wounds. He was in fact a Yorkshireman named Robinson. According to his biographer, his imitators included Ching Ling See, Ching Ling Sen, Chung Ling Fee, Ching Ling Fee, Ling Lang Hi, Chang Hi, Ching Foo So, Little Chung Ling Soo and Chung Lin.[62] It is unlikely that many of them were true Chinese.

Chinese sets and costumes were particularly popular in musicals, whose generous budgets made for gorgeous spectacle. However, shows like *San Toy* and *A Chinese Honeymoon* reflected China about as accurately as *The Mikado* depicted Japan. References to "Rhoda and her pagoda" and "the double chin" of "the mandarin" indicate the level of sophistication.[63] If they influenced public thinking, it could only have been to suggest that China was not to be taken seriously. Strangely, the most popular musical with a Chinese sounding title was not about China at all. From the end of August 1916 *Chu Chin Chow* ran for more than two thousand two hundred performances, a record not beaten for forty years. The story is in fact a version of Ali Baba, and the Chinese mandarin is one of the disguises of an Arab robber chief.

The disguise inspired a memorable poster, which was reproduced in large numbers. Posters made an important contribution to the collective memory. One observer remarked that "anyone... who saw much of politics in the winter of 1905–06 must have noticed that the pictures of Chinamen on the hoardings aroused among very many of the voters an immediate hatred of the Mongolian racial type".[64] These pictures were not aimed at the Chinese in Britain but were part of the row about Chinese labour in South Africa. In a different vein Sax Rohmer's biographers reported that when the first two-reeler Fu Manchu films came out, "In the underground stations, all over London, larger than life-sized posters depicted the leering visage and clutching hands of the Devil Doctor. The fame of Fu Manchu had never seemed greater than at that moment".[65] One of the main factors making the Chinese interesting was always the simple truth that they *looked* different.

Unfortunately, "different" could mean "ugly", and, according to long-established literary convention, "ugly" usually meant "wicked". The evil face of Dr Fu Manchu stayed long in the memory, not only from the film posters, but also from the films themselves. The books' descriptions of a "brow like Shakespeare and a face like Satan" do not justify this, although elsewhere Rohmer was ready to frighten readers with visions of "a hideous Chinese face, pock-marked, mask like,... pressed to the glass",[66] or "a pair of sunken, squinting eyes, set in a yellow face so evilly hideous that I was tempted then, and for some time later, to doubt the evidence of my senses".[67] Similar phrases were used in boys' literature – "Suddenly I saw an awful ugly yellow face peering through the glass"[68] or "there was another blinding flash of lightning that revealed a terrifying picture. It was the abrupt presence of a face – the face of a Chinese twisted demoniacally".[69] Often a Chinese with an ugly face also had ugly, claw-like hands, a convention perhaps derived from the long-finger nails worn at the Imperial court. This ugliness often went together with great age, which might be honoured, as the Chinese themselves honoured it, but more typically was played for melodramatic effect: "the face revealed was hideously ancient, wrinkled and withered like the skin of a baked apple... The man might have been a lifeless mummy, save for the steady nodding of his head and the twitch of mumbling lips over toothless gums".[70]

* * *

"He won't murder you; but he'll take his revenge – not in any obvious way, but in some subtle tortuous Chinese manner. He's a great gentleman in his own way" but "Hurt him in this – 'his point of honour' as he would call it – and you'll find him very different".[71]

Chu Chin Chow's poster had a dignity that the character himself belied. His depiction as a Li Hung Chang figure was misleading. In fact, the musical was still running in 1918 when the character most clearly based on the famous statesman was presented on stage. In "the Chinese Puzzle" which ran for more than a year from July, the point is even made explicit in the dialogue – "A Chinese diplomat! Like Li Hung Chang, I suppose?" "In a way – yes. He has certainly rendered equal service to his country".[72] He is the Chinese ambassador to Britain, who is involved in concluding a treaty to provide finance for the Chinese navy. The treaty is drawn up at the house of a young British diplomat, but his wife's mother, an adventuress, persuades her daughter to photograph it for a German spy. The details get into the press and the diplomat is forced to resign. The Chinese ambassador suspects the wife all along. Six months later he has proof of her guilt, but instead of denouncing her he takes the blame on himself. He makes it offensively clear to her that he is not doing it for her sake, but for her husband's. He owes a debt of honour to the husband's father, which he is determined to repay. One of the co-authors of the play claimed that "for the first time in European drama, [it] presented a Chinese gentleman in every way a peer of those qualified for that description in any other country".[73] Certainly, the diplomat shows an extreme sense of honour, and his values were those of a British audience, except for his very low opinion of women, which was seen as typically Chinese.

Five years earlier, in the very year of Dr Fu Manchu's first appearance in print, a Chinese protagonist appeared on stage with an equally developed sense of honour, but a more unsettling one. The eponymous *Mr Wu* was described by *The Times* as "an uncanny blend of Oriental ferocity and Western culture. He was at Oxford in his youth, and must, we think, have been a don there, for his English is far too carefully chosen for any mere undergraduate".[74] He is Hong Kong's most powerful mandarin, but his daughter has been seduced by the son of Mr Gregory, an English businessman. In revenge, Mr Wu lures the Gregory family to Hong Kong by bringing the Gregory Steamship Company close to ruin, and in the confrontation between the two men shows himself not merely the peer but the superior of his antagonist. Mr Wu is suave, polite, cultured, and masterful. Having had his daughter killed for her transgression and her seducer kidnapped, his target is now Mrs Gregory whom he induces to visit his house on the pretext that she will hear news of her son. When she arrives, he demands dishonour for dishonour. Her son will be killed unless she yields to him. This highly dramatic situation is ruined when, in her agony Mrs Gregory calls to her servant outside the house, and he throws her a phial of poison through a window. Mr Wu drinks the poison by mistake, and drops dead, leaving the Gregory family unharmed. In an earlier version of the play offered to the censor, Mrs Gregory tries and fails to poison Mr Wu. He gives up his attack on her virtue when young Gregory persuades him that he is an honourable suitor to his daughter, who has not been killed. It was safer not to depict an English memsahib as a would-be murderess, but Mr Wu's character is the same in both versions.

The play was such a hit that the star, Matheson Lang, entitled his memoirs *Mr Wu Looks Back*. He claimed to have been inspired by a visit to Shanghai where several highly cultured Chinese had discussed Shakespeare with him. As they sat in his dressing-room, "large, bland stout men most of them, with charming manners and an extraordinary sense of dominant personality", the idea came to him of getting a play for London about a Chinese of precisely this type. He argued that the character was innovative, as "up to then the usual stage Chinaman in our country had been a rather ridiculous, comical little figure of musical comedy, all shrugs and grimaces and squeaky noises, or a rather exaggerated monster of villainy in melodrama, the exact antithesis of these quiet, dignified cultured people".[75] Perhaps Lang's criticism does not apply to the other successful "Chinese" play of that year. *The Yellow Jacket* was supposedly staged according to the traditional methods of Chinese theatre, and comment on China or the Chinese of 1913 was not to be expected. However, along with the success of Mr Wu, it showed that 'The East has evidently a fascination' for the playgoer of to-day".[76]

Mr Wu's obvious superiority over his blustering English antagonists is linked to his role as a representative of China. Asked, "Why is

China so far behind today?", he replies, "Because China can afford to wait…. She watched the glories of Greece and Rome blossom into flower, fade and die – just as she is contemptuously watching Western civilisation today. All through the ages China has been waiting – waiting…. Soon she will wake, cast off her oppressors, arm herself, take her place among the nations".[77] At a time when China was so weak, "soon" had to be taken in the context of her unique time scale. The lines betray an underlying fear of her vast population and resources. "Soon", Mr Wu, declares, China will "pour her armed millions into Europe, dethrone kings, wipe out nations, change the face of the globe and establish the greatest World Empire ever known". For a moment he seems the Yellow Peril incarnate, which gives an extra dimension to the domestic drama.

There was talk of Matheson Lang playing Fu Manchu on screen, although nothing came of it. However, he played another masterful Chinese in *The Chinese Bungalow*, which started life as a novel, became a smash hit play when Lang toured it in the provinces, was filmed three times in under 15 years, twice with Lang as the star, and had a run in the West End. The protagonist, Yuan Sing, like Mr Wu, is determined to avenge the wrong done to him and his honour by the English. He is a man of great wealth, living near Kuala Lumpur with his English wife and her sister Charlotte. Once again the Chinese gentleman is suave, cultivated and courteous, but he knows that his wife is having an affair with a young Englishman, and he exudes menace throughout the play. When Charlotte exclaims, "You would not dare to kill – an Englishwoman", he replies, "I have no fear of, even as I have no respect for, your countrymen. They have no morals and no manners, no insight into life – no vision. They are imperfectly educated and unacquainted with the subtleties of the civilised soul". The English community has ostracised the wife for marrying a Chinese, but he says, "It is I who conferred a privilege on a barbarian and I have paid for my mistake".[78] Yuan Sing casts off his wife and has her lover killed, but he must also deal with the lover's brother, who, like him, wants Charlotte. In this case, though, murder is not appropriate; it is an affair of honour, and he offers his rival two glasses to drink from, one of which contains poison. The Englishman chooses correctly, and the play ends with the death of Yuan Sing. It was highly unusual for the public to be asked to accept a marriage between a Chinese and an Englishwoman, and it was necessary for it to turn out badly. One of the few works to breach this taboo was E Phillips Oppenheim's *Prince Chan* in which the eponymous Prince, the most powerful man in the world, destroys a Russo–German plot against Britain for love of the heroine. She is strongly attracted to him, and he carries her off to China as his wife. This novel was not particularly important in Oppenheim's vast output, but it is interesting that such a popular novelist tested his readers' prejudices in this way.

Like *Mr Wu*, *The Chinese Bungalow* offered its audience two possible conclusions. Either high caste Chinese had a moral code no less demanding but very different from that of Englishmen, or beneath the skin of even the most cultured Oriental there lurked something savage after all. The latter idea is very common in the fiction and drama of the period and it is stressed repeatedly that, however affable, charming and cultivated such characters may be, it does not do to push them too far. The moral judgement passed on them varies greatly from case to case, but, except perhaps in the very lightest of musical comedies, they are always formidable. In both *The Chinese Bungalow* and *Mr Wu*, the Chinese man has a genuine grievance. The Englishman has taken his daughter in the one case, and his wife in the other. We today, who are so familiar with the idea of colonial guilt, can see the parallel, perhaps more clearly than the playwrights, between the taking of the women and the capture of land and sovereignty from the Chinese.

CHAPTER 2:

Chinese Villains and Masterminds

"Imagine a person, tall, lean and feline, high-shouldered, with a brow
like Shakespeare and a face like Satan, a close-shaven skull, and long
magnetic eyes of the true cat-green. Invest him with all the cruel
cunning of an entire Eastern race, accumulated in one giant intellect,
with all the resources of science past and present… Imagine that awful
being and you have a mental picture of Dr Fu-Manchu, the yellow
peril incarnate in one man".[1]

All the qualities of Mr Wu and Yuan Sing are to be found in Dr Fu
Manchu, but he was conceived on a much more magnificent scale.
Like them, he was intelligent, sophisticated and urbane, highborn
and cultivated. Like them, for all his qualities, he was a deadly opponent.
However, unlike them, he did not enter into affairs of honour; he
operated in the political and not the personal sphere. He was determined to end the supremacy of the West, and, before the First World
War, this meant that he was above all, a danger to the British Empire.
For at least a quarter of a century he was one of the best known
characters in English-speaking fiction, and better known than any
real life Chinese. "An archangel of evil" he entered popular literature
as a negative racial stereotype.

No new Fu Manchu books appeared during the nineteen-twenties,
although there were many reprints of the three already published
by then. These were *The Mystery of Dr Fu-Manchu*, *The Devil Doctor*
and *The Si-Fan Mysteries*, issued between 1913 and 1917.[2] In their
descriptions of villainy they can descend to a nastiness, never reached
in the later works of the canon, which give more weight to the
Doctor's positive qualities. He is not only the greatest genius which
the powers of evil have put on earth for centuries but "a menace to
Europe and America greater than that of the plague". Although he
occasionally explodes into a terrifying rage, he is usually cold and
calculating, and, after all, "No white man, I honestly believe, appreciates
the unemotional cruelty of the Chinese". He is also repulsive to the
touch – "Never have I experienced a similar sense of revulsion from
any human being. I shuddered as though I had touched a venomous
reptile", and "I would sacrifice a year of my life to see his rat's body on
the end of a grappling iron".[3]

Nevertheless, Fu Manchu is also an extraordinary instance of
Western admiration for the Chinese intellect and for the great
Chinese tradition of learning. He is as great a scientist as he is an evil
genius. His researches have carried him far ahead of any Western
rival, especially his studies of poison and insects, which he uses to
deadly effect. He has also discovered the means of reducing his victims

to a death-like state and resurrecting them at will. This is an essential tool in his assault on world power. It enables him to cause the apparent death of leading Western authorities in every field, smuggle out their bodies to his laboratories, and then bring them to life. As a result they are working for him long after their supposed deaths. His victims are French, Russian and German as well as British, so emphasising that, as during the Boxer Rebellion, the whole of Western civilisation is under threat.

When there is no time for elaborate measures, Fu Manchu resorts to ordinary kidnapping. After he is shot in the head, the greatest brain surgeon of the day is abducted and made to perform the necessary operation. – "Virtually, Sir Baldwin, you stand in China; and in China we know how to exact obedience". Here is an echo of the famous occasion back in 1896 when the founder of the Chinese republic, Sun Yat-Sen, then still a rebel against the Manchu empire, was kidnapped in London and taken to the Chinese legation. As Sun himself told the story, he received the chilling greeting, "Here is China for you; you are now in China".[4] However, despite the historical reference, the early Fu Manchu novels take place almost out of time. There is no allusion to the First World War.

In these early stories, Fu Manchu's secret international organisation, the Si-Fan, is based in China. He himself mainly works from London, and has the resources of Chinatown at his disposal, a conventional but thrilling world of secret rooms and underground passages, houses with interconnecting cellars, floors which give way suddenly under the feet of intruders, and vessels waiting in the Thames in case a quick get-away is needed. If Fu Manchu later transferred his operations to the United States, this did not so much reflect a shift in world power as Rohmer's shaky finances. He himself moved to America to be in closer touch with his American readers and publishers.

The name of the evil genius is significant; recalling as it does the Manchu dynasty, which had ruled China until just before the first story was published. Fu Manchu is even supposed to be of the royal blood. Equally significant is the name of his antagonist throughout the whole saga, Denis Nayland Smith. This is only a letter away from Wayland Smith, the blacksmith of old English legend, comparable to Vulcan in classical mythology. Smith is the representative of honest Englishness in contrast to the fiendish Oriental. His sidekick, and the narrator, in these early stories, although he fades out later, is Dr Petrie, whose name is taken from that of the great Egyptologist, Flinders Petrie. Rohmer was passionate about Egyptology. *The Times Literary Supplement*, perhaps not well tuned to the delights of popular literature, unfairly called Petrie "even more fatuous than Watson".[5]

In fact the Smith-Petrie relationship is more equal than Holmes-Watson. The tall, lean Nayland Smith is similar to Holmes in appearance, and, like Holmes, he is an inveterate pipe smoker. However, Holmes is always confident that his mighty intellect will triumph. He never meets his intellectual superior, and only in the one story, which brings him up against Professor Moriarty does he admit to having at last met his intellectual equal. Nayland Smith never believes that he is the intellectual equal of Fu Manchu – "I am a child striving to cope with a mental giant". He is right. He is neither the leader of an immensely powerful international conspiracy nor the greatest scientist the world has known. However it was part of the philosophy of the imperial age that a British hero has more important qualities than intelligence. Typically British pluck and determination enable Nayland Smith repeatedly to fight a draw against a man so much more gifted than himself, and of course more gifted than Petrie: " 'Smith', I interrupted bitterly, 'what chance have we? We know no more than a child unborn where these people have their hiding place, and we haven't a shadow of a clue to guide us to it' ".[6] All this enhances Fu Manchu's status as a mastermind.

The senior members of his Si-Fan organisation come from all over Asia and the Middle East. When Petrie comes upon a top-level meeting "I was enabled to identify two for Chinamen, two for Hindus and three for Burmans. Other Asiatics there were, also … there was at least one Egyptian". Rohmer seems to be tapping into an underlying fear that one day the whole of the colonised world will rise up against its imperial masters. Fu Manchu also employs a variety of Asian hit men – Indians, Malays, Burmese. England had been seized by "a yellow octopus whose head was that of Dr Fu-Manchu, whose tentacles were dacoity, thuggee, modes of death secret and swift, which in the darkness plucked men from life and left no clue behind". Burmese dacoits usually form his personal bodyguard, and are depicted with such savagery that Burmese suffer even more than Chinese from racism in these books. Nayland Smith and Fu Manchu first met in Burma "the home of much that is unclean and much that is inexplicable".

On one occasion Petrie and Smith are chased by dacoits "more like dreadful animals they looked than human beings, running bent forward, with their faces curiously uptilted. The brilliant moon gleamed upon bared teeth". There is a lot of this animal imagery – "a repellent figure which approached, stooping, apish with a sort of loping gait … sprang like a wild animal on Smith's back. It was a Chinaman…".[7] In Rohmer's

The Golden Scorpion, where the "Scorpion", a Fu Manchu-like figure, is another Chinese scientist and evil mastermind, his brilliant yellow eyes are more like a tiger's than a human being's. They inspire the horror "which the proximity of a poisonous serpent occasions – or the nearness of a scorpion".[8] These bestial qualities are linked to the convention that wicked people must be ugly. The fact that it does not apply to Fu Manchu, with his brow like Satan's, presumably Milton's version, or to other Chinese masterminds, is a sign of their superiority to the run-of-the-mill criminal. Of course Smith's personal appearance – he was "lean, agile, bronzed with the suns of Burma – was in tune with the clean British efficiency which sought to combat the insidious enemy".

* * *

"Celestial though he was, and with no trace of white blood in him, he looked a man accustomed to command".[9]

Another Chinese super-villain leapt into print in the very month – June 1913 – that Fu Manchu first appeared in book form. This may not be a coincidence. *The Mystery of Dr Fu Manchu* was a reprint of stories which had already been published in a magazine, and they may well have been plagiarised for the creation of Wu Ling in the adventure weekly *Union Jack*. Wu Ling's antagonist was one of the great cultural icons of the twentieth century, Sexton Blake. Blake himself starred every week in *Union Jack* and later *Detective Weekly* for more than forty years up to the Second World War, not to mention the Sexton Blake Library and other outlets. He was a great detective but he owed much of his following to his prowess as a man of action rather than to his sharp brain. He is usually considered a boy's fiction hero, but many young adults read him, and also older adults of limited education. During the First World War *Union Jack* urged its readers to get copies of the paper to the men and boys at the front, which gives an idea of the target readership.

Blake has many encounters with the Chinese in Limehouse, and visits their country of origin amazingly often. The reader feels for his boy assistant when Blake tells him "We leave for China tomorrow, Tinker", and Tinker replies, "China, guv'nor. My aunt! It isn't so long since we returned from there. What's the stunt this time?".[10] On occasions Blake's faithful bloodhound Pedro accompanied them on the long and arduous journey.

Union Jack was determined to give Blake a very special Chinese opponent. Two weeks before the first story, it printed a whole page advertisement headlined: "The Chinese Peril. Birth of a Mysterious

Brotherhood. Rumours of a Wonderful Yellow Beetle. Will Sexton
Blake Probe the Mystery?" After arguing that the average Westerner
has a vague idea of the Chinese as a wrinkled, pig-tailed laundry
worker, the writer launches into a survey of the geography and history
of China. However, when he describes the current state of the country and the rise of secret organisations, fact soon slides into fiction
and Wu Ling is presented as "a man instilled with the wisdom of
thousands of years, steeped in the writings of Confucius, educated at
the best English, French, German and American universities, a linguist
of marvellous ability, ... shrewd, clever, unemotional, impassive patient
as the Sphinx and as inscrutable".[11] Much the same could be said for
Fu Manchu. When we learn that this mastermind is an enemy of the
white race, that he is head of a mysterious organisation, in this case
the Brotherhood of the Yellow Beetle, and that he is determined the
Chinese shall rule the world, the comparison is unavoidable.

   A few weeks later the magazine published a rare political article to
encourage interest in Wu Ling. Entitled "The Coming World War", it
posed questions which the author, Shaw Desmond, considered vital for
the twentieth century. They included "Is the Yellow Man about to
challenge the White Man's supremacy? If he does, who will win?
If the Yellow Man is victor what will it mean to the White Race?"
In Desmond's view the European powers had to withdraw from China
if catastrophe was to be averted. Since the Japanese defeat of Russia, the
yellow races had learnt the gospel of force for the first time. If the size of
the Chinese army were proportionate to Germany's, China would have
thirty million soldiers. The Chinese not only had grievances over the
jurisdiction enjoyed by the European powers in the treaty ports, but
against the United States over immigration, Britain over Tibet, and
France over Catholic missions. Europe's standard of living was threatened by the capacity of the Chinese to exist on tuppence a day. Their
"intelligence, endurance, adaptability and genius for taking pains" gave
them a supreme advantage over white workers.[12]

   By the time this mixture of shrewdness and alarmism was published,
Blake had already called Wu Ling "a foeman worthy of my steel", and
they had fought each other physically with no holds barred. Wu Ling
used a crouch and a lightning spring that drove his opponent's head
and shoulders upward like a battering ram. It was "much in favour
along the seaports of the East", but Blake was equal to it, having seen
"too much of the underlife of Canton and Shanghai" to be beaten.[13]
This is good action man stuff, but it detracts from Wu Ling's role as
an awesome mastermind. Dr Fu Manchu would never descend to
brawling.

The intellectual clash between the two men is more interesting. Blake tries to persuade Wu Ling to call off his anti-white crusade: "Build up your country. Teach them the great laws of the brotherhood of man. Instead of setting them at the throat of the whites, let them march shoulder to shoulder in the forward march of humanity". To which Wu Ling ripostes, "Did the whites march shoulder to shoulder with us when they bombarded our ports and ravished our lands while we were helpless to reply?" Blake seems nonplussed, and can only answer, "They made mistakes, Wu Ling. Man will always make mistakes and his greed blinds him to right".[14] Imperial guilt is something of a surprise in a pre-First World War adventure story. Nor is this the only example. Just after the end of the War Blake crosses "the roof of the world" to meet the grand lama of a remote monastery, who, now old and venomous, spent three years of his youth at a British university where he learned "how you white-skinned races despise us" and learned too "the rough uncouth ways of your young men. I learnt how to be laughed at and scorned – yes, and how to receive insults and blows from those young fools – with a smile, and I learned how to hate".[15]

There is a certain chivalry in the relationship between Blake and Wu Ling. The latter was "honourable in his methods", and, we are told, should not be condemned because they did not coincide with Anglo-Saxon ideas. "On that very point had Sexton Blake shown his deep insight into human nature". For his part Wu Ling tells Blake, "I would have you for my brother… You are really of the East",[16] but he continues in his nefarious ways for another twenty-five years. Of course inconsistencies arise in such a long running series of stories written by so many authors – a figure of more than a hundred has been mentioned.[17] There were also marked differences in literary ability.

To begin with, Blake is not fluent in Chinese, but he eventually masters several dialects. This enables him to disguise himself as a Chinese without being detected, helped by a wax which changes the shape of his face and a stain which alters the colour of his eyes to the necessary liquid brown. He can impersonate a mandarin or a coolie with equal ease. (He is recognised as a European only once, partly because he munches water-melon seeds one at a time rather than in twos and threes.) We are told on various occasions that his brain is as subtle as the finest in the Orient, he has formed one of the finest jade collections in Europe and only the most learned Chinese can rival his knowledge of Chinese culture. He stresses repeatedly that "there was a civilisation in China long before the Western world had emerged from savagery".[18] Yet, when provoked, he can descend to the racial abuse which was commonplace in the popular literature of the period, but which the Lord Chamberlain banned from the stage – "Blake jumped forward and grabbed the Chinaman by the neck. 'You yellow scum', he snarled! Out with it or I'll twist your neck as I would that of a rat' ". Tinker complains that "One of his beastly scum spat in my face when I was tied up". "Then go it, my lad", says Blake, "I'll see that you get a free run". And Tinker did. "He dealt out one of the most scientific beatings to the dope merchant that one could wish to see, and when he had hammered him to a sobbing pulp in one corner, he staggered back with the light of satisfaction in his eyes".[19] Such lapses are rare, perhaps attributable to a writer with different values from the rest. However, they are particularly unfortunate when it was being repeatedly suggested that the civilisation of the Chinese and other races was only skin deep – unlike that of the British.

* * *

"Now that events in the East have simmered down into at least temporary quietude, something of the inner history of the causes which
plunged China and Manchuria into a welter of warfare, and the part
that Sexton Blake of Baker Street played there can be revealed".[20]

It is a merit of the Sexton Blake corpus that readers were kept up to date with political developments in China. Wu Ling always continues to represent the Yellow Peril, but it is acknowledged that the idea of a Sino-Japanese conspiracy has been killed by the First World War. It survived the peace-time alliance of Britain and Japan, but in 1915 Japan is fighting on the same side as Britain and China has not yet committed itself. Wu Ling rails in vain at a high-ranking Japanese "Why is it that Japan is hand in hand with Britain? Is not her place with us?... I speak to you as to the Japanese nation. Answer me as you would have the nation answer". He does not get the reply he wants – "I grant you that the East was old in civilisation when the white man was a naked savage. But also the East stood still... The methods of the whites are faulty. They have made mistakes, and will make others, but the ultimate purpose is sound". And even more gallingly, Wu Ling's Japanese interlocutor refers to "Britain, the advance guard of the white, the nation which has always been the champion of the oppressed – the nation which is honest at heart, and which will stand by its friends to the death".[21] Two years later Wu Ling revives the old plan of setting the white races at each others' throats, but it is the Chinese armies alone who must do the rest.[22] A month after this story was published China declared war on Germany, and so became Japan's ally at last, but also Britain's. A belated attempt was made to revive a Sino-Japanese conspiracy in a story of 1933, not involving Wu Ling. By this time, although the Anglo-Japanese alliance was over, Japanese aggression against China made the old Yellow Peril alliance unbelievable.

However, in co-operation with some wicked Chinese, a sinister Japanese organisation tries to revive it. According to whispers, it was "the driving force behind the campaign that had brought the whole vast state of Manchuria under Japanese control" and, before it finished, "would drive every European west of Suez and every American west of Honolulu". Blake discovers the details of the conspiracy and lays them before the League of Nations in Geneva. We are not told if it takes effective action.

Contemporary China is linked with its nineteenth century past by Blake's mentor Sir Gordon Saddler. All traces of his British origin have been lost during more than fifty years in China, but, under his Chinese name, he works to thwart Britain's enemies. He has been part of Chinese history, from General Gordon's day to the Boxer Rebellion. "He had seen the glory of the court of the Great Empress; he had been a contemporary of the sagacious Li Hung Chang. He had seen the fall of the imperial Manchu house and the chaos which had followed".[23] In his romantic past Sir Gordon "had dared the wrath of the terrible Dowager Empress and had fled with one of the royal princesses from the Court of the Inner City of Peking".[24] After the 1911 revolution he moved to the Chinese quarter of San Francisco, but he is always available to Blake.

From the revolution on, and especially during the period between the two World Wars, the Sexton Blake stories reflect a China in turmoil. "Disaster after disaster had overwhelmed China. War had come, and famine. Bandits had ravaged the land… disease had continued the work they had begun. And now floods".[25] "The bandit scare", as it was known, was even introduced, as a topical element, into Ivor Novello's 1936 musical extravaganza *Careless Rapture*, although with Novello himself starring as a hero who, at one point, dresses up as a Chinese prince, Chinese politics are scarcely taken more seriously than on the musical stage of a generation earlier. In real life, bandits were exploiting a China torn apart by Japanese militarism and rival Chinese generals. It was easy to insert Wu Ling into such a confused situation as the greatest of all the warlords. In a particularly effective story a Canadian girl agrees to run guns for him because he persuades her that he is the man to cure China's ills.[26] He is woven even further into real-life politics with the suggestion that his Brotherhood of the Yellow Beetle is a parent organisation of the Kuomintang. The nationalist party founded by Sun

Yat-Sen is described as "the great 'Chinese Red' organisation" and its leader as "rabidly anti-British".[27] Much is made of the Soviet influence in the Kuomintang, which was real enough until Chiang Kai-Shek expelled the communists after Sun's death.

The comparative security of Hong Kong and the European enclaves in the treaty ports, which were outside Chinese jurisdiction, contrasted with the dangerous interior of China or indeed the dangerous Chinese districts of the treaty ports themselves. In the "native quarters" of Canton "the night life was teeming with the stealthy purr of a great yellow jungle"[28] and "right up to the gates of the concession is the teeming life of the great Chinese city, fully ninety per cent of which is hostile to the foreigner, and would if it dared sweep across the Shameen to loot and burn and destroy".[29] Europeans have a lot to fear. "There is probably no more unattractive city than the native quarters of Shanghai. Its streets are narrow, malodorous and ugly. It lies low, and reeks with an unhealthy miasma. Cholera, smallpox, dysentery and malaria all rage there at certain periods of the year".[30] A Chinese riot was frightening even though Westerners were not the target. "It might have been taking place in the Middle Ages. And yet it was in the present day, with modern Shanghai not a stone's throw away, and grey British destroyers, filled with complicated modern machinery, lying off the Bund".[31] In such conditions Blake is the gallant Englishman fighting to protect the peace and stability represented by the European presence in China, which, he believes, needs the guiding hand of Britain. He refers disparagingly to a Chinese girl who "like all the hare-brained youth of China, fondly imagined that they could get along without the foreigner".[32]

Blake fights Wu Ling all over the Far East. In Singapore he witnesses the reaction of the "bronzed Britons of the Empire outposts" when an attractive white woman enters a room. Their "gaze devoured her as they realised what still existed in the world which they so seldom saw, and then [their] steely eyes turned menacingly towards the half-castes and the Chinese with a promise of what was coming to them if one of them should dare to flicker a single lid of insult at the fair flower which they knew was of their own race".[33]

The Japanese installed the deposed emperor of China as head of their puppet state in Manchuria, and, in one story, Wu Ling has him kidnapped as part of his plan to re-establish the imperial throne for himself. He has Manchu blood after all. For his part, Sexton Blake repeatedly insists that he does not care whether Manchuria is a Chinese or Japanese province, or who rules China, provided it is not

Wu Ling. He has no qualms about accepting help from the Japanese. They lay on a special train for him, and he leads Japanese and Korean troops into battle against Wu Ling's men.[34]

The ex-Emperor was a romantic figure in his way, and his path crosses that of Sexton Blake on other occasions. There is a story in which he is kidnapped again, this time in London, where he has arrived for medical treatment. He is rescued by a young female ally of Blake's. When she points to the ivy outside his place of confinement as the only means of escape, he says, "Such monkey antics are not for the son of Heaven". However, knowing that he "had never lifted a hand to anything more arduous than a tiny cup of tea", she has anticipated his unheroic inertia, and sets the room on fire, so that he has to clamber down the ivy like an ordinary mortal.[35]

The turmoil in China was genuinely frightening for Westerners. In his thriller *The Rickshaw Clue*, Geoffrey Ellinger describes the fear of a young Englishwoman who has just been kidnapped. "Her captors had skins of a different colour from her own, and this difference permeated their whole beings. Their manners were different; their thoughts were different. Their actions were utterly incalculable". For once, there is nothing racist in this; it is merely an explanation of why it is particularly frightening to be abducted when the abductors are incomprehensible in every way. The chief kidnapper is treated with some sympathy. He is allowed to tell his British opponents, "we claim the same right as you claim, the right to make a mess of our own affairs". When the kidnapped girl meets him months after her release, she expresses admiration that he did his job as a kidnapper so well, even though in the course of the adventure he shot his thoroughly wicked rival dead at close range. She appreciates that he has his own morality; he might kill her, but would never lie to her; he knocked her out with a blow to the head, but, being a doctor, repeatedly tended the wound at some risk to himself. He is, she says, "a very decent kidnapper". Other Chinese in the book are more villainous, but Ellinger shows that such stories can be told with a restraint which most examples of the genre conspicuously lack.[36]

China offered such rich possibilities for adventure that even Billy Bunter and his chums of Greyfriars school were sent there by their creator, Frank Richards. Bunter is a decided liability when he and two of his friends are chased across country by Chinese bandits, as, apart from being so fat, he wants to eat or sleep at all times. Until the food arrives, the Chinese are "a race of heathen blighters who ought to have been exterminated". However, he is so enchanted by the cuisine, that after a particularly good meal he comments on Chinese xenophobia, "I dare say we should feel the same if a lot of foreigners came and bagged bits of England". The villain, in league with a powerful war lord, is allowed to say that thirty years ago a European army had marched on Pekin, burning and plundering, and he is determined it shall not happen again. In fact some attempt is made to explain China to a young readership, albeit in Greyfriars language. We are told, for example, that so many peasants are on the edge of subsistence that there is little room for "loafing or slacking". Reading Frank Richards' formulaic style enables one to understand that constant references to the Chinese, especially the wicked ones, being yellow is often the outcome of lazy writing rather than malice. It is mentioned with equally irritating frequency, for example, that Bunter is fat. Not all the Chinese characters are wicked as the boys are in China to rescue a Chinese school friend, whose father has defied the villain. In fact, the rescue is effected by a Baker Street detective with all the characteristics of Sexton Blake, except his name.[37]

* * *

"The very mildest can become fiends incarnate when anything upsets them concerning their religion, or their Josses, or any affront to the soul of their dear old ancestors".[38]

After *Union Jack* became *Detective Weekly* in 1933, it continued to be overwhelmingly a vehicle for Sexton Blake until 1935 when he had to share its pages with other heroes, who themselves involved themselves in Chinese adventures from time to time. By now the authors were no longer anonymous, and *Detective Weekly* proclaimed that "there is no better writer of Chinese stories than John G Brandon",[39] who had many other outlets for his work.

In *The Silent House*, based on his West-end play, which was filmed in 1929, Brandon introduces a rich young mandarin who comes to study at Oxford. He is a highly cultivated man, who declares "the passion for scientific knowledge is in the blood of our learned men just as the gambling fever is in our lower classes". This kind of general statement always seems to have been demanded from non-Anglo-Saxons whose foreignness was always a matter for comment. Back in the East the mandarin shows two English adventurers around the temple where his aged father is high priest. Their business is in trouble, and they are tempted by the temple treasure with dramatic results: "There before the rifled joss of his forefathers lay a feeble old figure, dead – strangled as he knelt in prayer... And over the stark body stood with cold stony eyes his son. With uplifted hand he swore an oath so terrible that men listening breathlessly shuddered as he spoke".[40] The oath was one of vengeance – for the sacrilege to the temple of his ancestors as well as for the murder of his father.

Two standard plots merge here. The first is what might be called the "Moonstone" plot. In Wilkie Collins's novel of the eighteen-sixties, an English adventurer robs an Indian temple of its priceless jewel. It is returned at the end of the story, and it is clear that Collins, less imperialist than most of his contemporaries, thinks this only right and proper. Similarly, many stories of this later period, centre on the theft, usually by an Englishman, of a jewel, a talisman, a scroll, a cylinder or a whole temple treasure, which Indians, or in many cases Chinese, are anxious to get back, for religious reasons, because it is the key to more riches, or because it will give the possessor political power. The theft, like the "theft" of the women in *Mr Wu* and *The Chinese Bungalow* can be taken as a symbol of colonial guilt. *The Silent House* also features the revenge plot featured in those plays, in which a Chinese suffers a terrible wrong and will stop at nothing to get back at his usually British enemy. He is sometimes treated with sympathy, due emphasis being given to the original injustice; sometimes his crimes are deemed too wicked to be excused. In *The Silent House* the latter is the case. Of the two murderous temple looters one dies in the East; the mandarin kills the other back in England, and commits more villainy in his determination to wrest the dead man's ill-gotten fortune from his nephew and heir. Grief and rage have transformed this learned young Chinese into such a monster of cruelty that the reader is supposed to welcome his violent death. In Brandon's novel *Yellow Gods* there is more emphasis on imperial guilt. The murder of the priest by a white man and the theft from the temple are repeated, as is the priest's son's arrival in England in quest of the treasure and of vengeance. However, although he kills and tortures, his original grievances are given greater weight. He is declared insane through brooding too long on his revenge, and, after being confined to an asylum for a while, is repatriated along with his entourage, and allowed to take the stolen treasure with him.

Brandon also created a sailor hero, Jim Hazeldene, who has a Chinese sidekick Wong-ti, described as his "faithful though fierce little henchman and slave generally". Despite the immense condescension the British admiration for Chinese intelligence shows through. He is not taller than an English boy of eight but "there was something of stoic wisdom in his small face that might have befitted a man of fifty". On board ship Jim's berth-mate does not like a "Chink" sharing their cabin, but Jim tells him that Wong-ti is "far cleaner than a good many whites". In another story Jim insists that Wong-ti is his friend rather than his servant, who waits on him because he enjoys it. On the other hand Jim addresses him, albeit affectionately, as "you wicked little rat". Similarly, Sergeant Sunyati of the Hong Kong police sometimes renders Sexton Blake great assistance, but Blake can still tell him, "You're a bloodthirsty little devil, Sunyati".[41] Sunyati is not unlike Charlie Chan, Earl Derr Biggers' famous Honolulu policeman, one of whose adventures was serialised in *Detective Weekly*, where he was advertised as "a quiet, smiling bland little Chinese talking a quaint style of English all hours" but also "patient, relentless, deadly on the trail".[42] However, in English fiction, Chinese who fight on the side of the law are subordinate to the white hero.

The Hazeldene stories contain some disconcerting animal images. Wong-ti is not only a "wicked little rat". "Ten tiger cats tipped out of a bag would be mild and reasonable animals compared with Wong-ti aroused". When he is, justifiably, angered by a villain, he is compared to a monkey, his hands are like an eagle's talons and he snarls "with the viciousness of a snake". When Jim is attacked by a Chinese mob – "Around him, like wild animals, they swarmed, and not even a mob of starving wolves could have torn at him with greater viciousness". It is all the more reassuring therefore that, as Jim cried out for help before losing consciousness, "the answering cry in a hearty British voice was the last sound he heard".[43]

Brandon also wrote full-length novels featuring Inspector McCarthy, who specialises in investigating the Chinese. He believes that, although their wall of silence is impenetrable, "taken as a whole they are far more law-abiding than any other section of a foreign population".[44] The point is confirmed by a white criminal who complains, "the Chinks are *too* damned honest; they cannot understand anyone who tries to make a bit over and above a bargain already struck. They haven't assimilated our Western ideas to that extent".[45] In fact, McCarthy finds the Chinese intimidating. In his view, a white man cannot read their thoughts but they can read his, almost before he has thought them. "Even the coolies seem to have the knack of making you feel that you're like a kid just out of school". When he meets a Chinese infant, it fixes him with an unflinching stare. "It made him feel that this amber-skinned morsel of humanity had, in some previous existence, garnered up a dashed sight more wisdom and knowledge of things in general than ever he had, and what was more knew it; hence that distinct look of contempt".[46] Nayland Smith's inferiority complex about Fu Manchu is extended here to his whole people.

As the title implies, the McCarthy novel *The Mark of the Tong*, involves the leader of one of those Chinese secret societies which the police found so hard to penetrate. Their secretive nature allowed writers to give free range to their imagination, so disgusting at least one old China hand. He argued that authors with at most a superficial knowledge of the East weave "a veil of gossamer nonsense about characters who would be very plain everyday folk in real life". Whereas the fictional Chinese remained inscrutable and calm "in the presence of anything from a street fight to a volcanic eruption", all residents of China knew, in his opinion, that the Chinese were "the noisiest people on earth".[47] Be that as it may, the tongs are an important element of popular fiction. They loom large in the Sexton Blake stories, where they often fight deadly battles against one other and an alliance with Blake being the best guarantee of victory. Sax Rohmer's investigation of a Limehouse tong inspired the Fu Manchu stories. He acknowledged that not all tongs were criminal, but was struck by the close relations between tongs in different countries which enabled, say, a murder ordered in New York to be carried out in London, where there would be no ostensible motive. He came up with the idea of a super-society, to which the tongs all over the world would be subordinate, and decided that its president would have to be a genius.[48]

However, by the 1930s, the tongs in Limehouse were declining, like Chinatown itself. Even those authors, who clung to the colourful old locale, had to reckon with changing conditions. In *Meet the Dragon*, a short story of 1936, a tong leader tells his men, "In the days before some of you remember anything, we in Limehouse did not like the ways of English law... It was not our way to seek justice in the courts of this country", but then, "we found the police of London too strong for us, we found we dare not oppose their laws, that unofficial executions were bad for us... For many years there have been no tong killings".[49] Admittedly, in this instance the criminal who is persecuting the Chinese has evaded the law for so long that the tong returns to its old ways and eliminates him.

The Mark of the Tong has a dramatic climax. Quong See is a medical doctor who tends the poor, both white and yellow, and is more likely to give them money than accept it from them. He is unobtrusive and shabbily dressed, but it is rumoured that he was once a great and powerful mandarin who had to flee China in the days of the Empire. Not only are the rumours true, but he is head of his tong, and, like his counterpart in *Meet the Dragon* decides that violence is necessary for the first time in many years. In a dramatic scene he has shed his dreary clothes, and bursts in on the Chinese villain "in a magnificent gown of Imperial purple, tied with a yellow cord of a prince of the blood".[50] He is accompanied by three men with sub-machine guns. At this dramatic moment the police inspector intervenes. He handcuffs the villain, and exclaims, "this man is my prisoner – the prisoner of that law under which you live. His death is not in your keeping". It appears that traditional Chinese values have been forced to yield to those of the modern British state, but not so. The villain dies in agony in prison, killed by a huge, bloated hairy spider. Not only is the spider the symbol of Quong See's tong but, as in the case of Wu Ling's Brotherhood of the Yellow Beetle, the creature itself is used as a deadly weapon.

The day to day weapon of fictional Chinese criminals was the knife, just as their heroic British antagonists preferred the sock on the jaw. The introduction of the sub-machine gun was a new development, betraying the influence of American gangsters and American crime fiction. Just as Chinatown was physically shrinking, its old ways were changing, despite the death by spider. Chinese bafflement at the peculiar British preoccupation with the rule of law recurs in many stories. Dr Quong See reappears in Brandon's *Yellow Gods*, and finds it necessary to tell a fellow countryman that in England the Chinese are not a despised race, and that the law protects foreigners and native born alike. This is admirable but a bit rich considering that Quong See has ordered death by spider in the earlier novel.

In a series of books published between 1928 and 1935, Roland Daniel fed the taste for Chinese villainy. His Chief Inspector Saville is pitted against a Chinese mastermind Wu Fang. More than the latter's name recalls Sexton Blake's adversary Wu Ling, and of course Fu Manchu is a literary ancestor. When Wu Fang makes his first appearance in *The Society of the Spider*, he is merely head of the eastern branch of the secret organisation of the title. The "Spider" himself who is in overall charge is an American. We are told that he is rotten but not cruel, whereas Wu Fang, who has tortured an informer, is "the devil incarnate" and, "perhaps more dangerous than his master".[51]

With the American disposed of at the end of the first book, Wu Fang becomes the protagonist of *Wu Fang An Adventure of the Secret Service*. Saville teams up with the American Secret Service man, Alec Williams, in an Anglo-American alliance against the forces of evil. Like Wu Ling, Wu Fang has Manchu blood in his veins, is virulently anti-white and wants to bring back the Chinese Empire with himself as emperor. Like Fu Manchu he targets various British experts to work for his nefarious international organisation. The novel has many stock elements. Wu Fang has the use of an opium den behind a Chinese laundry in Limehouse, where Williams arrives disguised as a drunken sailor looking for a smoke. This was a favourite ruse of Sexton Blake's. Like Fu Manchu, Wu Fang has a ship in the river to make good his escape, and while the heroes believe at the end that he has drowned in the attempt, they are, with good reason, not quite certain.

Daniel's *The Yellow Devil* provides an interesting variation on the "Moonstone" plot. It is not a British adventurer but a Japanese general who has desecrated a temple and brought away its most sacred object. The scene of the crime was Manchuria, where the general has earned himself the reputation of being the most hated man in China. The book seems to have been written while the notorious Japanese atrocities in Manchuria were being committed. Nevertheless the Japanese is welcome in Britain, as he has come to negotiate a big arms order which will give work to thousands of unemployed. Wu Fang is determined to relieve him of his loot, but the Chinese mastermind has not become the virtuous representative of an oppressed nation; he is as wicked as ever. Few stories of the period sympathise with Chinese victims of Japanese aggression. In *The Son of Wu Fang* the heir to the Japanese throne has arrived in London on a state visit. The eponymous villain intends to kidnap him and not give him up until all Japanese troops have been withdrawn from China. This time Saville does go as far as to say that "one can hardly blame him for wishing to rid his country of the Japanese. At the rate they are going on, they will overrun the whole of China before long". And the American replies, "I don't know that we in America are particularly anxious for them to do that". The Japanese prince is treated sympathetically all the same. He is cheered as he drives through London to lunch at the Mansion House, although he is kidnapped on the way. He joins in the fight that leads to his escape, and Williams calls him "a bit of a sport". He wants to make up as soon as possible for missing his lunch, and, although he has little English, Saville is delighted when he manages to say "I am damned hungry". Even the respected Chinese of London disapprove of the kidnap. Williams tells the elderly head of a powerful tong, "As an honourable Chinese gentleman, I know that you will be only too willing to help me, if possible, to prevent a crime being committed in this country by men of your nation against a very distinguished visitor from Japan". The old man speaks of his distress that some of his countrymen "are planning to take advantage of the liberty of this country to take an action which may cause considerable ill-feeling between Japan and England".[52]

In *The Green Jade God*, the robber of a Chinese temple is again an Englishman. He is the heroine's father who was "damnably tortured" by monks in Tibet and "wasn't very nice to look upon when he got back". Although this was in retaliation for the theft of the god, the hero tells her, "I don't think we need accuse your father of being a common thief, even if he did take the Green Jade God... I guess those Chinese at the monastery deserved to lose it after the way they treated him". His prejudices have already been revealed by an earlier remark, "I guess you have more right to that god than anyone else except, maybe, than those from whom it was first stolen; however, I ain't worrying about them – they were Chinks".[53]

Daniel often describes Chinese inflicting torture on their enemies. Wu Fang has a man's eyes burnt out with red hot irons; another's feet are beaten with bamboo rods. He himself is being subjected to the bamboo canes when he is found shrieking in agony, lying strapped to a table on his stomach, his bare feet supported in the air by cords from the ceiling. He orders boiling oil is to be dropped on a man's bare stomach, and, after another beating is graphically described, it is remarked that "no one but an Oriental could have witnessed the disgusting sight which now began to unfold itself without crying out in horror".[54]

In fact torture is a staple ingredient of crime and adventure stories involving the Chinese. It was generally accepted that it was one of the things at which they excelled, just as they were good at all forms of intellectual activity, family values, loyalty and keeping their mouths shut. This last virtue was linked with their alleged torturing proclivities, on the grounds that, without torture, no Chinese could be made to talk. However, the torturers were often supposed to enjoy inflicting pain. This was repeatedly the case in the Sexton Blake stories, where it is thought better for a man at the mercy of his Chinese captors to be killed; otherwise, "he'll be systematically and scientifically tortured for weeks, perhaps months, at intervals, and they will sit round and giggle softly while he squeals and squirms".[55] Another Blake story has a Chinese villain setting a species of large rat on his helpless victim. "It sent his nerves delightfully a-quiver to see the flesh nipped and gashed in crimson blotches where the teeth of the bandicoots had torn at their prey".[56] One of Blake's incursions into China is to rescue a man who has been tortured day by day for eleven months, during which many another victim was tortured in front of him to show him what was coming next. "In five minutes the poor wretch was screaming not as a human being screams, but as a tortured cat might. For a whole hour that went on". A suave Chinese, an Oxford graduate, is enormously helpful to the rescue attempt, but Blake takes a dislike to him – "His fat face may beam smiling at you, but I can fancy him beaming exactly the same smile if he was watching you being handled by his men in his own private torture chamber". Blake's companion reacts the same way, and stresses another quality widely attributed to the Chinese – patience: "I can understand that man waiting twenty years to get his knife into you; but when he did he'd give it an extra wiggle for every year he had waited, and take a scientific interest in watching you squirm while he ate his dinner". In fact the character never does anything to justify these judgements.

* * *

"No desire for personal aggrandizement inspired him, Nayland Smith had assured me. He aimed to lift China from the mire into which China had fallen. He was according, to his peculiar lights, a great patriot. And this, I knew, according to those same peculiar lights, he was scrupulously honourable".[57]

Dr Fu Manchu was not above torture, and he set no great value on human life, but by the time the Fu Manchu chronicles resumed in 1931 after a fourteen-year break, he had come to regard physical violence as unnecessarily crude. Hypnotism and brainwashing are now his preferred methods of bending people to his will. In that first book of the new series *The Daughter of Fu Manchu*, he does not appear until the end of the novel, but his appearance is all the more dramatic for being delayed. His daughter has taken over the Si-Fan and made a pretty good job of it, but, in her father's view, she has taken the organisation in the wrong direction, one that can only lead to world war. He drags himself from retirement to set things to rights, and, old as he is, the narrator tells us, "this frail old man radiated such power that I was chilled". His daughter, a commanding figure up to this point, can only kneel and give way.

From the next book, *The Mask of Fu Manchu*, the Doctor is a man transformed. He has used drugs to shake off the burden of years. It is hinted that he has done this many times, and that his real age is incalculable. "He carried no stick; his long bony hands were folded upon his breast. He was drawn up to his full height, which I judged to be over six feet. His eyes, which were green as the eyes of a leopard, fixed me with a glance so piercing that it extended my powers fully to sustain it".[58] He has always had a brow like Shakespeare and a face like Satan, but from now on his appearance is also compared to that of Dante, the Egyptian Pharaoh Seti the First and Buddha. Nobility and power rather than the evil are its outstanding qualities.

By now Fu Manchu is no longer rooted in Limehouse, and would not stoop to use members of the underworld as his tools. His operations take him to the South of France, Haiti, New York, and, in the last book, even China. He almost transcends being Chinese; like his organisation he has become an international brand. "The natives of the Pacific Islands are indirectly controlled by this group, I know for a fact; why not the negroes of West Africa?"[59] One of Nayland Smith's young assistants writes, "I had formed an impression of his greatness which, oddly enough, gave me a sense of security... I believed him too big to glance aside at one so insignificant as myself".[60] Nayland Smith compares him with a painter – "his canvas the world; his colours, the human race".[61] Smith has come to admire his antagonist as much as he fears him. Much of this is due to the character growing, as so often happens, beyond the author's original conception. It may also be that Rohmer regretted some of the racism of the earlier books. According to his biographers he found it necessary in later life to excuse their use of "Chinaman" rather than "Chinese", pointing out that the former had been the usual term when he began writing. In his view it took on a derogatory meaning because of the behaviour of Chinese in Limehouse and elsewhere, not all of whom were criminals but many of whom "had left their own country for the most urgent of reasons".[62] It also seems likely that Chinese official protests against the racism of Fu Manchu films made in the United States had an impact on the later novels.

In *The Mask of Fu Manchu* the great man takes on the role of a fanatical Islamic prophet fanning unrest throughout the Middle East and putting British interests there in danger. Nevertheless he is a man of honour who never lies or cheats. In this respect his behaviour is compared favourably with that of the archaeologist Sir Lionel Barton, in this and other books a Nayland Smith ally. Barton has the ancient relics needed by Fu Manchu, who has Barton's niece in his power, and when the necessary exchange has been carried out it is discovered that Barton has substituted copies for the originals. Fu Manchu would never stoop so low. He enters into several bargains with his enemies and always keeps them. When he is cut off from the elixir, which wards off death through old age, he trusts Dr Petrie to find the ingredients and restore him to his old vigour in exchange for the freedom of Petrie's daughter. With the coming of a more cynical age, such chivalrous arrangements would soon cease, even in popular fiction. There are occasions when Nayland Smith or one of his acolytes comes upon Fu Manchu, helpless in the grip of opium. Although they are convinced that his death will be of immeasurable benefit to the world, they cannot bring themselves to take advantage of him.

It is of course a problem that Fu Manchu's contests with Smith always have to end in a draw to make the next book possible. His reputation as a superman inevitably suffers from the repeated failure of his attempts to take over the world. On the other hand, he always survives to try again. As the later books are mainly set outside British jurisdiction, Nayland Smith, the only man who can thwart him, has to be given unlimited powers by the American government, and, even more improbably, the French.

The development of Fu Manchu's character is a strength of these later works, but his stature is diminished by the dictators who really were trying to take over the world. With all their absurdities, the Sexton Blake stories managed to incorporate interwar China into the Blake myth because anything could be presented as possible in a country where all was chaos and confusion, and a great deal went unreported. However, Fu Manchu, operating on a world scale, has to reckon with political leaders whose every move is reported in the press. Events in Asia are ignored until the last book, but great play is made with political developments in Europe and America. In *The Bride of Fu Manchu* of 1933, the terrible doctor says, "The imprint of my hand is on the nations. Mussolini has so far eluded me; but President Hoover who stood in my path makes way for Roosevelt". Fu Manchu, who is supposed to have engineered the great depression, apparently believes that he will find Roosevelt more amenable than his predecessor.

Strangely, Roosevelt is ignored in *President Fu Manchu*, although the book came out in 1936. The title is a misnomer. Fu Manchu cannot be president himself, as he was born abroad, but he plots to get his candidate into the White House. In addition, Mid-Western farmers, crippled by debt, are being subsidised by his organisation and sent to Alaska, where, although they do not know it, they are to become a nucleus of his future power. Australia, the Philippines and Canada are also targeted. All this works reasonably well, and there is some shrewd satire on American politics. The difficulties arise in *The Drums of Fu Manchu* of 1939, where the Doctor conducts a crusade against the politicians who are threatening to plunge the world into war. He eliminates a German warmongering dictator with straight hair and a black moustache, despite the efforts of Nayland Smith to stop him. (Regrettably the world does not notice, as the dictator's double survives.) It is Fu Manchu, not Nayland Smith, who seems to stand for civilisation, when he tells the dictator, "Your ideals cross mine.

You would dispense with Christ, with Mohammed, with Buddha, with Moses, but not one of these ancient trees shall be destroyed". The scene of the confrontation is Venice where the German has come to meet his Italian counterpart, and where Hitler and Mussolini held their first meeting in 1934. Fu Manchu urges Nayland Smith to help him – "I shall employ you to save civilisation from the madmen who seek to ruin it.... I am determined that there shall be peace; the assumption of the West that older races can benefit by your ridiculous culture must be corrected... What have your aeroplanes – those toys of childish people accomplished?... Poor infants who transfer your prayers from angels to aeroplanes".[63] This does not seem entirely unreasonable. However, Nayland Smith continues to be obstructive. He foils Fu Manchu's attempt to murder a leading French politician, who, nevertheless, is forced to draw back from putting France on a war footing.

The difficulty in an age of German and Japanese militarism of maintaining Fu Manchu's position as the greatest threat to the Western world is clear from a passage in *The Island of Fu Manchu*, published in 1941. The narrator is with Nayland Smith hunting Fu Manchu in New York: "In a moment of perhaps psychic clarity I saw [Smith] against a different background: I saw the bloody horror of Poland, the sullen sorrow of Czechoslovakia, that grand defiance of Finland which I had known, and I saw guns blazing around once peaceful Norwegian fiords. An enemy pounded at the gates of civilisation, but Nayland Smith was here, and therefore here, and not in Europe the danger lay".[64] This is unconvincing. It was beyond the reader's imagination to suppose Fu Manchu to be more dangerous than Hitler in 1941. Rohmer continued to offer new Fu Manchu adventures for more than a decade after the War ended, but it was not credible to suggest that "Hitler and Stalin were babes and sucklings compared to Dr Fu Manchu".[65]

In fact, Fu Manchu is as virulently anti-Communist as he is anti-Nazi. He repeatedly says in the late 1940s, that his mission is "to save the world from the leprosy of communism".[66] Perhaps Nayland Smith should have stopped persecuting him and lent a hand. True some of Fu Manchu's methods were unsavoury, but the same could be said of many an ally of the West. 1959, the year of Rohmer's death saw the publication of his last book, *Emperor Fu Manchu*. It offers the final absurdity of both Fu Manchu and Nayland Smith operating effectively within Mao's China. The former is not only determined to rid the country of Communism, but to banish "this Russian pestilence" from the whole world. He asks Smith, "In this purpose do we, or do we not stand on common ground?" Smith's reply is feeble – "As I am still employed by the British government … your question is one difficult for me to answer".[67] By the 1950s, Fu Manchu, a contemporary of James Bond, has lived too long, even though Bond's enemy Dr No might not have existed without him. His role as the greatest threat to Western civilization since Attila the Hun is not convincing in the age of the Cold War and the threat of nuclear conflict between the superpowers.

In the 1930s, a "Yellow Peril" really had existed in the shape of Japanese imperialism, but it had threatened the West in South East Asia rather than at home. Writers of popular fiction had ignored or underestimated it. The cliched phrase had become a joke. For example, one of a number of school stories of the period involving Chinese boys, *The Yellow Peril of Paxton* by Reginald G. Thomas, published in 1935, is about a Chinese public schoolboy whose affectionate nickname is "the yellow peril". His prowess at games and ability to see off bullies make him very popular. After the Second World War, the Peril facing Western civilization was not Yellow, but Red. Mao's China was considered a threat not because it was Chinese but because it was communist. It was no longer possible to contrive plots around Japanese generals visiting Britain to buy arms. In 1941 the Japanese had swept away the last vestiges of Western privileges in China, and they were restored only in Hong Kong. Sexton Blake could no longer use Shanghai or Canton as a base, let alone sally forth into Manchuria. In any case, *Detective Weekly* had died the previous year, officially because of the wartime paper shortage, but probably, too, because of reduced demand. The Chinatown of Limehouse was only a memory. Dr Fu Manchu had become a relic of a fascinating but extinct chapter in Britain's cultural history by the time of his last appearance. In fact, Sax Rohmer's freelance enemy of Western governments, with a shadowy international organisation at his back, is more relevant in the age of Osama Bin Laden, than he was then.

The Arabs

How Britain's stormy relations with the Arab world translated into popular fiction; burning issues which still burn today; the lure of the desert, and of the virile Arab male for British women; how the tabu of inter-racial sex was evaded.

CHAPTER 3:

Gordon and Arab Nationalism

"Cut off – abandoned at Khartoum
Far out in the Soudan,
One man against ten thousand stood;
And he – an Englishman!
For near one year the whole world gazed,
And praised him with one breath;
Think of it, Englishmen! – and know
What's meant by Gordon's death".[1]

Any popular novelist would have been proud to have invented Gordon of Khartoum. From his death in 1885 until the end of the First World War, he was always likely to be in the minds of British people when they thought about Arabs. Memories of his exploits in China were fading, but he was still a warrior hero, a deeply religious knight in shining armour, who had fought to put down slavery and impose the values of civilization – that is to say British values – on a savage and corrupt country, the Sudan. He made an impact on Egypt too, as Egypt, under British protection, had been struggling to maintain its authority over the Sudanese. On his return to the Sudan, he had stayed at his post under great danger, until he died the death of a Christian martyr, butchered by what would now be described as Muslim extremists. Gordon, surrounded by the Mahdi's forces at Khartoum, represented civilization against the Arabs, just as the Western legations, surrounded, 15 years later, by Boxer rebels in Peking, were to represent Western civilization against the Chinese. It is hardly surprising, then, that he loomed large in popular fiction.

In William Le Queux's *The Eye of Istar*, an extravagant tale involving Arab cruelty and slave trading, the Arab narrator describes how "the wild multitude heaped curses upon the last grim relic of the gallant, deserted hero of Khartoum, the man whose matchless bravery and dogged perseverance were alike admired by my own co-religionists as well as the infidels themselves".[2] "The wild multitude" does not seem to have admired Gordon much, but it was a common ploy of popular novelists to attribute to others the admiration, which the British public felt for their heroes and for themselves. The action of *The Eye of Istar* begins at Omdurman where, in 1898, a year after the first of the book's many editions, Kitchener was to avenge Gordon's death, thereby renewing the martyr's fame as well as establishing his own. In A E W Mason's *The Four Feathers* of 1902, a romantic novel still highly regarded a century later, the hero, who has been given the feathers as symbols of his supposed cowardice, decides to restore his reputation by acts of courage. So, with the involvement of a former servant of Gordon's, he takes enormous risks to retrieve correspondence between Gordon and the Mahdi. This is before Kitchener's famous victory, and he is imprisoned in Omdurman. According to Mason, England still knew nothing "of that squalid and shadowless town, of its hideous barbarities, of the horrors of its prison-house". In the same vein one character calls the Sudan "a callous country inhabited by a callous race". The hero redeems himself before the battle of Omdurman, but the preparations were already advancing "which would one day roll up the Dervish Empire and crush it into dust".[3]

Gilbert Parker, an Imperialist politician and a Conservative Member of Parliament as well as a popular author, used the Gordon name in several tales collected in *Donovan Pasha*. Donovan is one of those gallant British officials battling against a cruel climate and a not always grateful population, who feature more often in stories of black Africa than of the Arab world. The ruler of Egypt is said to like him better than any Englishman he has known "save Gordon". In *While the Lamp Holds Out*, Donovan meets an Englishman who has lost his gentleman status through being caught cheating at cards and now leads a life of degradation and self-contempt. "Gordon was a white man", he says, and invited him to the Soudan, but he is ashamed to go because "there was another fellow with Gordon who knew me, and I couldn't face it". However, Donovan and his colleague give him the strength to take up the offer, and he dies gallantly in a sortie into the Sudanese desert ordered by Gordon. These stories contrast the cruelty and corruption of Egypt with the idealism of Donovan who says, "I've tried to be of some use, and play a good game for England". He is prepared to help an Englishman he knows to be in the wrong because the man "was his friend as men of the same race are friends together in a foreign country".[4]

In Parker's novel *The Weavers* of 1907, Gordon is never mentioned because the action predates him, but readers could not miss the parallels with the hero, David Claridge. Claridge too is a devout Christian. He is offered a powerful position in the Egyptian government of the mid-nineteenth century. "Rapine, murder, tyranny, oppression were round him on every side, and the ruler of the land called him to his counsels. Here a great duty lay". "He felt that honesty and truth would be invincible weapons with a people who did not know them". His chief antagonist is not a Muslim but an Armenian Christian. Nevertheless this man is ranged with the East against the West, "with the reactionary and corrupt against advance, against civilization and freedom and equality". Gordon's two periods in the Sudan are merged into one when Claridge goes there to put down the slave trade, and is surrounded by an Arab army intent upon his death. A feature of the Gordon story was the slowness of the Gladstone government in sending a relief expedition, which eventually arrived too late. In *The Weavers*, although Claridge survives, it is no thanks to the British government which refuses to send troops. The dominant figure at the Foreign Office is an Earl who, having discovered that Claridge is his half brother and the rightful holder of the title, would be only too happy for him to perish. Claridge's survival leads to the book's conclusion that "Though the dark races might seek to hold back the forces which drain the fens, and build the bridges, and make the desert blossom as the rose, which give liberty and preserve life, the good end was sure and near, whatever of rebellion and disorder and treachery intervened".[5]

Two years later Hall Caine, one of the most popular novelists of the late nineteenth and early twentieth century, published *The White Prophet*. Its English hero is Colonel Gordon Lord and he shares his forenames – Charles George – with the hero and martyr. He is the son of the British Consul-General in Egypt, but, unlike his father, he loves Egyptians and speaks Arabic like his mother tongue. The novel opens with a ceremonial re-enactment of the battle of Omdurman in which Gordon Lord fought bravely and captured the enemy's flag.

Caine's use of the Gordon story is most interesting in his implied allusions to the Mahdi, the fanatical Arab leader whose forces had stormed Khartoum and killed Gordon. The White Prophet of the title is believed to be a new Mahdi, a dangerous demagogue, bent on ejecting the British from Egypt. Gordon Lord is sent to arrest him, but finds that he is an unworldly figure who preaches not so much against the British as against the corruption of modern life. He wants a reconciliation of East and West, and Lord compares him with Christ and John the Baptist, a reflection of the fact that Caine was dissuaded with difficulty from calling the novel *The White Christ*. Not only does Lord not arrest Ishmael Ameer, the White Prophet, but also he disobeys an order to close down Cairo University for being a hotbed of sedition. Even worse, he brawls with the general commanding the British Forces in Egypt, who has an unsuspected heart condition and drops dead. The general is the father of Lord's fiancee Helena. Disgraced and disgusted with the hard line policy of his own father, Lord joins the White Prophet in Khartoum. After yet more improbable complications he decides that the only way to avoid a bloody clash with British forces is to allow himself to be arrested, and he is sentenced to death. However, he is reprieved by the personal intervention of the King Edward VII, and the resignation, which his father had offered as a political manoeuvre, is accepted. Gordon Lord is given command of the British army in Egypt, where a new liberal policy is adopted.

The book was a commercial failure, the only one of Caine's novel's never to be reprinted – not, as the modern reader might suppose, because of the improbabilities of the plot, but because of its sympathy for Egyptian nationalism. Whereas Helena, very much the General's daughter, tells Gordon that "an Englishman's duty is to stand by England, whatever she is and whatever she does", he insists "Not for England will I do what I *know* to be wrong". "To carry the white man's burden into the black man's country for higher ends, than greed of wealth or lust of empire, he would die, if need be, a thousand deaths". This was the spirit of the real-life Gordon of Khartoum. Gordon Lord wants to be a link between East and West, while his father sees the situation in Egypt as one of conflict between them. The Consul-General is scornful of journalists and politicians at home who think that a free press can co-exist with foreign occupation. He despises religious milksops who suppose that all men are free and equal, and that great nations can be ruled according to the Sermon on the Mount. He wants to annex Egypt to the British crown.

An important sub-plot concerns the relations between the White Prophet and Helena. She is convinced that he has murdered her father and pretends to be one of his disciples, in order to betray him. He marries her to protect her from being molested in his camp but comes to regret the understanding that they will refrain from sex when he conceives a strong attraction for her. Her reaction shows all the prejudices of the period. "My skin was creeping, and I had a feeling which I had never known before – a feeling of repulsion – the feeling of the white woman about the black man. Ishmael is not black by any means, but I felt exactly as if he were". Nor does she hide her feelings – "Can't you see that you are hateful and odious to me – that you are a black man and I am a white woman?" She later apologises but does not heal his hurt. He had thought that where love is concerned "there was neither black nor white, neither race nor caste; but it seems I was wrong". Helena is only able to marry Gordon because the white prophet sacrifices his own interest by divorcing her. The Arab is as heroic as the Englishman.[6] However, Helena is no less the heroine because of her racist reaction to his advances. In Edwardian England she would not have been expected to feel differently.

A political row behind the scenes prevented the novel from being dramatised, as happened with several Caine novels. The actor manager Herbert Beerbohm Tree had agreed to direct and star, but hesitated when some of the civil servants in Egypt spread the idea that the book was seditious and gave an unfair impression of the country. Tree took Gilbert Parker to Egypt with him to find out for himself, and then withdrew from the project under the pressure exerted on him there. Bernard Shaw rallied to Caine's defence, but the second edition for which he wrote a preface never appeared, and the preface was published as a pamphlet.[7]

The White Prophet inspired a counterblast in the form of a novel, *The Tragedy of the Pyramids*. Its author was Douglas Sladen, a man of letters who was the first editor of *Who's Who*, among his other claims to fame. He was incensed by what he considered Caine's insults to the British army, beginning with a reference to Omdurman as an execution rather than a battle. It is true that an officer with a record of unlikely acts of gross insubordination could scarcely have ended up as commander of the British forces in Egypt, and other episodes in the book are equally improbable, However, Sladen's main objection is to the liberal position which Gordon Lord represents. Sladen shows how he thinks a British officer should behave when the Irish American millionaire of his story, who is plotting rebellion against British power in Egypt, offers Lord the hand of his daughter if he will in effect betray the trust of his superiors, and put love before country. He refuses immediately and with indignation. Even Sladen's Consul-General, who is portrayed as a deplorably weak liberal, behaves as an Englishman should, when his son is kidnapped and he refuses the kidnappers' demands. This character was a highly critical version of Sir Eldon Gorst, who had become Consul-General in Egypt two years earlier. In Sladen's view Gorst did not measure up to his famous predecessor Lord Cromer, on whom Caine had based *his* fictional Consul-General. Sladen thought that Caine had libelled Cromer, and wanted to show that only his policy of firmness towards Egyptian aspirations could succeed.

The two authors' different views on how Egypt should be ruled were based on their diametrically opposed attitudes towards the Egyptians. Caine's hero declares that "Ill usage may have made these people cowards in the old days, but proper treatment since has made them men, and there wasn't an Egyptian fellah on the field today who wouldn't have followed me into the jaws of death if I had told him to".[8] Sladen by contrast points out in his preface that he has made the leader of the anti-British conspiracy an Irish American because no Egyptian would be up to it, and the rebellion fails through the inadequacies of the rebels. The millionaire's daughter, although she begins by wanting independence for Egypt, "could not be blind to the unworthiness of the Egyptians. Each day brought some fresh proof of their rottenness, of their need to be saved from themselves by some strong, just people like the English".[9] Even her father ends up supporting British rule in Egypt.

A few years later Sladen published *The Curse of the Nile*, which describes in some detail the siege of Khartoum and Gordon's death, and keeps pace with historical events right up to the battle of Omdurman. The most interesting feature of this otherwise boring novel is the surprisingly sympathetic treatment of the Mahdi. Very many other writers contain brief references to the story in their fiction. They could always assume that their readers knew all about it. On the fiftieth anniversary of his death Gordon reappeared as the leading character in a novel, Marcus Maclaren's *Khartoum Tragedy*. Maclaren emphasises his stubborn idealism. "Administer the country for the people of the country", he says, "not for England and Europe. Native peoples have always been my friends". He complains that he gets on better with Eastern rulers than with the men in Whitehall, and declares that "We who profess to be a Christian country are worse than who we call coloured races". Criticisms of imperial orthodoxy are made by other characters too. The daughter of a War Office official remarks that her father "only works late when there is a little war on with the particular black people we last selected for slaughter and suppression". Lord Cromer is described as "the most efficient of all British public servants" but he is "thin-lipped, stony eyed". The author clearly sides with Gordon against his opponents, one of whom complains that the General "would never cast a tear for the British taxpayers or bond holders… but for these Arabs – for anybody whose skin isn't white".[10] In 1935, the future of Britain's relations with Egypt was a live issue, as was the drive towards independence for India. Against this background, Gordon's life rather than his death seemed particularly relevant.

The throes of Egyptian nationalism also feature in a novel of 1914, *Cairo* by Percy White, a teacher of English literature at Cairo University. When the hero Daniel Addington arrives in the Egyptian capital, he meets up with Abdul Sayed, a man he has known at Oxford. The literature of the period is full of assertive, sexually attractive and often sinister Arabs, who have acquainted themselves with British culture as undergraduates at Oxford – never Cambridge. It does not always do them much good. "'It's Sayed Bey', said Addington, 'an Oxford man, who talks English as well as you do.' 'Ah, that's what ruins 'em!' observed Mr Wright, re-echoing current opinion. 'They ought to be kept to the Koran.'" The author gives some support to this view because, as is the case with non-white characters in so many popular novels, "his culture was but a thin veneer that fell off in flakes, whenever shaken ... he was as ready to believe in witchcraft as to quote Huxley".

Sayed is intent on marrying Mrs Donne, an English widow whose free and easy ways are disapproved of by Cairo society, but who is not so cavalier as to consider marriage with an Arab. When she rejects him, the question is asked, "Under the pressure of a baffled passion, was he lapsing to an ancestral state of semi-savagery?" The reader is told that "thwarted love, when it rages in an Eastern bosom, is a more devastating passion than when it torments the better disciplined Western breast". In revenge the dastardly Sayed starts the false rumour that he got what he wanted without the need for a marriage ceremony. This is a particularly low blow as "if... her name were mixed up, even as a witness in such a case, might not the whole Empire be discredited?" The racial prejudices of Cairo are explored further through Andrew Kepple, a Greek, who despite anglicising his name and referring to himself as "a white man" and to the Arabs as "these Orientals", is nevertheless "barred as a complete bounder and sly Levantine". Once a character is labelled a Levantine in novels of this kind, it is clear that he is up to no good. "Levantines" and "Dagoes" were vague terms indicating people of Mediterranean origin of whom the speaker disapproved.* In view of all this, it seems a bit rich for the author of *Cairo* to complain of "the stupid racial prejudice that made the English unpopular, and drove leading Mohammedans, unbribed by office, to seek revenge in secret agitation".

Before his inevitable downfall, Sayed is allowed to express his nationalist views pretty forcefully: "You've given us police, dams, irrigation, drainage, and what you call justice. You repay yourselves for what you've done by wiping your boots on us". He points out that with the press gagged and the right of public meetings suppressed; there isn't much scope for constitutional agitation. He is the enemy of

---

* It is the attitude expressed in Agatha Christie's *Cards on the Table* of 1936. Whether the murder victim "was an Argentine, a Portuguese, or a Greek or some other nationality rightly despised by the insular Briton, nobody knew". He seemed to have relations in Syria. A Major says he would have enjoyed kicking him "because he was the sort of Dago who wanted kicking badly".[11]

"the domineering race who held his country in a velvet vice, concealing its purpose in a flattering pretence of teaching Egyptians the art of ruling". However, he eventually concludes that the anti-British conspiracy cannot succeed, and betrays it to the authorities. As a result the nationalists murder him. The political discussion continues until the final pages where Mervyn, an English radical, unpopular with his fellow expatriates, says, "We're capable of industrialising the whole world into a cinder-heap, and, if we gave the poor devils what we call a living wage…". However, the last word rests with Mrs Donne, who marries the hero, and asks rhetorically "Do you think any people did so much for the world as the English?"[12]

Although Percy White clearly supported British rule, he gave some weight to Arab discontent. He took Egyptian politics seriously. When the book was republished after the First World War he wrote a preface expressing disapproval of the direction they had taken since the strong hand of Lord Kitchener had been removed. Unfortunately, as in so many novels of the period, the plot is so extravagant, and many of the characters adhere so rigidly to romantic stereotypes, that the Egypt presented by the author fails to convince. However, one writer of the early twentieth century did succeed where White and others failed. The only extravagant thing about him was his name, Marmaduke Pickthall, which as Marmaduke Mohammed Pickthall, became even more extravagant when he converted to Islam.

By general consent, Pickthall's best work was *Said the Fisherman*, described by *The Times Literary Supplement* as "a novel of super excellence" and "a masterpiece".[13] First published in 1903, it had run to 14 editions just over 20 years later. The book chronicles the rise to wealth and subsequent fall of the eponymous hero, an Arab living in mid-nineteenth century Syria under the Ottoman Empire. There is a vivid account of the real-life Damascus riots of 1860, but the novel's chief virtue is its convincing presentation of events as seen from an Arab point of view. When Said enters the home of a Western missionary, he comes across "a picture of a girl, clad indecently after the manner of the Franks [Westerners] … he remembered that the Franks are but idolaters, who worship pictures and other forbidden things of their own making". Of the Western community he comments: "Here, by the mercy of the Sultan, the infidels are suffered to live apart under a chief of their own religion. It is their ancient privilege, and none grudged it them of old, when the dogs were meek and obedient to the law… But now that they grow fat and insolent, because of the Frankish consuls who pamper them, they are become loathsome as Jews in our sight". Said does not understand what he sees as Western prejudices about Arab customs – "Backshish is lord of all. A wise man does not fall out with the rich. It is the same the world over. They tell of countries where justice is for rich and poor alike; but that is all a lie!" Said has abandoned his wife to go on his travels, and the old beggar who adopts him says, "it seems to me thou didst well to get rid of her. What use, I ask, in keeping her since thou sayest she was barren". Dislike and disdain, where Christians are concerned is not disguised; after all, "they fall prostrate before pictures of women and sheep". Said becomes a rich merchant, but falls in love with a formerly Christian girl who decamps with her lover and his money. Then he hears of the great city of the English, and that their women are cold and difficult to men of their own race. "But they are warm and easy of access to foreigners, and especially to us sons of the Arab, whose blood is as fire in our veins, whose speech is impassioned poetry; so different from men of their nation, in whom the blood is a stagnant pool and the tongue a sluggard". This is such good news that Said travels to London, but when he gets there, sailors in a pub make him drunk and steal his money. What is more he falls into a huge culture gap – "He overtook the two women and walked at the young one's side, grinning into her face, and speaking words of love in Arabic. She shrank from him, pale with fright". Destitute he is sent home by charity workers and dies in Alexandria as it is being bombarded by the Royal Navy during the historic events of 1882.[14]

Pickthall's *The Children of the Nile* of 1908 also features the bombardment of Alexandria as well as General Wolseley's victory over Arabi Pasha at Tel-el-Kebir later the same year, both key events in the establishment of British control over Egypt. This is welcomed by an Indian doctor in the story: "Your Arabi Basha was no ruler, the land is left without a Government. By the Coran I am glad that the Inkliz – curse their religion – have devoured him quite". He says now that the English have won, the land will prosper. They are known to respect the rights of property. However, Arabi, who makes a brief personal appearance in the novel, is sympathetically treated. "The famous peasant-soldier was a tall, thick-set man, deliberate and something ponderous, but urbane and owner of a very pleasant smile". He speaks kindly to the hero who, like the other poor Arabs, thinks him "the noblest of all living men". This contrasts with the usual demonisation of Arabi by the British public and media. He was perhaps the first of a long line of Arab leaders to suffer this fate.

As with *Said the Fisherman*, the main virtue of *The Children of the Nile* is the ability to show events from an Arab viewpoint, rather than anything particularly interesting about the story. The hero believes that Western dominance in Egypt is being brought about because "The Franks, foul usurers, had persuaded the Khedive Ismail to contract huge debts – his slaves until they had him in their toils, and then his creditors". A sheikh deplores the Khedive's concession to the West in the matter of slavery – "To suppress the raids in the Sudan was one thing, but to interfere with our household arrangements is quite another. The Coran enjoins humanity towards slaves, and how can one be humane towards what is not?" A holy man hates Westerners, even though he acknowledges that the best are conscientious and well meaning. His complaint is against their civilization "which is a foe to all religion – theirs as well as ours. It extols the science of men's brains in place of God". Nor are Western marriage customs spared: "Imagine a betrothal lasting more than a year, with free intercourse between the parties! The men endure it, which shows how cold their blood is. And the women take advantage of their tameness and control them – artful there as here. A mad race!"[15]

Pickthall's main subject is the misunderstandings that arise between Arabs and British when they try to come to terms with one another. Even when the Arabs try to love the British, they are usually disillusioned in the end. The Arab peasants are always on the make, but their weakness and poverty make Pickthall sympathetic. In another novel *The Valley of the Kings*, the Arab Christians are pleased when a Christian mission arrives near them; it promises "escape from the repressive shadow of the Muslim", but they are soon repelled by "that cold priest, those bloodless women". The lack of passion in the British, as the Arabs see them, is a recurrent theme. Iskander, a young Arab, is anxious to be the friend of a sick Englishman who is in love with the female missionary nursing him. Iskander offers to make representations to her on the Englishman's behalf, and gets a beating as a result. It is not the beating which appals him but the refusal of his services. "Surely no man in love would question by what means he got his dear... Even in love – the fierce unreasoning passion of a youth for a maid – it seemed a Frank must differ from a son of the Arabs". Iskander and his friend lead the Englishman on a wild goose chase into the desert in search of gold, which does not exist. They half convince themselves of the reality of what began as an invention to impress him. The Englishman is understandably furious, but an Orthodox priest, an Arab, sees things differently: "The Franks will call thee sinful and a liar; but they, I think, have never known the youth which we experience – the warmth, the wonder and the dreams of it. The lad, who has been taught to read, or fed with stories, is dazzled by the vision of the world, its sovereignties, its wealth, and its strange encounters. He pictures himself a ruler or a lord of riches, and invents a store of marvels for his own delight; and that because he would admire himself, and cannot do so in the daily tasks and mean surroundings of his actual life". The trouble with the British, in this man's view, is that "they think all men should be on one pattern – the pattern of their wondrous selves, whom they esteem perfection. They suppose that what is good for their race must be good for all the others.... They know nothing of our beliefs and ways of thought, so call them wicked".[16]

The passionate friendship which Iskander offers the Englishman in *The Valley of the Kings*, and his subsequent disillusionment, are mirrored in Pickthall's short story *Between Ourselves*. Sir Charles, one of Egypt's rulers is approached by a young Egyptian who says, "At last I am permitted to be near to one of those noble and good men who have brought civilisation and all blessings to our poor dear Egypt". He is sincere. As Sir Charles, who tells the story points out, "We fail to make allowances for the capacity of young people of these sunstruck races for enthusiasm over anything or anybody". However the young man's passionate Anglophilia leads him to libel an Egyptian official, and he is duly punished. Determined to right what he sees as a great injustice, he travels to England where, despite having to live in a poor lodging in Bayswater, he calls himself "the representative of the Egyptian nation". In so doing, he falls foul of other Egyptians who are in London to plead their various causes, and they make sure that he gets nowhere. Love turns to hate, and he concludes that the British "had beguiled the Children of the Nile with talk of justice and civilisation into a bondage far more dreadful than the mere subjection to a foreign yoke, secretly undermining their religion and their nationality".[17]

Like Percy White, Pickthall deplored the development of Egyptian politics since the beginning of the First World War. However, whereas White thought British rule had been too lax, Pickthall was disillusioned for quite different reasons. He wrote in 1922, that "goodwill and geniality towards Eastern people could hardly flourish in the shadow of the Czardom which still lies over England's Eastern policy. May it be lifted and goodwill return".[18] Such was his sympathy for Arabs and Muslims generally – he was the first British Muslim to translate the Koran into English – it would be pleasant to record that he was entirely free of racism. However, he was first attracted to Islam through his love affair with the Turkish Empire, which of course ruled much of the Arab world until 1918.

Pickthall was so pro-Turkish that he was violently racist – towards Armenians.

Despite the sales of *Said the Fisherman*, Pickthall was more admired by the literati than by the general reader. His is a case apart from the reading public's taste for romantic stories about the Arab world. Norma Lorimer, sister of the distinguished Scottish architect Sir Robert Lorimer, wrote romantic novels but used them to make a serious attack on British racial attitudes towards the peoples of the Middle East. In *A Wife Out of Egypt* of 1913, the heroine is known as Stella in England, where she has been educated, but Hadassah in Cairo, where her family has its home. It is a family of Syrian Christians, and her lover Vernon Thorpe, whose Anglo-Saxon breeding is emphasised, only gradually realises that the woman he wants to marry will never be accepted by Cairo society. Not that he would have fallen in love with Stella, had her complexion been darker. "He belonged to the countless class of Englishmen who show all human beings who are not of the Western world that he scorns them". Stella has a dark skinned cousin, who is in love with her. He takes part in an assassination plot against Egypt's leading political figures, but withdraws when he learns that his rival Vernon would be blown up with the rest. This is very brave of him as his Moslem fellow conspirators distrust him for being a Christian, and one of them shoots him dead. Vernon assumes that the cousin entered the conspiracy in order to kill him, and even accuses Stella of being involved. "Don't lie to me, if your cursed race are capable of speaking the truth", he shouts. Stella breaks off the engagement and marries another Englishman who has no problem with her parentage. The Syrians are classed as "Levantines" rather than Arabs. "'Who are Levantines?' the girl asked. 'Speaking broadly we English, class the Greeks, Syrians, Maltese and Jews under the heading of Levantines'". Despite her stand against attitudes of racial superiority, Lorimer is not free of all the prejudices of pre-First World War Britain. The treatment of Stella is despicable only because she looks like a British girl. Making this point, the sympathetic older woman who is her mentor says, "Besides, Syrians are not a dark race. It is not as though coloured blood is to be feared". Vernon's sister, depicted as a virtuous character because she deplores his narrow-mindedness, tells Stella, "I hate the beastly stuck-up English people who can't see the difference there is between you, dearest, and all your clever family, and the ordinary common Levantines and natives whom both you and I abhor".[19]

Ten years later Lorimer returned to the theme in *The Shadow of Egypt*, in which, as was the vogue in the 1920s, there is a love affair

between an English woman and an Arab man. However, it is uncon-
summated because Lilian is faithful to her dull husband Harold. This
time, the Syrian – General Hassad – is not classed as a Levantine.
Early on Lilian finds it odd that he is "a *Syrian Arab* and proud of it
too". She soon appreciates his qualities, but Harold cannot believe
that his wife can be attracted by the General, "an awfully good chap,
of course, but he *was* a native. You couldn't get away from that". His
view of Egyptian nationalism is unequivocal: "Young Egypt and
Young India and Young anything else in the East, think only that
there will be more well-paid posts for natives when the British are
cleared out. They don't care a damn for their country's welfare".
Harold has brought Lilian to Egypt for her health, although he cannot really afford it, and when he finds a hoard of ancient treasure he
illegally keeps some items to pay expenses. The General saves him
from exposure to preserve Lilian's view of her husband as a man of
unflinching British integrity, and then saves the lives of both husband
and wife when they are endangered by a nationalist rising. In what
seems now a bizarre twist to the story, the General, a supporter of
British rule in Egypt, dies at the head of his Fascist fighters, who,
inspired by Mussolini's crushing of Italian communists, try to put
down the nationalists. However, when the book was written,
Mussolini had only just gained power, and, with his major crimes in
the future, was widely admired by people who later changed their
minds. It is more to the point that the General, who is a leader of
men and more intelligent, as well as more attractive than poor old
Harold, was taken for an Englishman during the novel's opening
scenes in London. This is why the prejudice against him is so
deplorable. His heroic behaviour leads Harold to apologise to his
dead body. The moral of the story is that, as the General has said, the
British abroad, in their attitude to other races, sell their country short.
It is not understood that "in spite of the cold manner of their children... Britain is the land of mercy and tolerance and justice".[20] It is
a fair point that the attitudes of the British to other races did their
own country harm. However, although Lorimer, in her attitude to
racial questions, was ahead of her time, she was also somewhat
behind ours.

CHAPTER 4:

French North Africa and the Lure of the Desert

"She rode over the hard dust-covered shadow-less roads, over the
weary sun-scorched monotonous country, over the land without
verdure, and without foliage, the land that has yet so weird a beauty,
so irresistible a fascination".[1]

Egypt was of course the centre of Britain's interest in the Arab world,
certainly from the 1880s, but the French had established themselves
in Algeria a half century before then. This enabled Europeans to visit
Algeria long before Egypt became a prime venue for rich tourists, and
even longer before Turkey's defeat in the First World War opened up
Arabia and Palestine. For this reason Algeria was the first setting for
desert romance and held its own when novelists eventually got to
know Egypt. The earliest best seller in which the Algerian desert
looms large, Ouida's *Under Two Flags*, dates from as far back as 1867.
Ouida shows little interest in the Arabs but her desert descriptions
point towards the future and towards works like William Le Queux's
Zoraida, published in 1895. The plot of this farrago is no more
comprehensible than that of *The Eye of Istar*, and, if the Arabs play a
greater part than they do in *Under Two Flags*, they are only the vehi-
cles for the ferocity and cruelty so beloved of melodrama. The
English narrator is fascinated by desert life, unchanged from ten centuries ago, "free and charming in its simplicity, yet with certain terrors
ever present". He declares that after three years in Algeria he has
learned to love the Arabs. Nevertheless, he meets some nasty examples, like the Grand Vizier whose "fierce brutal countenance,
hideously distorted by uncontrollable anger, broadened into a
fiendish grin". Then there is the robber band "who delighted in cruelty to their victims, and whose religious rites were practised amid
scenes of horror and bloodshed". Zoraida herself scarcely displays the
modesty associated with Arab women. She is dressed with her arms
bare to the shoulder, and when she receives the hero alone her jacket
is cut very low at the throat, exposing her white breast. With so much
on display it is surprising that she wears a veil, but she soon tears it
aside, and their lips meet in a passionate kiss. The hero witnesses
"scenes of relentless butchery... Men, women and children were
slaughtered out of the mere fiendish delight of the victors in causing
agony to their vanquished foe".[2] He is sold into slavery and has to
wipe the blood from the scimitar used to carry out a beheading. At
one point he is sent a severed hand. The publishers managed to find
a useful press quotation, laughably comparing *Zoraida* with Rider
Haggard's *King's Solomon's Mines* and *She*. Another puff claimed that
Le Queux showed "an insight into Eastern life which is obviously the

result of personal experience".[3] This, too, is hard to credit, although he had indeed travelled in North Africa.

Nearly 20 years later Le Queux published the *The Hand of Allah*, this time set in Egypt. It offers less bloodshed and a rather different mix of racism and melodrama. The latter ingredient is exemplified by exchanges between Marjorie, the English heroine and the Arab villain. "Taunt me, no longer, you fiend", she cries, and he tells her, "You are mine, remember, mine!" The villain, Amin Bey is, alas, another Oxford man. He has built up a fortune by swindling and embezzlement, and does not stop at murder. He has become so powerful in Egypt that the British wink at his shady dealings, unaware of his hatred for them. Worse, he has induced the heroine's late father to betroth her to him when she was a girl of twelve. For all his wickedness he is remarkably patient in allowing the situation to drag on for ten years, but until he commits suicide at the end of the book, this is the dark secret which prevents her from accepting the hero.

Marjorie asks Amin Bey, "How dare you come here to this hotel, and risk compromising me, you an Arab!" Nor is she alone in espousing the worst values of the time – the book first appeared in 1914. "There were men in that room, who knew Africa, who knew the Arab, and who hated the taint of black blood. To such men the sight of their own women introducing their daughters to that oily Egyptian sickened them, and they turned away in sheer disgust. They could have kicked him down the stairs". Egyptians are seen as belonging to Africa as much as to the Arab world. Amin Bey's "subtle African blood, bigoted by his religion, was aroused against the first Christian who had dared to defy him". Curiously, "the declaration that he was an Arab aroused his indignation. It was the worst insult that could be offered to that man who, despite his African blood, prided himself upon his English training and English education".[4] This attitude fits the worldview of the author rather than that of an anti-British Egyptian nationalist.

Le Queux's novels with an Arab setting form only a small part of his vast output. Once read, they were easily forgotten. It is hard to believe that they were ever taken seriously. The man who made a lasting mark on the public imagination and, in the wake of Ouida, established Algeria as the country of romance for early twentieth century readers was an exact contemporary of Le Queux's, Robert Hichens. His best-seller *The Garden of Allah* sold 800,000 copies from 1904 and was filmed three times. The heroine is 32-year-old Domini Enfilden, and "in the huge spaces of the Sahara her soul seemed to hear the footsteps of Freedom treading towards the south". Her

English mother ran off with a Hungarian musician, hence her dark gypsy good looks. She falls in love with and marries a mysterious Russian, but, when she finds out that he is a monk who has abandoned his monastery, she remembers that she is a good Catholic and persuades him to go back. He does not know that he has given her a child, which she has decided to bring up on her own.

Her relationship with the monk is less convincing than the liberation of her previously dormant emotions under the influence of the Arabs and the burning Algerian desert, "the garden of Allah". She "looked at the gentle Arab youth beside her, already twice married and twice divorced" and told herself that "these people, uncivilised or not, at least live, and I have been dead all my life". She learns how passionately a life can be led from the example of an Arab girl who stabs, then marries, then divorces her lover. In the desert she comes to realise that she wants "freedom, a wide horizon, the great winds, the great sun, the terrible spaces, the glowing shimmering radiance, the hot entrancing noons and blooming purple nights of Africa". (The nights were the same colour as Hichens' prose.) The freedom, which Domini associates with the desert, is of course freedom from the constraints of life in Britain, moral and physical, and this is one of the most influential aspects of the novel.[5]

To take one example of this influence, five years later Kathlyn Rhodes published *The Desert Dreamers*, in which, Richard, the hero, travels through the desert to a remote Egyptian village. "The scene was one of enchantment … moon-lit desert and palm-trees, a symphony in silver and blue which set the young man's quick sensitive blood racing through his veins with its suggestion of infinity and mystery". His blood is still racing when, learning that the friends he had come to meet are dead, he finds instead an attractive young Irish woman, Emer. They are the only Europeans in this corner of the desert, and their rides over the sands inflame her passion as much as his. After all, as the Edwardian author remarks, "We women as well as men are charged with passion; let the prudes and the ignorant deny it as they will". Despite all the efforts of these devout Christians to hold back, they fail. When they start for the nearest town where they can get married, she falls from her horse and is killed. Later in the novel he marries her sister, Diana, who finds out about the affair, and is convinced that he has seduced Emer. He protests that she had been as willing as he – "We were in Africa, in the heat of the warm desert, where the sun whips the blood into a flame, and the hot passionate nights excite one till sleep becomes an impossibility". She is not convinced, and he returns to Egypt to find Emer's diary, which will prove his point. This time he nearly dies in the desert, and curses "the great, haunted God-forsaken wilderness". However, by the time he has brought the diary home to his wife after many adventures, she has come to accept that it does not matter. "I too would have sinned", she says. She has come to accept the power, which the desert can exert over human emotions.[6] Its influence is as strong and wholly benign in Arthur Weigall's *Madeline of the Desert*. Madeline's husband tells her, "I'll take you away from the shams and insincerities of the existence you have known. You'll come with me into lands where no living man has trod, and where the air is pure of all taint; and we'll ride side by side over untouched ground in the splendid light of the sun, and we'll sleep together under the stars". Their marriage goes through a rocky period, but in the end they are reconciled when they return to the Sahara. "With him she rode out into the limitless desert and rested upon the soft, warm sand.... No longer should the cold rains of England drench her weary body, nor the biting gales freeze the very marrow in her bones".[7]

Another aspect of *The Garden of Allah*, repeated many times elsewhere, is the impression made by Islam on Hichens' devout Catholic, Domini. "'Allah! Allah! Allah!' Surely God must be near bending to such an everlasting cry. Never before, not even when the bell sounded and the Host was raised, had Domini felt the nearness of God to His world, the absolute certainty of a Creator listening to his creatures". When she comes upon men learning the Koran, she feels that "there was violence within these courts. Domini could imagine the worshippers springing up from their knees to tear to pieces an intruding dog of an unbeliever, and then sinking to their knees again while the blood trickled over the sun-dried pavement and the lifeless body lay there to rot and draw the flies". She admires what she sees despite her revulsion. "The tameness, the half-heartedness of Western prayer had no place here".[8] In Conan Doyle's *The Tragedy of the Korosko*, the kidnapped Western tourists have a similar reaction when they watch their captors at prayer. "It was with their backs to the sun and their faces to the central shrine of their religion that they prayed. And how they prayed, these fanatical Muslims".[9] In Caine's *The White Prophet*, Gordon Lord remarks that "No Christian nation nowadays believes in Christianity as these Moslems believe in Islam".[10] It is a paradox that pious Christians admired the fervour of worshippers whom they believed to be infidels.

Nearly a quarter of a century after *The Garden of Allah* was first published, a parody of desert romances, *Sheikh Bill*, appeared, in which the impressionable American girl exclaims that, like Domini, she wants the desert to take her. She wants to travel far beyond Biskra, "Mr Hichens's favourite pitch". A guide she meets, says of Biskra, in which much of *The Garden of Allah* takes place, "the great Monsieur 'Ichens make it the fashion of all the world". Claiming to have been Hichens' best friend, he says he practically wrote the novel for him.[11] When *The Garden of Allah* was dramatised, the vast stage at Drury Lane was admirably suited to mounting the desert scenes, but there was a drawback, as one critic noted: "The camels, the mules, the goats, the sand, the sandstorm, the apparatus of the East, are all so real that over against them the raptures and despair of the lovers seem almost artificial". In as far as the spectacle overwhelmed the charac-ters, the play was arguably a faithful reflection of the novel a third of which, it has been estimated, consisted of descriptions of the desert setting.[12]

Hichens' *Barbary Sheep* is also set in Algeria. The heroine Lady Kitty Wyverne is married to Sir Claude, whose nickname "Crumpet", far from having today's slang meaning, betrays his *lack* of sexual allure. She meets an Arab spahi, a cavalryman in service with the French, and sexual allure is his strong point. While Algeria's main attraction for Sir Claude is the opportunity to hunt Barbary sheep, "another hunting engrossed the Spahi, the sport that was the passion of his life, the consuming passion, as it is of the lives of so many Arabs". Lady Kitty is fair game, as after all, "the English were not like the Arabs. They let their women run loose. They let them talk and laugh with any man who came near". For her, he is a figure of romance, and she is captivated when he speaks "of the desert, of the strange life there, of the freedom, the adventure, the passion". He knows that she is attracted to him; he "read with the swift certainty of the Arab, always horrifyingly acute in summing up the character and flying thoughts of the European, all that was passing in her mind".

And yet she does not fall. We are told that "the love of money in an Arab is a passion of the heart, of the mind, of the whole being". In the final confrontation, his one hand takes hers but the other snatches at her diamonds. "The barbarian forced his way up into the light, splitting through the thin crust of civilised culture that had covered him". At that moment "her heart clamoured for the blessed protection of the commonplace which she had been rejecting, and the peculiar disgust which so many white-skinned people feel towards the dark races of the earth suddenly rose up in her, rose to the level of her husband's". The fact that this disgust is described with such detachment speaks for itself, and although the author clearly disapproves of the husband's more aggressive racism, he is not outraged by it. Arabs and black Africans were all the same to Sir Claude – "'blacks' or 'damned blacks'". As a result it does not occur to him that his wife could be attracted to an Arab. A Frenchwoman tells him never to let her have anything to do with one. "The Arab has a charm for women. I myself have felt it, I who speak to you. He calls and they come". To which Sir Claude replies, "My wife would as soon think of tryin' to fly as of havin' anything to do with one of these damned blacks. As a friend, I mean – as a guide, of course! What are you smilin' at?"[13] The crisis comes when Sir Claude, armed with a gun, comes across his wife and her would-be seducer. He cannot decide which of them to shoot, but a mad Arab hermit saves him from his dilemma by stabbing the seducer to death.

In *Bella Donna*, one of his greatest successes, Hichens switches the locale to Egypt, where Nigel Armine, an English aristocrat, comes with his wife, a louche gold digger, who has married him because she thinks he will succeed to wealth and a title. When she begins to lust after Mahmoud Baroudi, a powerful Egyptian millionaire, she proceeds to dose dull old Nigel's food with poison. In fact, Baroudi has Turkish and Greek blood as well as Egyptian, but he fits into the pattern of the many fictional Arabs who represent the lure of the East to susceptible Englishwomen.

Baroudi is virulently anti-British in politics, and he tells Mrs Armine that the Englishman despises as well as rules the Egyptians. "'He thinks us silly children. But sometimes we smile at him, though, of course, he never smiles at us, for fear a smile from him should make us think we are not so far below him. And then' – again he leaned forward, and his chair creaked in the darkness – 'there are some Englishwomen who like to see us smile, some who even smile with us behind the Englishman's back'". This is a more than usually open hint of what is touched on more obliquely in other novels – that the Arab antihero sees the sexual potency which makes him so attractive to Englishwomen as a compensation for his political impotence. Baroudi is "one of the many Egyptians who go mad over the women of Europe and of the New World, who go mad over their fairness of skin, their delicate colouring and shining hair". As for his attraction for Mrs Armine, it is possible for Hichens to be franker than usual as she is not a heroine but the kind of adventuress familiar from the melodramas of Oscar Wilde. "She felt cruelty in him, and it attracted her, it lured her, it responded to something in her nature which understood and respected cruelty, and which secretly despised gentleness. In his love he would be cruel... His eyes had told her that, had told it to her with insolence".[14]

In the end, however, when her attempts to poison her husband have been foiled by a Jewish doctor, she abandons their home and goes to Baroudi, who rejects her, leaving her all alone. When the novel was dramatised, one playgoer was particularly impressed by this scene. "On the left through a gate can be seen the desert, with the Nile and the dahabeeyah in the distance. She gives an agonising look at the house and very slowly goes through the gate out into the desert. I cannot tell you how dramatic it was".[15]

If Algeria was the land of romance, Morocco was the land of savagery, where the Sultan was a despot, and cruelty was the norm even after European control was formally established in 1912. Hall Caine opened a novel with this description of Morocco: "A land where government is oppression, wherein law is tyranny, wherein justice is bought and sold, wherein it is a terror to be rich and a danger to be poor, wherein man may still be the slave of man, and woman no more than a creature of lust – a reproach to Europe, a disgrace to the century, an outrage on humanity, a blight on religion!"[16] Caine was referring back to the Morocco of 1859, but, writing in 1891, he argued that nothing had changed, and this, in the main, was the Morocco presented to the novel-reading public. It was not, of course, incompatible with romance. According to A E W Mason, "nowhere in the world is there a land more vividly Eastern in spirit, its walled cities, its nomadic tribes, and its wide spaces".[17] Being "Eastern in spirit" also implied many of the negative qualities described by Caine.

Stories with a Moroccan setting were a speciality of the turn of the century novelist A J Dawson, another writer who had travelled in North Africa. His dislike of interracial sex and children of mixed race is even more obsessive than was the norm for the period. His *Bismillah* of 1898 is almost a tract on the subject. The villain, Richard Besanquin, is the son of an unknown Muslim and an Algerian Jew's widow. If the mother's origins are not entirely clear, she is certainly an unpleasant character, and we are told that in Besanquin himself "the Semitic strain preponderated". He was taken in by the heroine's broad-minded and tolerant father, and, of course, betrayed him. A subplot involves the love of a Moroccan boy, Salaam, for a beautiful Jewish girl. Although Morocco is described as a country which, according to "thoughtful foreign residents" contains "no really honourable and upright natives", Salaam appears to be an exception, especially when compared with the half caste. "The one, whatever its quality, was the blood of one race, one faith, one kind, undiluted, undefiled; the other was – that of Richard Antonio Besanquin". Besanquin's wicked designs on the heroine are eventually foiled with the help of a Swedish Baron. His high-handedness towards the Swede is described as "an unfortunate mistake that had its root in the man's blood". He gets off lightly, however, because "all the prehensile cunning, the facile intuitiveness which pertains to men of mixed blood" came to his aid.[18]

The city of Tangier had been the main centre of European settlement in Morocco for centuries, and its teeming and varied population symbolised the racial integration, which Dawson hated so much. "Here are all the vices, the diseases, and decadence, which are born of intermingled blood, and insistent disregard of the great fundamental laws of caste, race, colour and faith. Here may be seen in fullest working the process – none the less tragic because inevitable – by which men and women of a dozen races, relinquish, each their characteristic virtues, in their haste to acquire, each, the other's characteristic vices".[19]

Dawson also shared Hall Caine's view of Morocco's political system. Here too Tangier is the symbol; its famous Casbah is "that Bastille of Morocco, in which justice is unheard of, even as a pretence; where starvation, torture, filth and every form of corruption, rule paramount". In Dawson's short story *A Moorish Hero and Juanita*, the Casbah is "that curious abode of death, torture and filth, which is within gunshot, almost, of a British fortress". Dawson clearly wished that the guns of Gibraltar could destroy the Casbah and all of Tangier. As for Morocco itself, what it needed was European rule, "British for choice, as most Moors would tell you; particularly those among them who, with an eye for deductions, have visited Algiers and Egypt". Britain did not make way for the French in Morocco until a few years later.[20]

In Dawson's *Hidden Manna* the pious lessons taught to the heir of the great tribal leader known as the "Shareef" involve "racial exclusiveness, the aristocracy of pure Mohammedan breeding". Not surprisingly, then, good Muslims are said to hate Tangier, "one of the most racially corrupt cities on earth", as much as Dawson himself. From their point of view, it is "the Christian-ridden, where caste is forgotten of all, Babel is outdone, the Faith is befouled, and forbidden liquors and forbidden habits are a part of the daily life". The book is another polemic against inter-racial sex. At the centre of a curious plot is a wicked stepmother story in which the wicked stepmother is a Christian woman, married to the Shareef. She tries to make her own son his heir, supplanting his child of an earlier marriage. However, this young man of mixed race, is selfish and effete, a poor creature compared with the pure Arab. Of course the Shareef's marriage to a

Christian is unpopular with his followers, on both religious and racial grounds, but he is protected from criticism because they see him as a saint as well as a tribal leader. The strange figure working on the true heir's behalf is inhibited by his refusal to harm the wicked step-mother, as he is in Morocco as a penance for having seduced her years ago. This man who seeks to atone for the wickedness of his past life had a Spanish Jewish mother and a Christian Turk "of sorts" for a father. This makes him a half-caste and so irredeemable. Although he came to Morocco determined to do good, he dies feeling he has failed. The last lines of the book are "What a life was his! God save us all from mixed marriages, I say!"[21]

Twenty-five years later, in his thriller *The Man from Morocco* Edgar Wallace broadly endorsed Dawson's view of that country. The Casbah in Tangier is described as "a hell upon earth", and we are told that "murder isn't a serious crime in the Rifi Hills". Ralph, the villain, declares, "There is no law in Morocco: fix that in your mind". This encourages him to hire a Moroccan assassin, experienced in the use of knife and rope. Ralph's Moroccan wife has grown fat and ugly. "They go like that in Morocco. It is the dark of the harem, the absence of liberty and exercise. It is being treated like cattle, locked up in a hot-house atmosphere day and night, and exercised for half an hour a day under the eye of slaves". The heroine hates Ralph's Moroccan partner in crime "for the veneer of his civilization, his polite English, his ready smile". These are surely not his worst qualities, but the "native" was damned if he looked civilised, and damned if he did not.[22]

In Amy Gilmour's *The Lure of Islam* it is specifically Morocco which attracts the hero to the Islamic world, although, as it is described, the reader might not share his enthusiasm: "There was a sickening smell of drainless houses, camel dung and decaying fruit and vegetables, mingled with the smell of boiling oil in which many of the cloying sweetmeats of cocoanut, almond and honey were being fried in the open on primitive fireplaces. To deGray this was part of the fascinating life of Islam; the more than half Europeanised Egypt had no lure for him". Unfortunately he is also lured by the intoxica-tion induced by the kief pipe, which does him no good at all.

DeGray, an Earl's son falls in love with a young Moroccan girl, Zweema. He marries her and brings her to England, along with her maid. Zweema inherits her white skin from her English grand-mother, but she still has to endure the racism of deGray's sister-in-law, Lady Rupert, who is admittedly embittered by being crippled and unable to have the child she badly wants. Lady Rupert tells Zweema, "How I detest that horrid native of yours. Why don't you send her away and engage a maid who is white, not a nasty nigger". Despite having accused her of ensnaring deGray "by the artfulness of your race", she persuades her that she must not risk giving him a black child, and to do the right thing by him she must give him up. The Earl too, despite saying "I personally have known many good and great men of fine character who were Mahommedans", shrinks from the dread of colour. "Anything like colour would about finish me". The author distances herself from these sentiments, but she nevertheless, writes of "love greater than the Moorish girl could ever know – the deep, lasting love of the Northern woman, handed down to Zweema through her grandmother". After Zweema has fled back to Morocco for her husband's sake, he scours the country to find her. Having done so, he says, "You are greater a thousand times than all the lure of Islam".[23]

A big obstacle to taking the novel seriously, of course, is Zweema's light skin, which is a clear sign that the author plays with the issue of race without wanting to tackle it seriously. Popular fiction bred many Zweemas, characters who conveniently take their light skin colour from a grandparent, or even a remote ancestor. However, what virile Englishmen got up to with "native" girls was a less acute problem than the threat of the dark-skinned seducer to the chastity of the young Englishwoman. The reader may have noticed that in no example mentioned so far, did he get his wicked way. But what if she did not mind? This issue was raised for the first time, in 1919, in probably the most famous desert romance of all.

CHAPTER 5

The Sheikh and His Imitators

"She had fought until the unequal struggle had left her exhausted and
helpless in his arms, until her whole body was one agonised ache
from the brutal hands that forced her to compliance".[1]

Previous encounters between ardent Arabs and innocent English
heroines had never been as steamy as this. Now that nothing is too
explicit to be printed in a novel, it is hard to recapture the impact
made by Mrs E M Hull's *The Sheikh* when it was first published
in 1919. It exploited the familiar elements of the desert romances,
which had preceded it – the contrast between the simple life in
the desert and the murky compromises of civilization, the beauty of
the desert under the stars, and the exotic interest of a way of life
unknown to British novel readers. However, *The Sheikh* was read
voraciously by more readers than a desert romance had ever attracted
before, because it offered, as never before, the elements of sex and
sadism.

The beautiful Diana Mayo, slim and boyish in the taste of the
time, has insisted on riding into the Algerian desert beyond Biskra
without an escort. A free spirit, she has been scornful of women who
allow men to dominate them, but that is her fate when the Sheikh
captures her. "It was the handsomest and cruellest face she had ever
seen". His fierce, burning eyes "swept her until she felt that the boyish
clothes that covered her slender limbs were stripped from her, leaving
the beautiful white body bare under his passionate stare". The most
extraordinary aspect of the story is that the Sheikh repeatedly rapes
Diana. "She gave in suddenly, lying quiet in his arms. She had
touched the lowest depths of degradation; he could do nothing more
to her than he had done... Helpless, like a trapped wild thing, she lay
against him, panting, trembling, her wide eyes fixed on him, held
against her will". She asks when he will let her go. "When I am tired
of you", he replies.[2] Mrs Hull wrote this when her husband was away
during the First World War. He was, apparently, a dull pig-breeder
called Percy.[3] Millions of other women had also been lonely during
wartime, and, whatever the merits of their husbands, they eagerly
followed where Mrs Hull's imagination led them. If ever a book was
published at the right moment, this was it.

The Sheikh not only has a cruel face; he is cruel. He whips a
servant into pulp. His method of taming a horse is distressing. He is
brutally frank. "You didn't suppose you were the first, did you?" he
says. "She had never thought of that. In the purity of her mind it
had never occurred to her". His behaviour confirms all she has been
told about how Arabs treat women. Not surprisingly she hates him.

His only virtue in her eyes is his total lack of vanity. "He was as unconscious of himself as was the wild animal with which she compared him".

Diana tries to escape, riding desperately across the desert, but the Sheikh recaptures her. And as he bears her back, pressed closely to him on his horse, she realises for the first time that she loves him, "Her heart was given for all time to the fierce desert man… a lawless savage who had taken her to satisfy a passing fancy and who had treated her with merciless cruelty". Her brother would call him "a damned nigger", and a year ago "the thought that a native could even touch her had been revolting". Now she does not care. Anyone still taking the view that rape victims are really asking for it will be encouraged by this novel.

The Englishwoman's love of horses is of course a bond with the Arabs. However, Diana's determination to ride alone in the desert gets the better of her a second time and she is captured by another sheikh, very different from the man she now loves and who now loves her with an equal passion. "This was indeed the Arab of her imaginings, this gross, unwieldy figure … his swollen, ferocious face seamed and lined with every mark of vice, … bloodshot eyes with a look in them that it took all her resolution to sustain, a look of such bestial evilness that the horror of it bathed her in perspiration". He murders a woman, "his lips drawn back from his blackened teeth in an evil grin", and of course he tries to take Diana. "With a horrible loathing she felt his hand passing over her arm, her neck and down the soft curves of her slim young body".

Fortunately, *her* Sheikh arrives in the nick of time. There is a long-standing tribal hatred between the two desert leaders, but when he kills his rival with his bare hands, it is to save the woman he loves. "He choked him slowly to death, till the dying man's body arched and writhed in his last agony, till the blood burst from his nose and mouth, poring over the hands that held him like a vice". The sadism on her Sheikh's face is unmistakable. "It was a revelation of the real man with the thin layer of civilisation stripped from him, leaving only the primitive savage drunk with the lust of blood". However, there is a startling variation to this familiar theme.

This "primitive savage" turns out not to be an Arab. He is an Englishman, the son of an Earl. The Earl had abandoned the boy's mother, who fled into the desert and took refuge with the leader of a desert tribe. The latter took her in and adopted the son born soon afterwards as his heir. The Sheikh never knew his mother, who was Spanish, as it happens, but this does not seem to count. The son of an

English Earl is an Englishman. He adored the man he long believed to be his father, and inherited his position as tribal leader. Although educated in France and England, "it was the desert, not civilisation that called loudest to him". He is the least likely fictional descendant of an English noble house, except, possibly, for Tarzan. [4]

Diana, with whom he lives happily ever after, "could not think of him as an Englishman. The mere accident of his parentage was a factor that weighed nothing. He was and always would be an Arab of the wilderness". However, the fact remains that he is not an Arab. The only real Sheikh has turned out to be the horrible old man who gets murdered for trying to do precisely what the romantic hero gets away with. Readers prejudiced against inter-racial relationships could have it both ways. They could enjoy the thrill of the forbidden, but keep their prejudices intact after the Sheikh's true identity is revealed. Seven years later when the sequel, *Sons of the Sheikh*, was published, it even emerged that the Sheikh himself shared their views. He declares that, although Arab at heart, he is entirely against mixed marriages "and mixed entanglements for that matter". On the other hand, young women readers dreaming of desert romance, dreamt of being swept away by an Arab, not by an Englishman whom bizarre and unlikely circumstances had landed in the Sahara.

The sequel continues the rape theme into the next generation. The Sheikh has two sons; one brought up in England as a patriotic Englishman, and the other a child of the desert like his father. "There was the same great height and arrogant bearing, the same handsome face with its cruel mouth and piercing eyes... the Sheikh as he had been when she [Diana] had known him first". There is also the same propensity to take women by force. When his father reproaches him, he whispers with shaking lips, "how did *you* take the little mother?" He gets the answer, "God pity you if you ever experience the same regret and self-loathing that has been my punishment for twenty years". However, Diana herself, still slim and boyish-looking twenty years later, has a different view. "If he had not taken her as he had, if he had not forced her to a recognition of her womanhood, she would never have known the deep happiness that through him, had come to her in wifehood and motherhood". Diana has had sex with an Arab, but she has not; rape is a bad thing, but it is not. The moral issues are blurred and not allowed to get in the way of a good story. This is what made the book a triumphant success in its day, but is a factor in its lack of staying power since.[5]

The film starring Rudolph Valentino had a worldwide impact greater even than that of the novel. Although Valentino is rough in his lovemaking, there is no indication that the heroine is raped by him. However, the scene in which he rescues her from the real Arab rapist is faithfully reproduced. The Englishman prevents rape; the Arab tries to commit it. None of the Western cinema-goer's racial prejudices need be disturbed. Admittedly, the open sexuality of the film did not please everybody. In Nora K Strange's 1920s novel *Kenya Calling*, a woman says that only silly fools take the sheikh business seriously, but there are a lot of them. "They think it romantic, and all that sort of tosh. I was asked to go on the committee for censoring films in this country. They find me pretty thorough, I assure you".[6]

There are many such sneering references to both the film and the novel in the fiction of the 1920s. Hull's rivals had reason to be jealous of her print-run. P C Wren, who, as we shall see, had his own line in desert romance, portrays a cockney maid who has been bowled over by the book. "Oh Miss! I'd give anything in the world to be carried off by a Sheikh! They *are* such lovely men. I *adore* Sheikhs". She continues at length in this vein, and Wren comments that he almost wished the author "could herself have been carried off by one of the dirty, smelly desert-thieves, lousy, ruffianly and vile, who are much nearer the average 'Sheikh' of fact than are those of the false and vain imaginings of her fiction".[7] It is true that, when she wrote the book, Hull had never visited an Arab country. According to another jaundiced novelist, experienced travellers in the East will always tell you that "handsome and princely sheikhs never exist except in fiction, and that the genuine article is perfectly disgusting and primitive, eats with his fingers, etc, etc".[8] In lighter vein a music-hall song told the story of a girl who saw the film with her young man:

> "The girl in the [film] play, how she loved him,
> Though he knocked her about, and o' lor,
> My 'Arry he tries to make love like The Sheikh
> And that's why I'm feeling so sore".[9]

Alice M Williamson's *Sheikh Bill* was given over to satirising the story. A young American girl, addicted to the whole genre of desert romances, is bowled over by both the film and "the novel which had captured all flapperdom and spinsterhood!" She believes that men make fun of it all out of sheer jealousy, but English and American men are nothing to her now anyway. She drags her unfortunate father deep into the Algerian desert in search of an Arab sheikh who has featured in an American magazine article. "He would seize her in his arms, crushing her breath away, and kiss her with bruising kisses till she nearly fainted with love and pain". He turns out to be a timid, unheroic figure in horn-rimmed spectacles, who was a figure of fun in his student days – at Oxford, of course. Bill, a friend he met there, impersonates him and gets the girl, but by the end of the story she never wants to hear the word "sheikh" again.[10]

This is all good fun, the more so because the novel was taken so seriously by so many readers, mainly young and female. More than half a century later, one of them recalled, "We all saw ourselves in the role of Diana Mayo, we all longed to be abducted into the desert, and to be forced by sheer violence into obedience by an all-conquering male".[11] The writer of those words was another romantic novelist, Barbara Cartland, famous in her old age for her advocacy of chastity before marriage.

There are striking similarities between the Sheikh and Lawrence of Arabia. They burst upon the public in the same year. It was also in 1919 that the American journalist, Lowell Thomas, brought to London the illustrated lecture, which launched the Lawrence legend. If the Sheikh was pure fiction, the Lawrence propagated by Thomas was partly so. But both were Englishmen who wore Arab dress, were at home in the desert, were trusted by Arabs and led them into battle. Like the Sheikh, Lawrence could pass as an Arab, at a pinch, or at least as a man of the Middle East who spoke good Arabic. Even Lawrence's disinclination to sweep women off their feet was unknown at the time. He received 27 offers of marriage while in London in 1919, according to a newspaper reporting Thomas. Moreover, in his best-seller, *With Lawrence in Arabia*, Thomas extolled the romance of the desert and its bedouin warriors as enthusiastically as any popular novelist did. He also compared Lawrence with Gordon, as well as other English heroes, and threw in the Arabian Nights for good measure.[12] The debunking of T E Lawrence did not begin until the 1920s were over, and the story of his Arabian exploits made the desert a more romantic place for the British public.

Hull's other desert novels did not repeat the success of *The Sheikh*, or even its sequel, but the same themes occur. *The Shadow of the East* features another pair of Arab brothers, one Westernised and the other not. The English hero is in despair at the suicide of his Japanese mistress. Surprisingly, the Japan of the 1920s is far too Westernised for his taste, so he makes for the Algerian desert. He feels drawn to the brother who has rejected Western values, but this is because "here, too, was a man who for love of a woman sought death that he might escape a life of terrible memory".[13] Of course he does not find the death he seeks, despite risking his life recklessly in a battle between Arab tribes.

The hero of Hull's *The Desert Healer* is Gervase Carew, an Englishman who has also retreated to the desert to assuage his emotional pain, having divorced his unfaithful wife. He lives like an Arab, or, as one character puts it, "I don't mean that he's 'gone native' or anything horrid of that kind, he is *much* too dignified a figure. But … he wears Arab dress most of the time and would pass for a native anywhere". He is taken for an Arab by the heroine, when he comes to her rescue, and, although the misunderstanding is resolved, it reveals her feelings about Arabs. "And he was an Arab!… What did his nationality matter? It was the man himself who counted, the man who had shown her a nobler type than she had ever met". The heroine is married to a brutal husband, which contradicts the assumption that it is always the Muslims who treat their women badly. The hero hates him; this seems reasonable, but nowadays it is impossible to share his belief that, in so doing, he has succumbed "to the savagery and lawlessness of the people among whom he lived".[14] On the other hand, such thoughts are in line with the implication that in *The Sheikh*, the hero's brutality stems from his Arab upbringing and environment. A true Englishman does not behave that way. Therefore, in *The Desert Healer*, despite the hero's murderous thoughts, the killing which leaves the heroine free to marry him is carried out by an Arab.

No single book sold as many copies as *The Sheikh*, but the 1920s was the decade of the desert romance, most of the successful writers being women. *The Sheikh's* most remarkable single feature, its brutal treatment of sex was not particularly influential, although the book made it easier for novelists to contemplate the consummation of the relationship between the Arab man and the English woman. However, Hull's theme of a confusion of identity between English and Arab was repeated endlessly. It might come about through a European, usually an Englishman, impersonating an Arab, as in *The Sheikh*, or through the true birth of a character being hidden until the author chose to reveal it. One of the most popular examples of the former type of story was the musical *The Desert Song*. It was an American import, but, being set in the desert of French North Africa, did not seem like it. It ran for more than 400 performances at Drury Lane from April 1927, was revived several times in the West End, and never seemed to stop touring the provinces in the following decades. The main character is "the Red Shadow", the leader of a band of Arabs fighting French colonial rule, who turns out not to be an Arab but the son of the new French governor brought in to put down the rebellion.

Kathlyn Rhodes used the confusion of identity theme several years before *The Sheikh* was published. She was an established novelist before E M Hull, and had a much longer career; she was still writing desert romances after the outbreak of the Second World War. She must have influenced Hull, having herself fallen under the influence of Robert Hichens, whose early novels inspired her to go to Egypt in search of local colour. In Rhodes's *The Lure of the Desert*, which pre-dates *The Sheikh* by several years, Clive, who delights in the great desert spaces, marries Carol, and wants to take her to Egypt. However, she does not want to go – "You know, although I try to hide it, I can't bear coloured people". Nevertheless Clive gets his way when she is ordered to Egypt for her health, as many people were in those days. They are befriended by handsome, rich Mirza Bey, whose grandson, Ali, becomes Clive's best friend, and is the one Egyptian Carol can stand. Mirza Bey lures them to his palace in the desert, not to seduce Carol, but to tell Clive a story, of which the reader has already been given broad hints – "Just for a second Carol saw Clive as an Arab, wearing the burnous or some other native garment, and she was forced to admit unwillingly enough that his bronzed skin and slightly aquiline features would suit the alien attire". Later she is startled when "a tall native entered the room"; it is Clive in Eastern dress. The story Mirza Bey tells is that Clive's father "forgot that he was an Englishman and a gentleman and broke a woman's heart". He seduced Mirza Bey's married daughter, and returned to England. The daughter was murdered by her enraged husband, who then killed himself, but not before the birth of Clive.

Clive is not worried that he is illegitimate, and is pleased that Ali is his half-brother, but "the English blood in him revolted at the idea that he himself could claim only a mixed nationality". He is understandably concerned about Carol's reaction to the news of his Arab blood. The conflict between her love for her husband and her racism should have been the most interesting part of the book, but it is fudged. Clive also worries that "in him, it might reasonably be supposed, were to be found the worst, the least attractive traits of both nations". After all, "what is it they say of half-castes? The vices of both and the virtues of neither?" Given that he has behaved throughout the novel merely as an ordinary Englishman with a more than average enthusiasm for the Arab world, the deficiencies of this familiar theory could have been explored with advantage, but they are not. Instead we are given Carol's kidnapping and flogging at the hands of a black servant of Mirza Bey – "all her innate dread of Egypt, her atavistic hatred of the East and Eastern peoples justified at last".

Kathlyn Rhodes shies away from aspects of her story, which might have challenged popular prejudices in order to embark on a new episode, which seems to confirm them. Even Clive now has no regrets at leaving Egypt. "He shuddered at the remembrance of all the plotting, the intrigue, and the treachery, which had lurked behind the white walls of the magnificent palace".[15]

A decade later, in *Desert Lovers*, Rhodes returns to the same theme except that, instead of an Englishman who turns out to be half-Arab, she offers an Arab who turns out to be half English. He is Omar Bey – "so long had he mingled with English people, so kind and friendly had been the hands held out to him from his early schooldays, that the barrier of race seemed to him to be almost negligible". Nevertheless, he is still believed to be pure Arab when he asks to marry Sheila Raymond. Her uncle, Sir Henry, hesitates to give his permission, and discusses the problem with Kenyon Millward. Kenyon does not like the idea, although Omar is "a thoroughly good fellow". He points out that there would be "complications". "You mean there would be children?… Of course that does confuse the issue – the more so as one can't talk much to a girl beforehand on these matters". Omar seems an ideal prospective husband, except for the one big problem. "Sir Henry told himself that had this attractive and engaging young man been an Englishman, he would have given his dearly-loved niece to him without a qualm". Eventually, he overcomes his reservations, and agrees to the marriage. Then, however, it transpires that, like Clive's father in *The Lure of the Desert*, Sir Henry too forgot long ago about being an Englishman and a gentleman; Omar is his son. When he learns the truth, he withdraws his approval, not because his niece and Omar are cousins, but because of his own guilt.

There is a powerful reaction from Omar. "He told himself furiously that it was because of his illegitimacy, his mixed blood, that he was not considered fit to wed the English girl; and in the first transports of passion he cursed all English people, cursed the land which had given him of her best; and cried on Allah to witness that he had done with that perfidious race for ever". He rages furiously at Sheila, who is terrified. Her love for Omar had flowered when she saw him starring in a military tournament in the desert. She had been dazzled at his prowess in "the vast space of sand, gold and tawny … in the light of the setting sun". Now she sees him "dreadful in his rage, no longer the gentle, dreamy Omar, but an alien full of strange words and curses, his eyes flashing fire, his lips curled in a terrible sneer, his every gesture eloquent of the savage, beautiful, barbaric desert". Ironically, as soon as it is revealed that he has an English father, he seems to confirm all the familiar prejudices about Arab barbarism under the civilised veneer. Sheila decides that her love for this half-Arab had been shallow, and becomes engaged to the very English Kenyon Millward. The unfortunate Omar retreats to the oasis, where his beautiful garden had captivated Sheila. Kenyon casually dismisses him with the thought that he will "steep himself in the traditions of the land of his birth and ... forget the Western world which had brought him only a deep and abiding sorrow".[16] This is a flowery way of expressing a widespread view at the time, that it would be convenient if people of mixed race could be dumped in the desert and forgotten.

No writer exploited the desert setting more relentlessly than Kathlyn Rhodes. In *The City of Palms*, the heroine says, "I never dreamed the stars could be so brilliant. But the whole desert is a revelation for me. I didn't expect so much. I feel like the Queen of Sheba when she saw King Solomon's treasures".[17] Her counterpart in *The Relentless Desert* takes the title to heart at first, but then "the desert was no more a vast unfriendly waste, but a many-hued magic garden, in which glowing fruits, sweet-scented flowers grew in profusion for those who were courageous and cared to gather them".[18] In *A Daughter in the Desert*, "an undertaking which at home in quiet England would have seemed too good to be true, seemed out here to be merely in keeping with the setting of moonlit desert, of tufted palm trees, and the whole entrancing, ancient, intriguing land which is Egypt".[19] There is more of the same in such titles as *Desert Justice*, *Allah's Gift*, *The Will of Allah*, *Desert Nocturne* and *Under Desert Stars*.

Yet of all the women writers of desert romances, it was probably Joan Conquest who wrote the lushest prose. Conquest shot to fame in 1920, only a year after E M Hull had done. As Hull was known as the author of *The Sheikh*, she was always the author of *Desert Love*. Jill, the heroine of that story, falls in love with Hahmed, an immensely wealthy camel king from Southern Arabia. He has "a width of shoulder rarely found in an Arab", but also the familiar "aquiline nose, thick virile, hair, sharp pointed beard". As *The Sheikh* bore Diana Mayo to his desert encampment, so Hahmed carries off Jill. "He sprang towards her, and sweeping her into his arms, tore the covering from her breasts, until indeed like a lotus-bud she lay silent upon his heart... then he flung her upon the bed of cushions and stood above her with blazing eyes and dilated quivering nostrils". He tells her, he is "of the desert, O! my woman, of the sandstorm and the winds, the rocks and the heat". After they marry, they quarrel, but the quarrel ends when Jill "laid her arms in utter submission upon the man's breast, and sighed again in perfect content beneath the kisses which covered them, and her arms and breasts and her beautiful mouth... verily was her heart glad when she was carried into the inner chamber and passed into the keeping of her master for ever".

However, it seems at one point that it is not "for ever". Like Sheila in *Desert Lovers*, she tires of the desert; she longs for Cairo, and, in a stroke of bathos, eggs and bacon, presumably the most English and un-Arab dish she can think of. Hahmed follows her to Cairo, and flies into a jealous rage when he sees her with a young Englishman, with whom she has a merely platonic relationship. Jill cannot understand his jealousy. "The independence of Western womanhood had clashed with Eastern ideas on the seclusion and privacy of the gentler sex". This seems to be a major crisis, but she changes her mind again. Her passion, like his, is too strong for them to stay apart. Jill knows that back in the desert, she will not be allowed to escape again. Her life will be a limited one, but she does not care. "Silently she held out her hands with a little movement of utter submission, as a sound twixt a sob and a moan fell gently on the soft air". The story ends with her giving birth to a child on the desert sand, according, we are told, to the custom of his tribe.[20]

Desert Love spawned a sequel, taking the original story into the next generation, as Hull had done in *Sons of the Sheikh*. In both cases a son of the lovers of the first book has been educated in England. However, whereas Hull tells us nothing of any problem with racism which her character may have experienced there, Conquest's Hugh Carden Ali, eldest son of Hahmed and Sheila, has fallen in love with a beautiful Englishwoman who taunted him by asking, "Do you think that any white woman would marry you – a *half-caste*?" Seared by this experience, Hugh throws up Oxford and returns to Egypt.* He is "The Passionate Lover or The Hawk of Egypt" of the title, and, in contrast with *Desert Love*, this is not a book in which love conquers all. A mutual passion is born between Hugh and the heroine Damaris, who curiously is half Italian, but this does not seem to matter, and she is treated as English throughout the novel. She is clearly ripe for an Eastern adventure when she tells her father, " 'I've *got* to go to Egypt

---

* As few Arabs lived in Britain, serious treatment of their experience is rare. However, in 1937 a black author had his black protagonist meet an Arab student who hates his dark skin, and asks him "Where is the pride of your race... we poor negroes have been almost as much under your heel as that of the white man and you are if anything more cruel". The Arab agrees, but says "today is for the European – and we, you and I, live today".[21]

sometime or another, Dads. I've got to see the desert and the mosques and the whites and blues and oranges and camels', and she thumped her night gown above her heart".

Despite the strength of his passion, Hugh's experience in England has taught him that there are problems ahead. He tells her, "I am a half-caste. I am nearer white, truly, than my father, but – but my son, although he might be white or dark – a – a native as you say in England – would only be a half-caste lying on your white breast, if you were my wife". He can only offer Jill the life in the desert, which his father offered his mother. He knows that there would be no life for them together in English society. "Such a faint line, this one of racial distinction, yet which rises as a barrier higher than the Himalayas, deeper than the ocean and stronger than steel".

As it happens, Damaris has another admirer, Ben Kelham, who was at Harrow with Hugh Carden Ali. It seems that the stolid Englishman cannot compete with the romantic qualities which Hugh has inherited from his Arab father. However, when Ben follows the lovers into the desert, worried that the young Englishwoman is being compromised, the two friends confront each other, and Hugh sees in a flash how the triangular relationship must end – "By the sound of his friend's voice, the way he moved, the whole western look of him, Carden Ali had understood that the man born of the moors, the bracing climate, the cold skies, the snows and springs of England, was the true mate for beautiful English Damaris". And so it proves. When the two men are attacked by a lion, Hugh rushes forward to save Ben, who shoots at the lion, and kills Hugh by mistake. This gives Damaris the opportunity to realise that she had been only infatuated with the "hawk of the desert", and it is her lot to marry an Englishman.[22] Conquest has retreated from her position in *Desert Love*, where marriage between an Arab and an Englishwoman is allowed to be successful, although not, of course, in England.

Margaret Pedler also explores the theme of confused identity in *Desert Sand*. The heroine, Toni, meets the mysterious Ryan Strode, while she is staying on Dartmoor, which "gives one something of the same feeling of space and freedom, of being right away from modern civilization as one finds in an Eastern desert – although in a quite different way of course". They have a mutual interest in horses, which, in his case began in Egypt where he has been living. Although they are attracted to one another, and both are unmarried, he shies away for some reason. However, when she visits Egypt, Ryan follows her. He saves her from an Arab band intent on holding her to ransom, much to the annoyance of a member of the party who has his eye on Toni and does not like Ryan: "Probably he's more than half-Arab. These damned natives appear to regard him as a personal friend". He later apologises for this outburst, but it has revealed the truth. Ryan confesses, "I am half an Arab". He turns to Toni. "Now … *now* do you understand?" She is devastated. "She found that she had given her whole heart and love into the keeping of a man in whose veins ran Arab blood. Native blood. A violent sense of repulsion seized her… Every instinct that had been bred in her for generations recoiled at the bare idea".

Ryan recalls the moment when, at 17, he discovered he had an Arab mother. "He had been so proud of being English – boyishly proud. And now – why, he wasn't even a white man! He remembered how something had died – withered within him – at that moment". One of the worst aspects of the racism of this period is that is often shared by its victims. Ryan believes that, however well he behaves, he cannot compensate for his mixed blood. This view is echoed by the companion of Toni's aunt who asks, "Why didn't God make such a splendid man an Englishman?" Toni's father would have liked to have had Ryan as a son-in-law, but it is impossible. That no one guessed there was a problem is not the point. "His Eastern blood will predominate over the English strain in him. It always does". Another character remarks that "Race prejudice is a wall that has never yet been satisfactorily climbed or broken down". At this period, "Prejudice" was not always a word of condemnation, as it is now.

Eventually Toni's love for Ryan, overcomes her racism, which, however, does not entirely disappear. "I wish to God there was no Arab in you. But I love you so much … that if you were all Arab I should still want to be your wife". However, Ryan will not marry her. He is determined not to have children, and reminds Toni of their meeting with a drug-ridden beggar, half-French, and half-Arab. He does not want a child like that. With his assumption that the beggar's degradation must be a consequence of his mixed blood, Ryan is arguably the most racist of all the characters. His father, yet another earl's son had disappeared to Egypt, after being told by the earl, "Go to your damned niggers and stay there!" He did, and the aristocratic family does not know that they have a half-Arab for a potential heir. Ryan is determined that they never shall: "I can't foist native blood on the Chetwoods – leave a half-caste to carry on the name".[23] What the author presumably saw as an attitude of noble self-sacrifice on her hero's part will be seen by the modern reader as a product of snobbery as well as racism. However, he ends up with both the girl and the title, when it turns out that his mother was not an Arab after all. The usual cop-out gives Ryan a happiness, which, from today's perspective, he does not deserve, but many readers of the book when it first appeared in 1932 will have thought differently.

Saada, the heroine of *A Daughter of the Sand*, by Mrs Frances Everard, looks white and has converted to Christianity, but is obliged to tell her boyfriend that although her mother may have been European, her father is an Arab sheikh. She is aware of the problem this brings to their relationship: "We shall never be happy in England, Lance. An Englishman with a native wife is always the object of scorn". As it happens, Lance is in the Diplomatic Service, and is posted to Tunisia, where Saada joins him. She is disappointed by the Tunisians, and tells her father, "To me they appear indolent and dirty, with no desire in life but to sleep the hours away. The girls seem to live only for love-making and fine clothes; the men drink and smoke and gamble from sunrise to sunset". Her father admits that she is right. "Except for the better classes, there is little real work done".

The British community in Tunisia refuse to recognise Saada, and Lance is subjected to pressure to abandon his marriage plans. He resists, and she is happy in the knowledge that he is trying to overcome "the prejudice which most white men have for people of another race". However, he does wonder if after their marriage she will "lose her veneer of Western civilisation and become again one of her own people". He hesitates; "always pride of race had held him. To be regarded as an object of pity or derision … was it more than he could stand?" The greatest pressure is applied by a friend of his father, a general who has served in India. He has strong views about Arabs, whom he compares unfavourably not only with the British but to the yellow races. The latter are highly moral, witness Confucianism and Buddhism, whereas the Arabs are "a lascivious, sensual passion-loving people. It is in their blood". The general then launches into his theory of race: "Each individual is representative of the whole. That is why all whites hang together and array themselves against blacks, brown and yellow. We belong to a race which possesses, and always has done, an instinctive repulsion against the order of colour". He tells Lance that with a coloured wife he will be a broken man in six months.

Meanwhile, the Sheikh reveals to Saada that she is only his adopted daughter, and that both her parents were English. She does not tell Lance immediately; it will be a nice surprise for him after they are married. They duly are, despite his reservations, but as soon as the ceremony is over, and before she has a chance to give him the good news, a telegram arrives from his ambitious mother. He has just inherited a fortune and an ancestral home, where an Arab wife will be a grave embarrassment. He must back out of the wedding at all costs. It is too late for that, of course, but he nevertheless leaves immediately for England on a pretext, which Saada does not believe, because she has read the telegram. She is not surprised when he eventually writes to say that he is not coming back and the marriage is over. In fact, Lance, half regretting his decision, does return, but he perishes when his ship catches fire off the Tunisian coast. This leaves the way clear for Saada to marry another Englishman, who has saved her from being molested in a bazaar, and subsequently conquered his drug addiction for love of her. The belief that Saada is an Arab has never affected his love. As he puts it, "the man who really cares for a woman gives himself body and soul. He isn't affected by race, creed or colour".[24]

A Daughter of the Sand is a refreshing change in that the author herself does not share the racism of her characters. In Margaret Pedler's *Desert Sand*, the conventional device of mistaken identity is used to end the unhappiness which the hero and heroine have brought on themselves through their horror of Arab blood. In *A Daughter of the Sand*, however, the mistaken identity trick is used to test the would-be hero's love for the heroine. He fails the test, and the reader is pleased that she ends up with a better man. Ten years separated the publication of the two books, which is not to say that the literary world was becoming more enlightened. It is the earlier novel, which is more acceptable today.

Thora Stowell's *Strange Wheat* is another novel of the period, which has some merit. The heroine, Fay Lorraine, is madly in love with Abd el Hamid, a charismatic Egyptian political operator, who is half-French, which seems irrelevant, and Oxford-educated, which seems inevitable. "To her crude young judgment the Egyptian's facile love-making, with its sensuous hint of hidden depths she could not fathom, yet that mutely stirred her pulses, was the one golden love of her life". The dull Englishman, Peter, whom her family want her to marry, cannot compete. Her sister raises the usual objection of Hamid: "He's quite a decent youth, I admit, and has a topping backhand at tennis. But he's black for all that and your kids would be half-castes all right". She adds, "I expect he's quite a Sheiky sort of lover, while poor old Peter…". Stowell is brave enough to have Fay marry the Egyptian, despite the protests of her family, and to explore the real difficulties which the clash of cultures bring to the marriage. The action is set in a believable political context, a far cry from the fairy-tale desert world of *The Sheikh*. There is an ironic if inaccurate reference to the latter in an American woman's enthusiasm for "a perfectly wonderful book about a girl who married an Arab".

This marriage, however, suffers badly from the husband's involvement in an anti-British plot, especially as Fay's father, an important official, is wounded. He begins by being sympathetic to Egyptian nationalism, but eventually concludes, "You can't say a country like this is fit to rule itself when their only means of showing they disagree with you are to shoot you in the back". On the other hand Abd el Hamid, who had a brilliant career in England, became a nationalist plotter when he returned to Egypt and "met with the usual cold-hearted official friendliness that is all the Englishman extends to the educated Egyptian". More significantly Saad Zaghlul, the leading nationalist politician of the time, makes an appearance in the novel as "a tired-faced, kindly old man, suffering visibly from the ravages of the disease that was sapping his life, full of courage, ambition and hope". The book was published in 1925, when Britain had recognised Egyptian independence, but the action predates this.

Fay betrays the conspiracy to the authorities, but such is her love for her husband, that she does not do so lightly. They have a son, and Fay fights desperately to hold on to him, rather than give him over, as Abd el Hamid wishes, to his female relatives. She fails, as the law is on the husband's side, but she cannot hate him. "I can't help remembering how perfect he was to me – if he called to me, I'd go back even now". However, a doctor's view that "the children of mixed race are very delicate" is borne out in this case, as the little boy dies, partly due to neglect. Fay is pregnant again, but now husband and wife both see divorce as the only option. Their ideas of marriage diverge too far, and his political ambitions have become paramount, "It does not look good for one who wishes to stand for Parliament to have an infidel wife, or for one who is trying to oust the foreigner to possess a foreign woman". Fay goes to Italy to bring up her new baby, as life with a mixed race child would be made hell for her "in Watford or Ealing". When Abd el Hamid says goodbye to her for the last time, "Fay knew then that he loved her in spite of all he had done, under the crust of ambition and lies and lust and cruelty. Something good, something fine, all that still was decent in the man leapt up suddenly then and the memory of that would never leave her". The death of his son has made him reflect: "Allah has opened my eyes, Fay. I see that in taking the child from you I did wrong and I have been punished".[25]

Although Abd el Hamid hates the British, and treats his wife badly by Western standards, he is too complex to be a mere villain. Egyptian nationalism, while not endorsed, is not condemned either. The heroine's family and the young Englishman who wants to marry her are proved right in their belief that marriage with an Arab will fail, but there is no nonsense about inferior blood; cultural differences and politics as well as character play a part. The book is subtler than most of those considered here; perhaps as a consequence it sold less well.

The works of P C Wren have a pre-First World War flavour. His subject matter, the adventures of Anglo-Saxons in the French Foreign Legion, and his setting, the Algerian desert, derive from Ouida's *Under Two Flags*, although the American characters introduce a more modern element. The romance of the Algerian desert inspired Wren as much as it did his pre-1914 predecessors, but he overworked the vein, which he found so profitable, and the quality of the books declined. The first in the series *Beau Geste* evokes tales of "desert warfare, of Arab cruelties and chivalries, of hand-to-hand combats wherein swordsmen met swordsman on horseback as in days of old, of brave deeds, of veiled Touregs, veiled women, secret Moorish cities, oases, mirages, sand-storms and the wonders of Africa".[26] *Beau Geste* also has a feel of Mason's *The Four Feathers* of 20 years earlier in that in both novels a young Englishman has unjustly lost his reputation, and seeks to recover it by distinguishing himself in desert warfare.

It is the masculine feel of Wren's works which makes them stand out among the desert romances of the inter-war period. Most of his competitors were women, who put the love interest first and foremost and told their stories very much from a woman's point of view. Wren gives the greatest prominence to fighting, and, increasingly, to the masculine relationships between the legionnaires. The warfare is of course waged against the Arabs, which makes them the enemy, savage opponents in a conflict between East and West. However, due credit is given to their bravery, and there is a surprisingly sympathetic approach to their methods. When the Arabs stab a band of sleeping soldiers to death, an Irish legionnaire defends them against the indignation of his comrades. "Would a bunch of us dare walk into an Arab camp one night, odds a hundred to one, and bayonet twenty-nine of them and get away with it?" The narrator agrees: "If we could kill them in the light of day with our superior weapons – grenades, machine-guns, aeroplane bombs and high-explosive shells, why shouldn't they kill us by night with their inferior weapons?"

This is very modern, but Wren shares all the old prejudices against inter-racial marriage, which, in his view, must always be a failure. An Englishwoman, a nurse in the French army, marries an Arab farmer – "I fell in love with him. I used to be a great one for those Sheikh novels". She lives in a hovel, and is now terrified of her husband. Wren comments, "What an unthinkable life for a girl, even if she came from the poorest sort of English home... Her Sheikh! And yet I suppose she wasn't so much worse off than some of those English girls who marry young Indian students of the baser sort, in England, under the impression that they are as soulfully and romantically gentle as they look, and that they are the authentic Rajahs they profess to be".[27]

The old theme of confused identity also appears in Wren, but he uses it to comic effect. The Emir in *Beau Sabreur* appears to be a conventional leader of desert tribesmen, and is given to provocative remarks about Western values – "'The blessings of civilization!' he mused. 'Drink ... Disease ... Unrest ... Machine guns ... Has the civilization of the *Roumis* [Westerners] always proved such a blessing to the dark races who have come into contact with it?'". However, it emerges that this is all a game, and that the Emir and his vizier are American adventurers who appeared as Foreign Legionnaires in an earlier novel. It is not, after all, a romantic Arab who has swept the heroine and her maid away into the desert. The plot does not adhere to the usual convention, but is a satire on it.

The better novels of P C Wren continued to be popular after the Second World War, by which time the vogue of the more feminine desert romance was dead. It took a long time to die, however. Kathlyn Rhodes, its longest-lasting practitioner, published *A Daughter in the Desert* as late as 1940. By this time, the British position in Egypt was under threat, but the novel betrays no sign of this. There is a new theme, the war against drug dealers in Cairo, but many familiar elements remain in place from the fiction of earlier decades. The heroine asks whether a particular Arab can be trusted. "He won't carry me off to be the... er... wife of a handsome Sheikh, will he?" There are references to "the better class of natives". The hero sees that fellow diners at his hotel are "greasy Levantines, Greeks, Syrians". He does not like the way they look at the fair-haired girl. Foreigners' admiration for the English is grudging, but all the stronger for that. They are "a barbarous people, always they do as they choose, no one can stop them, turn them aside when they make up their minds. Every one knows it – kings, emperors, dictators – mad Englishman is a match for them all". Above all, "an undertaking which at home in quiet England would have seemed too good to be true, seemed out here to be merely in keeping with the setting of moonlit desert, of tufted palm trees, and the whole entrancing, ancient, intriguing land which is Egypt". This was the last throw of the desert romance. Riven by war, Egypt gave birth to a new kind of adventure story. The desert lovers gave way to the Desert Rats.[28]

1. *The Vengeance of Li-Sin* by Nigel Vane. One of many examples of the selling power of the sinister Chinese.

2. *The Yellow Danger* by MP Shiel, see page 14.

3. *The Yellow Claw* by Sax Rohmer, see page 23.

4. *Limehouse Nights* by Thomas Burke, see pages 25–7.

5. *Bella Donna* by Robert Hichens, see page 81.

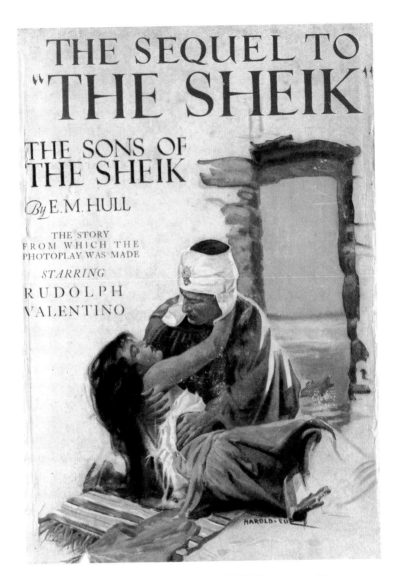

THE SEQUEL TO
"THE SHEIK"

THE SONS OF
THE SHEIK

By E.M. HULL

THE STORY
FROM WHICH THE
PHOTOPLAY WAS MADE

STARRING

RUDOLPH
VALENTINO

6. *The Sons of the Sheikh* by EM Hull, see page 90.

7. *The Passionate Lover* by Joan Conquest, see page 97.

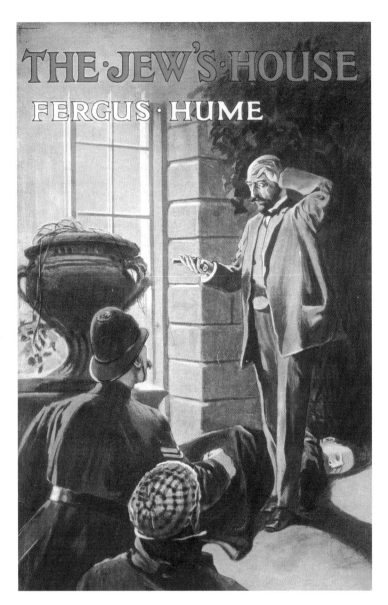

8. *The Jew's House* by Fergus Hume, see page 145.

"Britannia: I can no longer offer shelter to fugitives.
England is not a free country."

The Aliens Act at work.

9. The Alien Act of 1905 led to a decline from the highpoint
of Jewish immigration.

SPECIAL SUPPLEMENT TO "THE SPHERE"

OUR ALIEN IMMIGRANTS

How the New Alien Act Operates.

10. The Jewish immigrant who, unwittingly, made a big impact
on popular literature.

11. *Captain Kettle* [Adelphi Theatre programme, 1902]. Kettle's
racism was no detriment to his adventures being dramatised
or his appearing in advertisements. The proprietor of *Pearson's*
attributed the early success of his magazine to Kettle.
See pages 170–2.

12. *The Missing Mayor* by T Stanleyan King. A crude example of
the black man as a big, strong thug and henchman of criminals.

SANDERS OF THE RIVER

Edgar Wallace

PAUL ROBESON AND **LESLIE BANKS**
IN THE "LONDON FILM" PRODUCTION OF THE STORY.

1/- NET

13. *Sanders of the River* by Edgar Wallace. Paul Robeson dignified the film but his character was far from dignified in Wallace's original version. See pages 173–4.

The Jews

The ghetto and the traditional Jewish villain; Jewish pride of race and the impact of Zionism; how Jewish stereotypes were used by novelists; who were the antisemitic authors? How Jewish writers saw their own people.

CHAPTER 6:

Ghettoes and Stereotypes

"They are not pleasing to the eye, with their predatory noses and features which the word 'alien' describes with such peculiar felicity".[1]

The most famous Jewish character in English fiction – Shylock – was, of course, a villain. The second most famous Jewish character – Fagin – was a villain, too. And at the start of our period, a third Jewish villain – Svengali – was created, who was also imagined vividly enough to give a word to the language. Svengali is the fearsome musician whose hypnotic power makes a concert singer of Trilby, the eponymous heroine of George Du Maurier's 1894 novel, even though, without him, she cannot sing at all. Du Maurier was already famous as a cartoonist for *Punch*, where his depiction of Jews did not depart from traditional stereotypes.

Svengali is described as "of Jewish aspect, well featured, but sinister... His thick, heavy languid, lustreless black hair fell down behind his ears on to his shoulders, in that musician-like way that is so offensive to the normal Englishman". Du Maurier seems to suggest that what meets the disapproval of the "normal Englishman" is abnormal, and that this includes his Jewishness as well as the external qualities associated by the inartistic English with musicians. He goes on to refer to Jewishness in terms of "blood", "that strong, sturdy, irrepressible, indomitable, indelible blood which is of such priceless value in diluted homeopathic doses"; it is like that Spanish wine "which is not meant to be taken pure" but which sherry needs as an ingredient if it is to keep its flavour. "Fortunately for the world, and especially for ourselves, most of us have in our veins at least a minimum of that precious fluid, whether we know it or show it or not". This preference for "mixed blood" was highly unusual in its day, and welcome in itself, but Du Maurier loses the sympathy of the modern reader in suggesting that it is Svengali's "pure" Jewish blood, which makes him a bad man.

Svengali is also "very shabby and dirty", while the friend and pupil who posed for him was "a dirty, drabby little dolly-mop of a Jewess". In 1894, with Jewish immigration into the slums of the East End continuing apace, many Jews lived in unhygienic conditions. Readers would have had the East End in mind, even though *Trilby* is set in Paris. Svengali also sounds as bad as he looks. His French is "pronounced with a Hebrew-German accent, and uttered in his hoarse, rasping, nasal, throaty rook's caw, his big yellow teeth baring themselves in a mongrel canine snarl". Only to be endured for the sake of his music, he is "always ready to vex, frighten, bully or torment anybody or anything smaller or weaker than himself". His external characteristics therefore reflect his true character. Svengali is kind to

Trilby, an artist's model, but he has his designs on her. She says after his death that she "could never be fond of him in the way he wished – never! It made me sick even to think of!", although the question of whether she yielded when under his hypnotic spell is tactfully avoided. In any case, it is established that he is physically, morally and sexually repulsive – so much so that he is like the evil spirit of a fairy story rather than a real human being. At the end of the book even readers inclined to believe that hypnotism can make a great singer of a tone-deaf young woman, must acknowledge that *Trilby* is not a work of realism. The dying Trilby, whose voice has left her since Svengali's death, gazes at his photograph and launches into a last glorious rendering of Chopin's *Impromptu in A flat*.[2]

A year after the novel was published; *Trilby* reached the West End stage, where it was just as successful. Svengali was made more prominent in the play than he had been in the novel. The villain is usually the most interesting character, but the actor manager Herbert Beerbohm Tree ruthlessly expanded his own part, as actor managers were wont to do. He himself wrote a scene making a melodrama of Svengali's death, which had been mentioned only briefly in the book. He not only borrowed from Marlowe's *Dr Faustus* – "let me live, another year, another month, I will repent" – but, as he had done throughout, rammed home Svengali's Jewishness – "Oh God of Israel".[3] The critic William Archer wrote that Tree's conception of the part was "sheer untrammelled fantasy",[4] but his was the interpretation everyone remembered, although new productions continued to be staged for another three decades.

The role of Svengali also left its mark on Tree. When he played Fagin, *The Times* remarked, "After Svengali, of course, Mr Tree was sure to give us a wonderfully fantastic Fagin. Give him a monster to play and he is always happy, always at his best". And when Tree played Shylock, *The Times* said that he was "unable and perhaps unwilling to forget previous states of existence in which he was Svengali and Fagin".[5] As Tree played the three parts, they seem to have been remarkably alike – almost a composite Jewish monster.

The Jewish community in Britain at this time was divided between long-established families, mainly middle class and successful, and, since the early eighteen-eighties, poor immigrants from Russia and Poland who settled mostly in the East End of London, particularly Whitechapel. Svengali emerged against this background, as indeed did Tree's Shylock, who was a far cry from the dignified Jewish merchant created by Henry Irving a quarter of a century earlier. As few outsiders penetrated Whitechapel, it was possible to imagine it populated by Shylocks, Fagins and Svengalis. On the other hand, the exotic community which came into being there received a great deal of attention from journalists, and its most successful literary chronicler was Israel Zangwill, an assimilated Jew who, although unsparing of its faults and foibles, was a highly sympathetic observer.

Zangwill's masterpiece was *The Children of the Ghetto*, published in 1892. Its most interesting feature is that it makes the same criticisms of Jews that were made by unsympathetic Gentiles. Zangwill's criticisms are extremely frank, but frankness is tempered by affection. As Zangwill puts it, "Jews are very fond of telling stories against themselves ... but they tell them within closed doors, and resent them from outside. They chastise themselves because they love themselves, as members of the same family insult one another". He adds that, unlike outsiders, they understand the limitations of the criticisms. What is published in a novel can hardly be described as "behind closed doors", and when, in the second half of the book, Zangwill discussed the lives of longer-established Jews like him, "the grandchildren of the Ghetto", some took his criticism badly. The "children of the ghetto" themselves were not novel readers, and in many cases not readers of English at all.

In his description of these poor Jews, Zangwill refers to "the uncleanliness which was so generally next to godliness in the pious circles round them" and to the Ghetto itself as "where cleanliness, so far from being next to godliness, is nowhere in the vicinity".[6] One might compare these remarks with the account of the Jews of Austro-Hungary and Russia published in the same year by Joseph Pennell in *The Jews at Home*. He describes Hungarian Jews living in filth, and, while criticising the Russian authorities, adds that "no one who has seen the Jew in Russia can wonder that they want to get rid of a creature so dirty". Pennell claims to be neither a Jew hater nor a Jew lover, but his opening remarks do not entirely bear this out – "What may have made the Austro-Hungarian or Russian Jew the most contemptible specimen of humanity in Europe it is not my purpose to discuss ... what makes him loathed by people of every religion, and what makes him despised by his fellow religionists of the better class who live with him and know him, I have no intention of entering deeply into". It comes as no surprise when Pennell writes that although the individual Polish Jew may be a desirable citizen, "brought away in families and colonies, as the Austrian or Hungarian knows, he is as serious a demoralising factor in the community as the Chinaman and to be kept out at any cost". The title becomes loaded; *The Jews at Home* implies that he is an alien anywhere outside Eastern Europe.[7]

References to Jewish lack of hygiene in *The Children of the Ghetto* may have offended some Jews, but were less offensive from a sympathetic Jewish author than from a writer like Pennell. Zangwill's description of the divisions within the East End Jewish community are similarly bitter sweet: "Next to a Christian, a Dutch Jew stood lowest in the gradation of potential sons-in-law. Spanish Jews ... are a class apart, and look down on the later imported Ashkenazim, embracing both Poles and Dutchmen in their impartial contempt. But this does not prevent the Pole and the Dutchman from despising each other". But, Zangwill adds, there is a brotherhood between them, which makes it all bearable.[8] "Next to a Christian" is a reminder that Orthodox Jews were just as fiercely opposed to marriages with Christians, as any Christian could be to marriages with them. Indeed the narrow-mindedness of the devout is one of the themes of the novel. It is most movingly expressed in the story of Hannah who is prevented from marrying the man she loves because a friend has jokingly put a ring on her finger and recited the formal marriage speech. When the rabbi, her father, insists that this constitutes a marriage, divorce seems the obvious solution to the problem, but the friend is a Cohen, who, according to Orthodox belief, is a member of the priestly caste and may not divorce. The rabbi rules accordingly. Hannah arranges to elope with her beloved, but, when he calls for her, she realises that her roots in the Ghetto are too strong to escape. Zangwill is critical of the severity of the religious law, but deeply impressed by the fervour of its devotees. A few years later a reporter for *The Pall Mall Magazine* visited a great East End synagogue and wrote, "You may like a Jew or not ... but he is intolerant indeed who cannot yield a small tribute for such unbounded faith".[9] Religion, as practised by poor Jews and the emotional power of Judaism are closely linked in *The Children of the Ghetto*. Even Esther, who goes out into the wide world and becomes a successful author, experiences this emotional power when she returns. "The race instinct awoke to consciousness of itself. Dulled by contact with cultured Jews, transformed almost to repulsion by the spectacle of the coarsely prosperous, it leapt into life at the appeal of squalor and misery". *The Children of the Ghetto* was the first Anglo-Jewish bestseller and is a minor masterpiece because Zangwill not only conveys what he describes as the "tawdriness and witch-like ugliness" of the immigrant community, but also its "indefinable touch of romance and pathos".[10]

Popular fiction tended to show the Jews of Russia in a better light than Joseph Pennell's reportage. The Russian Czar was considered the greatest tyrant in Europe, a hate figure for British liberal opinion. Russian persecution, after all, had instigated the Jewish flight to Britain. In addition, the contemporary anarchist and nihilist attacks on the Czarist regime made for exciting stories, in fiction and on the stage. As the anarchist and nihilist revolutionaries included many Jews, a Jew was often presented sympathetically, and could even be a hero or heroine. Joseph Hatton's *By Order of the Czar* will have to represent this sub-genre of romantic fiction. Hatton accepts that Russian Jews live in squalor and that "in every village there is at least one rich Jew – a local Shylock – who lends money at usury... The child of a thousand years of ill-treatment, it is not to be expected that he will deal any more charitably with the Christian than the Christian deals with him". In taking Czarist persecution as his starting point, Hatton is sympathetic to the suffering Jews. After all, "what kind of miracle would it be that – in spite of persecution, stripes, murder, enforced penury and hunger, with debarred constitutional, social or any other rights, except now and then to see the light of heaven – should raise a people to the level of the masses of free countries, such as England and America?"

Anna, the Jewish protagonist of *By Order of the Czar* is beaten just short of death, and raped by a brutal Russian governor, who has her fiancé killed and her father sent to Siberia. She marries a noble anarchist sympathiser, inherits his fortune and turns up in England as a Countess. She has her persecutor assassinated in Venice, and, after rejecting the love of an English artist, finds happiness when she returns to Russia and is reunited with her father. Anna is beautiful, brave and entirely sympathetic, but the Jews do not escape criticism. "As a rule the Jew is good to his people, but in London the English Jew seems to take advantage of his foreign brother; the sweated and the sweater in the East End are mostly Jews". Anna "remembered the sufferings of her race" and did all she could to help the poor Jews, but "why England should allow these waifs and strays to be cast penniless upon her shores was one of the questions that puzzled Anna in her studies of English freedom". In more positive vein, a Jewish character states that, among European cities, "it is only in London where it may be said the Jew is equal to the Christian".[11] No contradiction was recognised between a desire to keep poor Jews out, which was shared by many well-established Jewish families, and pride that on the whole Jews were treated better than elsewhere.

One of the most popular authors of the first decades of the twentieth century had been born in Hungary. She wrote a novel about her native land which reflects its antisemitism, and in which the Jew conforms to the worst racial stereotype. Baroness Orczy published *Children of the People* in 1906, the year after she had shot to fame as the creator of *The Scarlet Pimpernel*. *Children of the People* features Rosenstein, a miserly Jewish moneylender, whose first appearance sets the tone for his character: "The next moment the Jew, with doubled spine and obsequious bow, entered humbly into the room. As the Countess sailed majestically past him, he tried to stoop still lower and to kiss the hem of her gown". He is equally obsequious to her husband, Count Bideskuty: "He rubbed his thin, claw-like hands incessantly together, and his watery blue eyes were fixed on the floor, all the time the noble lord deigned to converse with him. Only from time to time, when he thought himself unobserved, he threw a sharp malignant look at the Hungarian, then his thin lips almost disappeared between his teeth, and there was that, in his colourless eyes, which would have taught a shrewd man to beware".

Rosenheim acts as intermediary between the Count and a rich peasant money-lender. He prepares two documents for each loan, so that neither party knows that he has added an exorbitant rate of interest for himself. Arguably, the Count deserves to be cheated. He treats Rosenheim with contempt, and his idea of fun is to take him to the castle kitchen and make him eat pork in front of the servants, who enjoy watching him squirm. One chapter in the book is called 'Pride of Race', and, although this phrase, so common at the time, usually referred to the English or the Jews, the pride here is that of the Hungarian nobility. "Tall and powerful, with proud-looking eyes and noble bearing, Bideskuty stood as the very personification of the race, which for centuries had buffeted, tormented, oppressed the Jews, denying them every human right".

However, Rosenheim also cheats the virtuous young peasant. "His deceit, his astuteness had profited him, beyond the dreams of avarice; never for a moment did remorse enter his grasping soul at the hideous way in which he was deceiving an honourable man. The Jew in Eastern Europe stands at war with the rest of the population; beaten, buffeted, derided, often injured, his only weapon is his money; with it, he gets revenge on peer and peasant … the hideous advantage he was taking of the peasant's sense of justice was not aimed at the individual, it was race against race". This contrasts with the very personal act of revenge that the heroine of *By Order of the Czar* commits against the man who has wronged her so grievously. Rosenheim, who has no friends or relations, does, it is true, bequeath the peasant money, but in all other respects he is like Tree's version of Shylock. The novel is likely to have confirmed any prejudice the reader may have held against Jews, although the Hungarian aristocracy come out of it badly, too.[12]

South Africa was another part of the world which featured largely in early twentieth century fiction, and in which dislike of Jews was common. The Boer War had harmed the reputation of Jews in Britain owing to the widespread belief that it had been stirred up by Jewish financiers on the Rand, anxious to protect their profits. Even before that war, Jewish fences were alleged to be heavily involved in I. D. B. or illicit diamond buying. In fiction, they were descendants of Fagin. A short story in *Pearson's Magazine* featured one such, although his appearance belongs to a different stereotype – "his fleshy, pendant under-lip trembled every now and then with the movement of his heavy jaw, and his fat, lavishly jewelled fingers kept alternately drumming on the dirty table and wandering through his black and rather greasy locks".[13] Recourse to the long established tradition that wicked people are ugly gives the stereotype villain two sets of undesirable characteristics, physical and moral. In *A Mistaken Marriage*, one of many novels set in South Africa by F E Mills Young, a Jew who seems to be implicated in I. D. B. and to lack any redeeming quality, lusts after the heroine throughout the book in the most open and disgusting way. His was "the ugliest smile she had ever seen distort a human face". The other wicked person in the story, the mistress of the heroine's husband, is "very striking in appearance – dark and of a pronouncedly Jewish type".[14] The popular writer of detective stories, Freeman Wills Croft, featured a Jewish trader in illegal diamonds in *The Grote Park Murder* of 1924. "Moses Goldstein was dark and oily of countenance, with semitic features and a pair of furtive, shifty eyes. He greeted his visitor obsequiously".[15] At least he was not the murderer.

The fiction of the period also reflected the widespread dislike of Jews in the Arab world. A J. Dawson went further by adding his own prejudice. In *Hidden Manna*, Jews are "greasy and gaberdined, hovering ever betwixt spittle-licking and tyrannical oppression".[16] In one of Dawson's short stories, an 18-year-old Arab is in prison for debt, most of which was "pure usury" owed to a Jew. The narrator turns aside from "the greasy Israelite", "from very loathing of him and of his works". The Jew "scraped and bowed his evil head, as his like in Barbary have been doing these many years, and doing to great profit".[17] In another story, Dawson remarks that "as schools of villainy begat by persecution and cruelty, out of avarice, servility, and immorality, the Barbary Ghettoes are probably unique. They supply Northern Africa and the Levant, and the most virile and prospering of their spawn eventually reach the capital cities of Europe, there to die at the last of it in the odour of sanctity and solid wealth". The Jew of the story is described, accordingly, as "the vilest mortal, I believe that ever came my way".[18] It is noteworthy that the most antisemitic passages are found in works by authors, like Dawson, who have other hang-ups about race. Douglas Sladen, who wrote so harshly of the Egyptians in *The Tragedy of the Pyramids*, created an unsympathetic Jewish couple in the same novel. On the other hand, Hall Caine, so sympathetic to Egyptian nationalist aspirations, hated antisemitism, was converted to Zionism by Israel Zangwill, and wrote a novel in which a Jew is 'The Scapegoat' of the title.

The virulence of an A J Dawson is rare, and it is hard to find a novel set in Britain centring on an evil Jew. John A Steuart's *The Hebrew* is such a book, however. It was published in 1903, the year when there was stone throwing, looting and serious injury in a riot at "Jew's Island" in Bethnal Green, and when the flow of Jewish immigrants into the East End of London was at its high point. Steuart's Israel Herstein is a slum landlord who is ruthless towards his tenants. When one of them hangs himself, Herstein is indignant that he has not paid his debt first. Jewish slum landlords have existed, of course – Peter Rachman became a national hate figure as late as the1960s. However, the problem is that Steuart identifies all Herstein's evil qualities with his Jewishness: "His eyes glowed, the craftiness of his face deepened; the immemorial expression of his race, older than Jacob's deception, overspread his countenance" and, again: he gave "a knowing Hebrew smile ... mantling and curling about that hard mouth and the crooked nose, that wonderful nose...". The law is on the landlord's side against the tenants, and Herstein declares "I stand by the law. It was not made for me. It was made by Englishmen for Englishmen... Let them remember that, and let them abide by it as I do". There is an echo of Shylock's "I stand here for law" in the trial scene of *The Merchant of Venice*. Herstein himself is well aware of Shylock, who, in his view, was a fool to endanger his own interests by seeking revenge. "He was no son of Abraham to do that". Herstein also resembles Shylock in having a virtuous daughter for "despite the inflexible laws of heredity, Rachel Herstein has the right sort of heart". One of the most long-lasting legacies of *The Merchant of Venice* was that so many authors since have given the wicked Jew a virtuous and beautiful daughter. Few novels were as unpleasant as *The Hebrew*, but it provoked little indignation. It is an anachronism to expect indignation at this period. *The Times Literary Supplement*, in its brief summary, did not raise the question of antisemitism, merely informing its readers that the novel was about "the overcrowded slums".[20]

In 1905, the flow of Jewish immigrants into Britain was slowed by an Aliens Act. The intense public debate which preceded the passing of the Act was carried on in terms of immigrants and not of Jews specifically. Everyone knew that most of the immigrants causing concern were Jews, but it is worth emphasising that antisemitism in Britain was more disreputable than in most continental countries. On the other hand, antisemitism, or indeed racism in general, was no bar to popularity. The racism of Cutcliffe Hyne's popular Captain Kettle stories relates mainly to black people, but in *Further Adventures of Captain Kettle*, the eponymous hero describes the passengers he takes on board from a wrecked emigrant ship as "Austrians, Bohemians, wild Poles, filthy, crawling Russian Jews, bestial Armenians, human *debris* which even soldier-coveting Middle Europe rejected". When Kettle is sacked by a Jewish ship-owner, he calls him a "knock-kneed little Jew".[21]

It is also true that during these years when Jewish immigration was at its height some remarkable fantasies about Jews found their way into print. M P Shiel's novel *Lord of the Sea*, published in 1901 imagines a Europe of the future in which most Prague Jews have been massacred, and Jews have been expelled from France, Russia and Austria, in the last case because "the Jews had acquired one half of the land of the Empire, and had mortgages on the other half". These Jews have come to Britain in huge numbers. "There was no time now for prohibitive law-making; before the nation could gather its wits, the wave had overflowed it". The press has failed to sound the alarm, because nearly every newspaper is owned by or in the pay of Jews. Jewish influence has become so powerful in politics that the old labels of Liberal and Conservative have been replaced by Jewish and anti-Jewish, the Liberals mainly belonging to the former party and the Tories to the latter.

The reader soon learns that the protagonist of the book, Richard Hogarth, is Jewish. He himself does not know this, and says that if he were King of England, he would send all the Jews packing. He concedes that "the Jews have been the noblest people that ever breathed", but that was in the past. "They are shepherds doing money-lending, and not doing it with that natural grace which natural products have. That they do it successfully is a proof of their immense racial worth. But they have got spoiled by Europe and they have spoiled Europe".

There is a stock Jewish villain, who, in the Shylock tradition, has a beautiful and virtuous daughter, with whom Hogarth is in love. Through the villain's machinations, Hogarth is sentenced to life imprisonment for a murder he did not commit, but escapes, and becomes immensely rich when he finds a meteorite encrusted with diamonds. He adds to his wealth through his financial acumen, a product, it is implied, of his Jewish heritage, and then builds a number of huge, heavily armed and impregnable island fortress ships. Strategically positioned in the world's main seaways, they enable him to levy tolls on the shipping of every nation, and become the all-powerful Lord of the Sea.

Hogarth also becomes the de facto ruler of Britain and the Empire. He is now able to carry out his plan of expelling all the Jews. They are packed off to Palestine and "that vast hinterland of Palestine called Turkish Armenia" which somehow gets confused with Mesopotamia or modern Iraq. The population of the region is airily dismissed – "the whole was an uninhabited land, as it were reserved, ordained, and waiting for inhabitants". However, the Jewish villain, with the help of a renegade Catholic priest, engineers Hogarth's fall from power, at about the same time that he learns that he is really a Jew called Raphael Spinoza. He moves to the Middle East, and becomes the ruler of the new Jewish state, the first civilised state in history. Jewish scientists make great discoveries there; "within forty years mighty works had been done: ports, irrigation of deserts, resurrection of the Dead Sea"; Corinthian cities arise in "that charming land of Mesopotamia"; "Jerusalem had become the recognised Academy for the wealthy youth of Europe, Asia and America".

The novel is prescient in foreshadowing actual developments of the twentieth century – the virtual elimination of Jews from Central Europe, the founding of the state of Israel. It is also a product of its time. Ridding Britain of its Jews was doubtless the realisation of a dream for those obsessed with the immigration issue, and for those who disliked Jews playing a prominent part in British life. However, the ending of the book reflects another strand of thinking – admiration for the achievements of Jewish intelligence, and even for traditional Jewish moral values. The Jewish state is a success because "in the Jewish race – the fibre of its soul – was an innate genius for Righteousness". The stock Jewish villain is balanced by the Jewish Raphael Spinoza. He has used his power as Lord of the Sea to try to establish a sort of world socialism and international government, before eventually becoming the benign ruler of a Jewish state, which is to be a model for the world. The fantasy has much to offer pro- and antisemites alike. [22]

Three years later Violet Guttenberg in *A Modern Exodus* also conjured up a future in which the Jews are expelled from Britain. The requisite act of parliament is driven through the Commons by an antisemitic prime minister. It has features in common with the early Nazi decrees. No Jew is to own property, be a money-lender or have a position in public life. Unlike the Nazi decrees, however, the Act allows the Jews to assimilate as an alternative to emigration. A Jew may obtain a Certificate of Assimilation by renouncing his religion, mixing freely and abandoning the reading and writing of Hebrew. Jews must marry only Gentiles and bring their children up in the Gentile's faith. The passing of the Act is helped by two events – the collapse of a company, in which the small investors lose their money, but the Jewish directors do not, and an unemployment march in which the slogan "boycott foreign Jews" features prominently.

The Jewish author makes a number of accurate observations in the telling of her tale. She points out that by and large "the number of faithful Jews increased as one descended the social scale", and she highlights the lack of concern among some affluent Jews for the plight of their poorer brethren. One of them asks whether the new prime minister "may direct his spite against the upper and middle classes of Jewish society as well as the sweaters and aliens of the East End". The hero is Lionel Montella, descendant of a well-established Jewish family, and a Member of Parliament, who of course has to give up his seat. He marries an English aristocrat, Lady Patricia, and, like the 'Lord of the Sea', makes for Palestine. Many Jews from England do the same – "they were very aristocratic, these exiled English Jews. Like many English people who travel abroad, they considered themselves vastly superior to all the foreigners with whom they came into contact".

Lionel becomes Governor of Haifa, but the Chief Rabbi hates his free-thinking liberalism, and demands that he divorce Lady Patricia, who, having tried and failed to take to Judaism, has been seen going into the Anglican cathedral. She returns to England three years after leaving it, and finds that without its Jews, the country is in a parlous economic state. The prime minister has aged and become depressed, because he knows he made a disastrous decision. When his daughter contracts diphtheria, he finds that the most eminent specialist, being Jewish, has left the country. When Lady Patricia nurses her back to health, he has the Act against the Jews repealed and declares antisemitism dead. It is a savage and retrograde movement, incompatible with Christianity and "our advanced state of civilisation". Shylock's speech in which he asks, "Hath not a Jew eyes…" now adorns a wall of his house. When Lionel, too, returns to England, because the Chief Rabbi has established strict religious orthodoxy throughout Palestine, he and the prime minister become friends.[23]

In M P Shiel's fantasy, the expulsion of the Jews is seen as beneficial. It does not harm Britain, and the Jews themselves flourish in the Middle East. For Violet Guttenberg, however, it wrecks the British economy, and Jewish society in the Middle East is oppressive to any but the strictly Orthodox. Her story is designed to justify the standpoint set out in her short preface: "It is a matter of congratulation and deep thankfulness to both Jew and Gentile that the attitude of our country towards her Jewish subjects is that of justice, toleration and friendliness. At the same time, the poisonous seeds of anti-semitism are so subtle and so easily instilled, that a warning – even in the form of fiction – may not be out of place".

William Le Queux's vision of the future in *The Unknown Tomorrow* was mainly designed to denigrate socialists but Jews do not escape his lash either. The story is set in 1935, a quarter of a century into the future, when there are great demonstrations of starving people, "men from whose mouths the Jewish greaser has taken the bread". British power has drained away, the turning point, Le Queux asserts, being Lloyd George's budget of 1909, the year before the book's publication. It is now seen as a pioneering landmark of British history, but reactionaries like Le Queux hated it. He describes a revolution, brought about by the socialists, which is bloodier than the French revolution. The Home Secretary is strung up on a lamppost and the British Museum is burned down. The wife of the protagonist of the story, the socialist leader Henry Harland, "with that baseless prejudice which so often possesses a woman, was fond of declaring that the downfall of England had been due to the Jews". Some are friends of hers, of course. Henry thinks she is a bit hard on the Jews, but "in his heart he knew that there was much common sense in what she said". Many agree. After a mass meeting in Whitechapel, thousands of immigrant Jews, both men and women, are massacred "in those dark evil-smelling East End streets which the alien Jew had transformed into a quarter of his own, while many honest English men and women, being mistaken for Hebrews by the mob, were ruthlessly put to death". Rich Jews in other parts of London are also murdered. Harland has lost control of the revolution to an extremist demagogue. He is powerless to stop the bloodshed and ends a broken man when socialism is seen to be a failure, and the old government returns. The catastrophe that falls on the Jews is described with relish, but the book's antisemitism is only one aspect of a world view which was reactionary in every respect. [24]

Le Queux was a best selling author, but no single book of his approached the sales of Guy Thorne's *When It Was Dark* in which a

Jewish millionaire M. P. tries to destroy Christianity. The story begins
in a Lancashire town, where rich Jews have given up their faith. "It
was people of this class who supported the magnificent concerts in
the Free Trade Hall at Manchester, who bought the pictures and read
the books". However, they get little credit for this. "They had brought
an alien culture to the neighbourhood... In their luxurious houses
they lived an easy, selfish and sensual life beyond [the vicar's] reach,
surrounded by a wall of indifferentism, and contemptuous of all that
was not tangible and material. At times the rector and the curate
confessed to each other that these people seemed more lost than any
others with whom the work of the Church brought them into
contact". However, the story centres on a single North Country Jew,
the immensely rich Constantine Schwabe who has conceived a hatred
of Christianity. "His features were Semitic, but without a trace of that
fulness, and sometimes coarseness which often marks the Jew who
has come to the middle period of life". He is good looking in a way
until "the beauty of his face went out like an extinguished candle. His
features grew markedly Semitic". The other Jewish character is
Gertrude, a performer in light entertainment, whose room is one of
"gaudy and lavish disorder. The most sober-living and innocent-
minded man, brought suddenly into such a place, would have known
it instantly for what it was, and turned to fly as from a pestilence".
Gertrude is the mistress of the British Museum's leading archaeologist, who has spent so much money on her upkeep that he is deeply in
debt to Schwabe. This enables the millionaire to persuade him to go
to the Holy Land and fake an inscription saying that Joseph of
Arimathea moved Christ's body without the knowledge of his disciples. The story of the Resurrection is therefore false. When the
news of the discovery spreads around the world, "in a moment all
was changed. The brute in man was awake, unchained and loose.
The fires of cruelty and lust were lit". A great revival of Islam spreads
from Jerusalem; the native regiments in Bengal become difficult to
handle, and there is a great outburst of Moslem hatred for
Christianity. In Britain and the United States crime figures soar. The
old horror of slavery has disappeared, and in Rhodesia "it was
proposed openly that slavery should be the penalty for law-breaking
for natives".[25]

Of course the curate, who is the hero, knows in his bones that the
inscription must be a fake. He exposes the plot with the help of a
journalist friend and of Gertrude who has learnt its details from her
lover. She is slowly dying and wants to reform. The story, which
struck such a chord with the public in 1903 and 1904, now seems

absurd, not least because of the difficulty of equating morality with religious belief. *The Times Literary Supplement* called the book "unreal" from the beginning. It referred to Schwabe as "a satanic millionaire", but did not mention that he was Jewish, although Thorne referred to "the strong forces of Unitarianism and Judaism, always active enemies of the Church".[26] *The Bookman* declared that the novel contained a situation which "is one of the widest importance and deepest significance", but recanted 18 months later when it referred to a mixture of "cleverness and silliness", adding tartly: "It was recommended by bishops and others".[27]

Was Thorne an antisemite? The answer seems obvious at first. We read of "the little group of Jewish millionaires" who sit in the office of a newspaper owned by Schwabe, deciding how to exploit the havoc he has caused. The journalist visits a music hall where he is repelled by the hard faces he sees there. "One elderly Jewish-looking person reminded him of a great grey slug". This remark is all the more offensive through its gratuitousness. On the other hand, Schwabe's great parliamentary antagonist is a virtuous Jew, although this might have been better expressed than by "The oriental strain of cunning in his blood had sweetened to a wise diplomacy". In her desire to change her life, Gertrude becomes a Mary Magdalene. The curate even says of Schwabe, "He is no longer a Jew, Judaism is nothing to him – one can reverence a Montefiore, admire an Adler".[28] Ten years later, Thorne published *Not In Israel*, in which Sir Henry Leon, a wealthy Jewish art collector, who hates Christianity but not Christians, is not the Schwabe he seems at the start of the novel. " 'How can a Jew love England?' they asked enviously… In reality he was a genuine lover of the country which had given him birth". Sir Henry's elder son, Sebastian, abandons Judaism to become a Roman Catholic priest. "The revelation of something infinitely higher than the Jewish faith had increased his quiet joys". Although he sees the Jewish religion as a misfortune, he says, "no one shall ever persuade me that the Jews are not the salt of the earth". The novel is hostile to the religion, but not the people. Sir Henry is described as "Judaism incarnate, the highest noblest expression of it". He refers sadly to Jews who "assume something of the Gentile in the effort to be genteel. It's a subtle form of snobbery in a country where 'Jew' is still a term of reproach among the common people". The woman who eventually marries Sebastian, says, "I think I have always been *glad* to be half a Jewess, but never proud of it. In my work, the work of the stage it is a great passport…. But the other side of me has perhaps unconsciously felt the disesteem in which so many Jews are really held in England, despite titles, royal friendships and all sorts of honours. The English bourgeoisie hates the Jews still". These remarks are complaints against antisemitism, not an endorsement of it. Sebastian's brother, a theatre impresario, does not care about money as such, "but it was in their blood, ineradicable, to care about the processes by which money is gained or lost;... if honest people did not watch and scheme for money, the dishonest people got it all".[29]

It seems likely that Thorne, rather than being consciously antisemitic was guilty in *When It Was Dark* of the lazy use of a racial stereotype, that of the Jewish millionaire whose wealth gives him power. The character who wanted to destroy Christianity had to be of a different religion, and in Britain at that time, Judaism was the only possibility. This is not to defend racial stereotyping, but *When It Was Dark*, for all its faults, is less unpleasant than Le Queux's hate-ridden fantasy. The Jewish capitalist was of course a stock figure in popular literature, a useful puppet for authors who wrote to a formula. Sax Rohmer in *The Sins of Severac Bablon* at least used the puppet in an inventive way. Several unpleasant Jewish capitalists appear in the novel, the worst of whom, Julius Roscheimer, established his fortune in South Africa, and is rumoured to be involved in illegal diamond buying. He is "an octopus whose tentacles were fastened upon the heart of society". However, Roscheimer and his associates are at the mercy of Severac Babylon, also a Jew and as handsome as Roscheimer is ugly. His "sins" of the title are the blackmail, robbery and kidnap he uses to force them to donate huge sums to good causes. He is indignant that "the Jews as a race bear the stigma of cupidity and meanness. It is wholly undeserved". In his view, it is the fault of these very few immensely rich men. They have a very public reputation for making money and keeping it to themselves. Bablon is determined to make them improve the image of the Jews by their apparent generosity. He feels that he has achieved something when a *Times* leader declares that "the Jews are the backbone of British prosperity, and truer patriots than any whose fathers crossed with Norman William". Rohmer also makes clever use of the slur that Jewish plutocrats are a malign influence in world politics by turning it on its head. Severac has, by his "sins", established his sway over the group of Jewish financiers who control the economies of Europe He avoids the war which is brewing by forcing them to refuse the loan which certain countries are trying to raise in order to launch an attack on Britain. Ironically the novel was published in January 1914.[30] A similar group of powerful Jewish financiers is equally benign in *The Jewess of Hull*, by Reginald Glossop. These men would abolish war, if they could. "They are the only level-headed community on earth".[31] The story is mainly about Jewish financial shrewdness operating on a more restricted scale. The narrator is a Gentile who recounts how he followed advice he was given to marry a clever Jewish woman, how he took the advice, and how she vindicated his decision by making a fortune for them both in the antiques trade.

The Jewish capitalist as caricature appeared nearly 20 years later in Osbert Sitwell's *Miracle on Sinai*. Various types from British society are satirised when they visit the Holy Land and imagine they see tablets of stone on which ten new commandments are written. Each character sees a different set because they are projections of his dearest wishes. The Jewish capitalist representative is Sir Levy Lollygo Bart M. P. who "resembled a very fleshy and aged wild-boar, save that his countenance lacked the expression, peculiar to that animal, of brutal courage". But perhaps his appearance was more like a rodent or reptile: "A huge blunted nose with wide-winged nostrils; and little twinkling dark eyes peering through a great mask of crocodile skin, sprinkled here and there with black bristles, and inevitably smeared across with a horrible sneering smile, that revealed two pointed ivories". His outward appearance is not deceptive. He was the kind of capitalist "who, by his megalomaniac materialism and blatant irresponsibility, had helped to ruin capitalism". A journalist of the party reflects that he has many Jewish friends whom he loves and admires, but Sir Levy is very different. He wonders if "as a race, the Hebrews tend less to establish an average, are inclined to produce individuals who are higher or infinitely lower than the average citizens born of other nations". This is often suggested about the Jews, and has the advantage for the antisemite that, while concentrating on "the infinitely lower", he can claim to believe in the existence of the "higher" without paying them any attention. As Jews were often blamed for the evils of communism as well as capitalism, the satire extends to Sir Levy's son, founder of the Love the Soviets as Yourselves Association. Father and son have a furious political argument, which is compared with "the noxious and obscene battle which is sometimes witnessed between a giant cuttlefish and a shark". They are both killed after the whole party is captured by an Arab sheikh, and a war breaks out in the Middle East leading to the murder of Jews in Berlin. According to the *The Times Literary Supplement*, "whether we make wry mouths or not, we cannot help being shaken by laughter at the Hebrew financier, Sir Levy Lollygo, engaged in throaty, lisping polemics with his fanatically Bolshevik son".[32] The book was published in 1933, the year Hitler came to power.

The difficulty of whether to class an author as antisemitic is exemplified by the case of Robert Hichens. It could be argued that a Jewish villain is less a proof of hostile intent than a single gratuitous insult. For example, in *The Yellow Man* by Carlton Dawe, a character says, "I once saw a Jew financier tap his nose and... thought immediately of fat pork. It is curious, when one comes to think of it, how the sight of a fat middle-aged Jew will conjure up the picture of a pig".[33] This is the only mention of a Jew in more than 300 pages. In *The Woman With the Fan*, a novel which garnered good reviews, Hichens is guilty of this gratuitousness at greater length. It is said of Mrs Wolfenstein, who is quite extraneous to the plot, that she is "a daughter of Israel; coarse, intelligent, brutal to her reddened fingertips. I'd trust her to judge a singer, actor, painter and writer. But I wouldn't trust her with my heart or half-a-crown". Her eyes "would be lovely if they hadn't that pawnbroking expression". "Like many clever Jewesses", she is "a ruthless conversationalist, and enjoyed showing off at the expense of others, even when they were her guests". If anything, the description of her family is more offensive still. Her husband is "shocking to look at: small, mean, bald, Semitic and nervous, with large ears". He is said to have earned his ill health "by sly dissipations for which he had paid enormous sums". Their two children are "small, swarthy, froglike, self-possessed. They already spoke three languages, and their protruding eyes looked almost diseased with intelligence". These remarks are all the nastier, because even positive qualities like intelligence and sensitivity to the arts are made to seem unpleasant.[34]

However, in Hichens' *Bella Donna*, already discussed in the context of its Egyptian setting, it is the Jewish doctor who travels to Egypt to save his friend from his murderous wife, even though "every day he spent out of London was loss of so much money". He is a sympathetic figure; "only the unyielding Jew-hater hated him". His friend tells him, "I have always looked upon you as one of the most fair-minded, broad-minded men I have met". In Dr Isaacson love of the arts is admirable – "He cared for beautiful things, and he knew what things were beautiful and what were not. The second-rate never made any appeal to him... And to music he was almost fanatically devoted, as are many Jews". In Isaacson's case, cleverness is not sneered at, as it was in the earlier novel, "that cleverness which came from the Jewish blood within him".

Admittedly, the novel is not devoid of prejudice. Although "one could not conceive of [Isaacson] doing anything low", this makes him unlike the "men of his type" one might meet "in the course of a walk down Brick Lane, or the adjacent thoroughfares". As in so many novels, the Jewish character, even if born in England, is associated with the East, and with oriental qualities. "As he sat alone there in the small room, so dimly lighted, holding the long, snake-like pipe-stem in his thin, artistic hands, he looked like an Eastern Jew. With a fez upon his head Europe would have dropped from him". Once arrived in Egypt, he feels at home. Improbably, a cry from a minaret thrills his blood and sets his pulse beating.[35]

Hichens emphasises the qualities that set Isaacson apart from the other characters and attributes them to his Jewishness, but in the successful stage version of the novel, the part was played by an actor manager who was not Jewish and did not try to look it. It was observed that only the character's religion marked him out as different. "Some critics said that Sir George Alexander did not look the part of the Jew! Can you beat it? Because Sir George Alexander didn't have a hooked nose, and did not lisp, he wasn't playing the part of a Jew!"[36]

Isaacson has little in common with the Jewish characters in *The Woman With the Fan*. In *The God within Him*, published in 1926, Hichens goes further. Two rich socialites, Imogen and Hugo, are antisemitic. The former says, "I love what Jews can do in a thousand ways but I've always disliked them… It's hopelessly unreasonable, but I've never been able to help it. I've been like Hugo. He never says 'Jew'. He always says, 'Damned Jew' ". She complains about all the Jews at St Moritz. Since the war, it is as bad as Brighton. On the train there "the faces she saw repelled her. In not one of them did she find any indication of lofty thinking, of strong imagination, of idealism", qualities not too common among Gentiles either. In the course of the story Imogen meets a Russian emigre who dislikes the Jews even more than she does, as he blames them for the Russian Revolution. "They're bloodthirsty vermin! They've ruined my country. They've drowned my country in blood. Surely – but I know in England you are free from our Russian prejudices. All Jews love England, I believe". When Imogen suggests that Russia has treated its Jews pretty badly, he replies, "You don't know them as I do".

Yet the antisemites are all converted by Peter Kharkoff, a Jew and a holy man. Imogen goes to him for spiritual guidance, after Hugo is crippled in a riding accident. He helps her to devote herself to Hugo at great personal sacrifice, but the hitherto equally selfish Hugo cannot accept this sacrifice, and commits suicide to set her free. Even the Russian is transformed by Kharkoff: "I told him of my Jew hatred – everything. And now it's gone… I couldn't hate now". When

Imogen's aunt asks her, "Do you realise the Jewishness of another power which once tried to save the world?" she answers, "Surely you do not connect the two". However, she later realises that there is something Christ-like in Kharkoff, a reminder that Christ was a Jew. The drawback, however, is that Kharkoff lives apart from society, and the antisemitic characters are never seen accepting ordinary Jews in conventional situations.[37]

If Hichens' best sellers are mostly forgotten now, *The Paradine Case* has an afterlife in Alfred Hitchcock's film version. The protagonist, Sir Malcom Keane is defending a client accused of murder, and falls in love with her. He labours under the additional disadvantage that the trial judge lusts after his wife and hates him accordingly. Keane is given great support by Sir Simon Flaquer, "the cleverest and most celebrated solicitor in England, a devout son of Israel, and the repository of the deadly secrets of practically the whole of London Society". He resembles Sir George Lewis, the best known solicitor of the late Victorian period, who was also Jewish, and on whom he may have been modelled. In the nineteen sixties, Lord (Arnold) Goodman was another Jewish solicitor known for keeping the secrets of the rich and famous.

Flaquer, a frequent and generous host, is "like so many Jews, an ardent lover and supporter of music and the theatre", and "a devoted family man". He is valued "for his extraordinary astuteness and discretion by many members of the English aristocracy, who made friends with him and his wife and daughters" and by the artists, to whom, provided they have real talent, he offers legal advice free of charge. "Like many Jews, he had a sentimental side, though as a rule he carefully concealed it". If Flaquer has a flaw, it is that on a couple of occasions he has got his client off, despite suspecting him to be guilty, but lawyers rather than Jews are being targeted here. He often discusses his cases with his daughter, a shrewd legal brain, and a good friend of Keane's wife, who is attracted by her "energetic zest for life, her gaiety, her artistic flair, her Jewish acuteness and the rock-bottom goodness of her heart". Nearly 30 years after the publication of *The Woman with the Fan*, Hichens created two entirely sympathetic Jewish characters.[38]

Unlike Hichens, Hilaire Belloc can be pinned down as antisemitic. His contemporaries recognised him as such, despite his denials. In the first decade of the twentieth century, he wrote a quartet of novels in which a Jewish financier appears. His original name is not disclosed, but it has become Barnett, before his elevation to the peerage as Lord Lambeth, and then the Duke of Battersea. The tone of the novels is ironic, as the viewpoint of the narrator is being continually satirised. For example, when in *Emmanuel Burden*, he says that Barnett has shown him "the little room in the Albany where he began his long and difficult struggle with fortune"; the point is that the Albany is one of London's most exclusive addresses. When the narrator condemns "a venomous article" suggesting that the interest paid by one of Barnett's companies could only have come out of new capital, we are to believe that the accusation is true. When he denies that Barnett has bought up the press, we know that he has. Barnett is the driving force behind a shady company set up supposedly to mine gold in Africa. Emmanuel Burden joins against his better judgement and against the advice of his friend Abbott, who, in detesting Barnett and all his works, represents Belloc.

In *Mr Clutterbuck's Election*, Barnett has become a Duke, although he is more often referred to as "the Peabody Yid", an ironic comparison between his charitable activities and those of the famous philanthropist. He gives money to both political parties, and is a friend of the prime minister. It is observed ironically, of the terms on which he gains control of ruby mines in India that they were "no more than was necessary to tempt a private venture". The book also introduces the bluff, hearty Englishman, William Bailey, who sees Jews everywhere. "Every widespread influence, from Freemasonry to the international finance of Europe, was Israelite in his eyes, while our Colonial policy, and especially the gigantic and successful struggle in South Africa, he twisted into a sort of petty huckstering, dependent upon Petticoat Lane". Put that way, it seems that Bailey's antisemitism is being condemned, but as the narrator is being satirised, this is just a clever way of giving vent to Belloc's own views.[39]

The third book in the series *A Change in the Cabinet* adds little to what has gone before, but *Pongo and the Bull* is the most venomous of the four in its spleen against the Duke of Battersea, as a representative of Jewish financial and political power. The prime minister, known as Dolly, is forced into asking Battersea to make the government a huge loan. He thinks he sees in Battersea's reaction "a little note of sneering patronage" and "a suspicion of a smile upon his thick lip". He realises that Britain is experiencing for the first time what other nations have already undergone, the humiliation of being in thrall to the international financiers. Battersea will lend the money, but only at a crushing rate of interest; he "held Dolly between his spatulated forefinger and his gross thumb. But then he did not understand blood which was not his own, nor what sympathies might arise between men of one race and one society". Most of the story is about how the prime minister shakes free of the Jewish financier's tentacles by getting the money from an American multimillionaire called Smith, who is presumably "of one race and one society" with Dolly, as Battersea can never be. More satire is provided by Smith's obsession with collecting Disraeli memorabilia, a dig by Belloc against what he saw as excessive admiration for a Jewish hero. Having successfully negotiated the loan, Dolly sweeps to victory in a general election, and Belloc ends the story this way: "The Duke of Battersea understood certain things in the English character which had hitherto escaped him; and, as is often the case with men of the Duke of Battersea's kind, he respected Dolly for having thrashed him soundly – but he could not forgive the house of Smith, Fischer and Co… and their commission rankled in his mind for three long years, at the close of which I am exceedingly glad to say the Duke of Battersea, having lost a good deal more money, died". *The Times Literary Supplement* reacted to all this by observing sarcastically "We all know that England is governed nominally by alternate gangs of politicians who keep up an amusing farce of going in and out of office by mutual arrangement; while actually behind all, in all and over all looms the tremendously sinister figure of the Jew". It added that the book is at its best "when politics and antisemitism are forgotten for the moment".[40] Once again, antisemitism is not condoned, but does not provoke indignation.

Belloc's novels were not best sellers, but they mattered because he was a public figure and a prominent journalist, like his friend G K Chesterton. Chesterton was less hostile to the Jews than Belloc, but he endorsed the 'Battersea' novels by drawing the illustrations. A decade later, Belloc wrote *The Jews*, a work of non-fiction, in which he argued that there was a Jewish problem "of the gravest character", and that what a Jew wanted was security, not "the proud privilege of being called an Englishman", something he could never be. Along with the Boer War, "openly and undeniably provoked by Jewish interests in South Africa" and the Russian Revolution, so many of whose leaders were Jews, this Jewish attitude was creating a majority in the country prepared to act against the Jews. Belloc, himself, was trying to help them by drawing attention to the problem, as disaster would befall them if nothing were done. They should be segregated from the rest of the population because eliminating them was the only alternative. As a start, disputes between Jews, and possibly between Jews and Gentiles, should be tried by special courts. He would welcome suggestions from the Jews themselves of further practical measures to make segregation work.[41]

At least Belloc was not able to invoke *The Protocols of the Learned Elders of Zion*, supposed evidence of a Jewish world wide conspiracy, which had been exposed as a fake in 1921, the year before his book was published. In fact, his polemic was out of date. It is true that the Russian Revolution increased hostility towards Jews, but, as one historian put it, "the manifestation of antisemitism in the context of post-war anti-Bolshevism, apparent in the publishing activities of a few groups and individuals, ceased during the early nineteen-twenties".[42] Some Russian Jews refused to fight in the First World War as Britain was the ally of their Czarist oppressors, but the Revolution invalidated this argument. Many Jews fought loyally and were respected for doing so. Belloc's *The Jews* reflects a pre-1914 mind-set, that of his 'Battersea' novels. Between the Wars, although antisemitism persisted, Jews in fiction often received favourable treatment, the more so as so much was written by Jewish authors.

CHAPTER 7:

Jewish "Pride of Race"

"He knew that the hope of Judaism lay in the new generation, and it was his aim to encourage in the minds of the young pride of race".[1]

As early as 1900, *The Pride of Race* was the title of a novel by the Jewish author, B L Farjeon. He had already used the novel form to fight antisemitism in his *Aaron the Jew*, although the propaganda content weakens the book. "The history of nations", Farjeon writes, "furnishes the proof that the Jew, fairly treated, is a good citizen, that he is obedient to the law, and loyal to the head of the State and in his support of lawful authority. In his love of family life…" All true no doubt, but likely to bore the reader looking for a good story. Moreover, Aaron himself, like Eliot's Daniel Deronda of a quarter of a century earlier, is unbelievably virtuous: "'You are always right', Mr Moss once said to him. 'How is it?' 'If I form a correct opinion', he replied with a smile, 'it is because I exercise my common sense. I do not judge from my own standpoint'".[2]

Farjeon's *The Pride of Race* of 1900 is also a propaganda exercise. The warm-hearted Moses Mendoza is no gentleman by his own admission, but has every other virtue. He scrimps and saves to pay for his son to be educated at the best possible school, but he also needs incredible persistence to persuade the headmaster to accept the boy. The latter feels that he is "in the power of a human octopus that had fastened its suckers upon him, and would not let him go". This kind of language was often used to describe the stock figure of the Jewish money-lender, and it is witty of Farjeon to apply it to a Jew's virtuous behaviour. Mendoza later becomes so rich that his son, Raphael, is able to marry Lady Julia, the daughter of yet another fictional earl. All over England, "millionaires from Chicago and Jerusalem" are joining the aristocracy. "What becomes of pride of race, and what is to be the end of it all?" a cabinet minister is asked. He replies gloomily, "The survival of the fittest".

Raphael stands for parliament in a constituency where anti-Jewish feeling is strong. However, he overturns a big majority when it is announced on polling day that his father has financed the building of a battleship and presented it to the nation. Not even these crude but effective tactics impress Lady Julia, who continues to make it clear that she despises her father-in-law and all his works. When an orator at a public meeting begins a speech thanking Mendoza for the battleship with "Belonging as you do to an alien race", Raphael immediately contradicts him: "We of the Jewish race are most heartily in sympathy with you in all that affects the welfare and prosperity of the nation. We are part of the nation". Later, Mendoza loses his money, and Raphael has to resign from parliament, as M. P.s were unpaid in those days. He makes a great success of a newspaper that a mystery backer has launched specifically for him to edit. It turns out to be Lady Julia, who, after separating from him, has repented of her racial snobbery. "Yes, Julia was changed. Through her husband and her husband's father she had learned that the world was not made solely for her class, for her race". The Gentile aristocrat's "pride of race" has been humbled for not respecting that of the Jew.[3]

The Dominion of Race by C J Silverston, published a few years later deals with relations between Jews and Gentiles in a very different spirit. Two years in Germany have made Rachel Stern an unbeliever, and after returning to her provincial town, she marries Arthur Lanyon, a Gentile. This greatly distresses her parents, and her father says to Arthur, "You think that you can ask anything of us Jews. You are mistaken. We have a pride that goes back further than yours". Although not a religious man, he tells Rachel that she is worse than dead to both her parents, as "dead we should think tenderly of your memory". However, he comes round at last when a baby is born, and he is tricked into taking it in his arms.

Rachel and Arthur have a loving marriage, but Rachel says, "Perhaps it is something racial.... I feel that there is that which connects me with almost any of our own people, and yet which does not exist between Arthur and me". To which her cousin Bertie replies, "It is the dominion of race". He says that the Jews may resemble the English more than any other nation, but the differences are unmistakable. In distinguishing between Jews and English he is typical of his time, but the message of this novel goes much further. It is that, broadly speaking, race hates race. The average Englishman and the average Frenchman hate each other. The average Englishman hates the average Jew, not because of commercial rivalry or jealousy of Jewish intellectual achievements. It is independent of reason, and "a pure race hatred". Love between man and woman can overcome it, but only for a time. "Death, should it step in, will give Race full play once more". Death duly steps in. Arthur dies and Rachel, albeit unenthusiastically, marries cousin Bertie. After all, for a Jew "when he comes into the presence of another Jew his heart goes out to him in a way which is called forth by no other person on earth".[4] In fact, Rachel does not hate Gentiles. The story does not bear out the author's pernicious doctrine, which nevertheless makes the book an unpleasant read. There was an antidote available in Violet Guttenberg's novel *Neither Jew Nor Greek*, which proclaims that love breaks all barriers, including racial ones. Jewish Celia eventually marries a vicar's son, and her

Jewish half-brother Herbert weds a Gentile aristocrat despite his previous opposition to mixed marriages. He would have yielded earlier but for the existence of a wife who had vanished on their wedding day. As experienced readers will have expected, she reappears only to die and set him free.[5]

A quarter of a century later, the question which dominates Mary Ashton's novel *Race* is – what kind of marriage between Jew and Gentile can succeed? That of Ivan Schenstein's parents has been a failure. His Jewish father is a domestic tyrant who has forced his mother to put aside her Roman Catholicism and sacrifice her identity to his. "This was a matter concerning that ancient battle-ground for the oldest of disputes, that most enduring antagonism, a question of race". Mrs Schenstein tells Ivan that to his father religion is not so much a question of belief as "something racial, in-bred". He doesn't care whether Ivan holds it sacred or whether his future wife does, but she must follow Jewish custom. A Jewish mother was not thought necessary to be considered a Jew at this period, so it is Ivan's choice to side with his mother and not think of himself as Jewish. He too falls in love with a Gentile girl, but having seen what has happened in the previous generation, and knowing that Ivan is financially dependent on his father, she refuses to marry him. Mr Schenstein dies, but tries to extend his power from beyond the grave. The family business is left to Ivan, but if he marries a Gentile he gets only £1,000. However, at this point, "Ivan, master financier from all generations, came proudly into his own". He builds up the business, but then resigns and uses the £1,000 to make a fortune for himself. He has made himself independent of his Jewish background. The novel reflects the increasing integration of middle-class Jews into the wider community which was taking place by the 1920s.[6]

Integration had already begun by 1891 when Leonard Merrick published *Violet Moses*. The heroine's father says, "The Jews are everywhere today… they are intermarrying more every year. You can easily meet one and get quite thick with him without suspecting him to be a Jew at all". Admittedly, he is trying to persuade Violet to marry a rich Jew, and she is eventually bullied into doing so. This enables the Jewish author to describe a particular Jewish milieu through the eyes of an outsider. It is the world of Maida Vale, overwhelmingly the most popular residential area for middle-class Jews in London, a world obsessed with gambling on cards, where the women are particularly unsympathetic.[7] They play all night for more than they can afford to lose, and gobble down the rich food to rush back to the card tables. *Neither Jew nor Greek* expresses much the same criticisms of

Maida Vale society, again as seen by a young woman outsider, Jewish this time, who does not play cards. Celia wonders "why they spoke to each other as if they were all deaf", and says, "there seems to be so much money-grubbing, and match-making and card playing about it. Can you wonder that I prefer to be with my Christian musical friends?" Although Gentiles exaggerate, there is "some foundation for the unfortunate reputation we bear". However, the author remarks that she could not yet see "the real goodness of heart underlying the apparent self-interest and occasional vulgarity of the average Jew of her acquaintance".[8]

In *Violet Moses*, the Gentile protagonist, married to a typical member of this Maida Vale set, finds a Jewish friend in Mrs Benjamin, who is a wise and cultivated woman. She says "I'm not proud of that class of my co-religionists, though I'm proud of my religion". She stresses that "an instance of a Jewess bringing disgrace to her family hardly ever happens". This is a relevant issue because Violet has met up again with an attractive Jewish man whom she rejected years ago. In those days, the admission that he was Jewish had not come easily to him – "It sounds very cowardly to say so, but one is always afraid the genial faces will harden, and the cheery smiles grow chilly and fade away. We have seen it so often. You Christians aver that your prejudice against us has grown less; we Jews endeavour to persuade ourselves it has, but it is all rubbish; you are as bitter as ever". He now wants Violet to elope with him, and, unhappy in her marriage, she is sorely tempted. However, Mrs Benjamin sends him packing. Despite the limitations of the marriage, it would be an outrage on Jewish pride to destroy it.

The revival of Zionism by Theodore Herzl at the turn of the century led to a reassessment of what constituted Jewishness and what there was to be proud of. In Winifred Graham's *The Zionists*, Herzl even makes a brief appearance as "the Viennese playwright, the celebrity of the hour, who had done so much for the cause in hand", and Israel Zangwill, a leading Zionist as well as an author, is described as "a distinguished English litterateur who might be called the New Moses". In this story, a Jewish woman, Rebecca, marries a rich and powerful English aristocrat, possibly modelled on Lord Rosebery whose wife was a Rothschild. The marriage is "an outrage to the whole Jewish race", according to her friend Esther, to whom Jewishness is everything. "'Even if Rebecca's religion is nothing to her', said Esther, 'even if she loved this man with all her heart and soul, she should sacrifice herself for the sake of her race'". Her emotional commitment is alarming when it chimes in with antisemitic fantasy: "She was sure Israel was strong enough to spread eventually a net over the world, if all opportunities were successfully employed. Frequently she told herself the hour was approaching when the world would exclusively belong to the Jews". She even tells Rachel that she prays for her not to have a child as it would not be wholly Jewish. For ten years the prayer seems to work, but then Rachel has a son, Alexander, who is handsome as well as rich and heir to a title. This golden boy is not brought up as Jewish, but Esther is determined he shall be a Zionist. He resists many blandishments until he is captivated by the beautiful Ruth. Thereafter he takes enthusiastically to the cause of "restoring the people without a country to the country without a people", a description of Zionism rather dismissive of Palestine's small population. He sets up a company to develop the economy of the Holy Land, and having proved himself in the service of Zionism, is at last accepted by Ruth. Alexander's lack of belief does not worry her. Pride in being a Jew is independent of religion.[9]

* * *

"The Jew was in a great many ways superior to those who maligned him; but it would be a noble thing for him to go back to the land in which we would harmonise better, yes, go back, and if need be, fight in order to get back to that land".[10]

By offering the Jews a national home, the Balfour Declaration of 1917 gave substance to what, in *The Zionists*, had only been a dream. Such a huge change in the fortune of the Jews naturally found its way into literature, even lightweight thrillers. In *Angels in Aldgate*. The Foreign Secretary, "a Jew and a gentleman", is found murdered in the Jewish restaurant of the title. He was due to make an important statement on Palestine aimed at protecting Jewish traders from attacks by Arabs. His secretary, Teddy Felton-Slingsby, who also works for the Secret Service, sets to work to solve the crime. When he died, the eminent statesman was holding a message from a shadowy figure accepted by many Jews as an incarnation of Elijah. He was also sitting with a Jewish dancing girl, the proud inventor of the "Yiddisher Charleston". However, the Elijah turns out to be a fabrication of Soviet intelligence, the suspected Jewish skulduggery is an illusion, and most of the Jewish characters are virtuous, notably three East End rabbis, who help Teddy clear up the mystery.[11] In another thriller, Carlton Dawe's *Leathermouth*, the all-action hero whose nickname provides the title, argues the pros and cons of Zionism with his friend from Scotland Yard. Leathermouth approves of the Balfour

Declaration on the grounds that Britain has a duty to keep the peace and look after the holy places. The policeman disagrees, saying "The imposition of a hated minority on a people who have owned the country for centuries can only mean one thing – disaster". What is more, the belief that "death at the hands of an infidel" is a passport to Paradise creates "an exceedingly difficult problem". The modern relevance of these remarks hardly needs stressing, but it is also significant that the Zionist issue could be debated in a thriller of 1931, even though it is soon forgotten in the search for a solution to the mystery.

If the Balfour Declaration identified the Jews with the interests of British foreign policy, it also exposed them to the argument that their home was not in Britain, as it had been provided for them elsewhere. *A Singular People* by Sydney A Moseley* takes this line, although the story is set before 1917. The protagonist Avrom is the son of a Jewish woman and a Russian count who have fled to the East End of London. Moseley writes that the Jews have improved the East End because they do not get drunk like the Gentiles. Nevertheless Avrom is determined to escape. He joins a socialist organisation where Jew and Gentile work together. He finds that the Jew of British birth, "reared in a world of tragedy", invariably made an effective speaker, although "any opponent, at a loss for argument, could point to him scornfully and say 'You're a Jew! Why don't you go back to your own country?' " Avrom comes to think this is a reasonable question. Although he was an English patriot as a boy, thrilled when England won a test match, he has now changed. "We have done our best to hide our Jewish traits. We've dropped the lisp; we've cleaned our nails", but Jews cannot be Englishmen…. "We put on frock-coats and hob-nob with the superficial unimaginative British aristocracy as if it was the alpha and omega of culture. I tell you it's damned moral cowardice".

After arriving in Palestine as a journalist, Avrom expresses himself even more forcibly: "What these lisping, long-nosed Jews of English birth and wealth want is to achieve the impossible – they want to be of English stock and society when they're just foreigners". He will always love England, but as an outsider. He is not an Orthodox Jew – "modern Jewry could be just as devotional after a hair cut and a shave" – but he is an out and out Zionist by now. "He returns to England, but gives freely to Zionist funds; at a big Zionist meeting, he listens to Jewish hymns sung by boys who could no more be regarded as

* No relation to Sir Oswald *Mosely.*

English boys than a Japanese could". At the end of the novel a society woman reports a friend saying to her, "'I hope they do give the Jews Palestine so that we can send 'em all back!' Isn't she a scream!"[12] If so, Moseley is a scream too. He refers to Jewish virtues from time to time and, unlike Silverston in *The Dominion of Race* does not claim that race hatred is inevitable, but his message is the same as Hilaire Belloc's – that the Jews are different from the British, and can never be anything else.

* * *

> "The Jew had so many hard things said about him that by now he must be getting used to it".[13]

The above quotation from *The Bookman* was a comment on a polemic by Moseley, entitled *The Much Chosen Race*, which was published the same year as Belloc's *The Jews*.

Moseley was advertised as "the journalist who dared tell the truth", and his name was well enough known to appear on newspaper placards. In *The Much Chosen Race* he no longer tries to make his views more acceptable by putting them into the mouth of a Jewish character.

He claims that Jews in general accept that they should go to their own country; only the "'British' Jew" intends "to hang on here till the Messiah comes". He thinks antisemitism is wrong, of course, and pays the Jews a lot of compliments, mostly backhanded. They are "dreadfully sober" and "ridiculously law-abiding". "The Jew is a great debater" but this is because "for sneering, slashing, cutting cynicism he has no equal". The Jewish woman is beautiful, but "by the time she is thirty she has despoiled her beauty". She will be faithful after marriage but, not wanting to attract men, will let herself become "bulky, gross and coarse". There is a sting in the tail, too, when Moseley defends the Jews. It is not true that they always stick together; on the contrary, "there is much more *esprit de corps* among apes". They have been oppressed, but oppression has brought out their worst characteristics. His only true concessions are that Jewish mothers are admirable, that Jews fought loyally in the First World War, and that they love their wives and children. Perhaps he even goes too far when he adds that "there are no family feuds in Israel".

The tone of the book is set early on when Moseley declares that he will use the word "Yiddle", to identify Jews who have deceitfully anglicised their names. In fact this device is mainly deployed against "Mr Yiddle Zangwill" "who could as easily be mistaken for a Britisher as Gorgonzola cheese could be mistaken for a rose". Moseley not only hated Zangwill's insistence that he was an Englishman as well as a Jew and Zionist, but also his affection for the piously Orthodox. For Moseley they are particularly objectionable. The atmosphere of synagogues is "the same putrid air one has breathed in many mosques out East". The Orthodox Jews are "priggish, boorish and unmanly". "Just as the ridicule which the fat boy excites is due to his gluttony, so the mocking laughter which greets the 'profound' Jew is a result of mental gluttony".[14]

Moseley, like the more famous Belloc, did not prove very influential with his anti-Jewish diatribes. The popular fiction of the 1920s is full of unpleasant Jewish stereotypes, but the characters are usually minor. Novels are rare, which, like John G Brandon's *Young Love* are dominated by an out and out Jewish villain. Whereas in *The Hebrew* he was a slum landlord, in Brandon's story of nearly a quarter of a century later he is an Oxford-educated financier plotting to increase his fortune by manipulating the share price of an oil company. The older generation is represented by his father, who, despite being "this illiterate old Jew of Poland", has for 40 years "battened, leech-like" on the financial needs of the great, from an office in Bond street. The hero is Bill Dennett, an American who, although a rich man, becomes the heroine's chauffeur in order to get near her. At first he does not get as near as the "yellow-faced, hook-nosed swine", as he describes the villain. "His heavy eyes were feasting upon the purity of her neck and shoulders…. His hands gripped about her white shoulders, his lips pressed to hers. And she, with her ashen face, was fighting at him, beating at his sleek black head, with her delicate hands clenched in a wild and helpless terror". Bill beats him up. "A horrible gurgling sound came from him as the second blow took him". It split "the red leering lips clean to the gums".

It transpires that this villain, who has tried to have Bill murdered, is so desperately in love with the heroine that he wants to marry her, although he is married to a beautiful and virtuous Jewish girl. She is the daughter of Mordecai, who works for the Bond street money-lender. Bill thinks she has "a *good* face – that type of exotic beauty is so often quite the reverse". Mordecai, who does not know of the marriage, becomes distraught when he thinks his daughter is the villain's mistress and then full of self-reproach when he realises that he has wronged her. The love of family and strict code of sexual morality, often ascribed to Jews even by their enemies, comes into play here. It is a turning point in the story. For the first time Bill sees some good in the villain: "Whatever the depths to which his passions had dragged him, he had both affection and respect for this hoary old man [Mordecai], down whose seamed and furrowed cheeks great tears were streaming". This is Shylock's love for his daughter without Shylock's vices, as Mordecai only works for a money-lender and is not responsible for his rapaciousness. The latter too is now seen in a more favourable light as "the forms of villainy to which his son had given his hand were totally abhorrent to him". He shows none of "that money-haggling propensity as ascribed from time immemorial to his race" and wants the proceeds of his son's crimes to be returned. He himself holds a mortgage on the heroine's home, fairly obtained from her profligate father, and now gives it to her as a wedding present. "'When you know more of my people', he said quietly, 'you will know one thing. Always it is that Israel gives everything to her children'".[15]

We have already come across Brandon's recourse to racial stereotyping in relation to the Chinese, and this is not a pleasant novel for Jews to read. Nevertheless, the ending makes *Young Love* less nasty than *The Hebrew*, which reflects the fact that, on the whole, Jews in Britain had a better time of it in 1925 than in 1902. However, in an age of intense patriotism and social conformity, people who were different could seem alarming. In a novel of 1928, a young Gentile woman has quarrelled with her Jewish lover. "She had that strong superstition of race that seems to be so common among English people. If Meyr had been an Englishman she might have been very much afraid of him; but she would not have credited him consciously with such diabolic powers…. He became in her eyes a mixture of Don Juan and of the scoundrelly heroes of her vernacular literature".[16] On the whole this literature did the Jews few favours, but all but the very worst credited them with some virtues, and even showed some sympathy for their "pride of race".

CHAPTER 8:

The Jews and Some Famous Authors

"The two others were Jews; a little flashily dressed, distinctly addicted to cheap jewellery… as the door opened their conversation ceased abruptly and they looked up at the newcomers with the keen, searching look of their race".[1]

In the thriller, one of the dominant genres of the interwar years, villains are very wicked indeed, as the more wicked they are, the greater the thrills. This makes racial stereotyping of the villain particularly damaging. As a key author in the development of the thriller, John Buchan has not escaped the charge of racism, and antisemitism in particular. A famous quote at the start of *The Thirty-Nine Steps*, his best-known novel, is often held against him: "If you're on the biggest kind of job and are bound to get to the real boss, ten to one you are brought up against a little white-faced Jew in a bath-chair with an eye like a rattlesnake. Yes, sir, he is the man who is ruling the world just now". However, this remark is made by an American who "had a lot of odd biases, too. Jews, for example, made him see red. Jews and the high finance" – that is the Permanent Secretary at the Foreign Office talking, and, in a Buchan novel, such a man is to be believed. In any case, the hero, Richard Hannay, has already concluded, "The little man had told me a pack of lies".[2] Buchan repeats this technique of allowing a character to make objectionable remarks which are later discounted in *The Three Hostages*, where the policeman Macgillivray sounds off against the Irish before he is dismissed as a prejudiced Ulsterman.

Admittedly, in *Greenmantle* the same Permanent Secretary briefs Hannay on Turkey, and says, "You will ask how a Polish adventurer, meaning Enver, and a collection of Jews and gypsies should have got control of a proud race". And in *Mr Standfast*, Hannay finds that "Aranson, the novelist, proved on acquaintance the worst kind of blighter…. The creature was tuberculous in mind and body, and the only novel of his I read pretty well turned my stomach". Aranson gets no further mention. This is a real lapse, but the case for Buchan is not that he was devoid of prejudice or took the care to avoid offence which would be taken now. The case is that his overall record shows that he was a decent man, even though the standards of his time were not the standards of today. In *The Three Hostages*, "the American banker who had done a lot of Britain's official business in the war" is an admirable character, "the whitest Jew since the Apostle Paul".[3] In fact, when an M. P., Buchan was an ally of the Zionists in the House of Commons and chairman of the Pro-Palestine Committee. He wrote, "When I think of Zionism, I think of it in the first place as a great act of justice. It is reparation for the centuries of cruelty and

wrong which have stained the record of nearly every Gentile people".[4]
He also admired "my master in fiction" E Phillips Oppenheim, who
was Jewish.[5]

Admittedly, for a thriller positively favourable to the Jews, one
must turn from Buchan to *The Jew's House* by Fergus Hume, who is
best known for *The Mystery of the Hansom Cab*. Although Hume
belonged to an earlier generation of best selling writers, this book
was published only four years before *The Thirty-Nine Steps*. It features
Mr Ben-Ezra, a wealthy Jew, who "was looked upon as a sort of
pound-of-flesh Shylock in the suburb he had created, and was
regarded more as a vampire than as a benefactor". When he is accused
of murder, there is delight at the prospect of his being hanged.
However, he turns out to be a virtuous man who has been given no
credit for his many good deeds, and he did not murder anyone. It also
emerges that his sister had married a Gentile, who "grew weary of her
within a year of the marriage, and taunted her, the coward, with being
a Jewess" The grounds on which his enemies hate him personally are
shown to be false, and their hatred of Jews is exposed as the product
of ignorance and prejudice. Ben-Ezra is philosophical about his difficulties, saying "Jews are used to harsh judgments" and "England is the
one place in the world where a Jew can get justice" He can be harsh
and unforgiving, but suffers enough to be excused his moments of
asperity. When someone says, "'I don't like seeing a man kicked when
he is down", he replies, 'You differ from your fellow Christians then".[6]
The section of society in which the novel is set is deeply prejudiced,
but the author himself is on the side of the angels.

Sapper is the thriller writer whose prejudices have received the
most attention. His first books were stories of the First World War,
and his famous all-action crime-buster, *Bulldog Drummond*, is a
product of the war. Having enjoyed fighting in the army Drummond
looks for opportunities, to unleash his aggression in peacetime.
Because of the war, he hates Germans, so he hates German Jews;
because of the Russian revolution, he hates Russian Jews. Any Jews
who are not Russian or German are near enough, and he would probably have hated them anyway because he is a good hater. During the
First World War Jews were sometimes associated with Germany.
When Sexton Blake used the word "wanderlust" to his chum Sir
Richard Losely, "'Don't talk German', said Sir Richard sharply,
'unless your name is Mosenstein, or Ikey or something else sounding
like a bad attack of catarrh'".[7]

Drummond, like his creator, is obsessed with the revolution in
Russia because he is terrified of a rebellion by the British working

classes. Any Jew might be a revolutionary, if not a criminal or, just as bad, a money-lender. Two Jews in *The Black Gang* are white slave traffickers, which gives Drummond the excuse to have them flogged within an inch of their lives. The Jews fling themselves on to the floor, grovelling for mercy, and the sadism is as unmistakable as in *Young Love*. On the other hand, who does Drummond treat kindly? – Only Anglo-Saxons and beautiful women. Sapper's other heroes are little better. In *The Island of Terror*, "a small obese Jew almost concealed behind a vast cigar rose at Jim's entrance". "I don't like your trade, Isaac", Jim tells him, "as you know very well; but you remember that day in Marseilles when I saved your worthless life… Some of the inhabitants of Marseilles had suddenly decided that a thousand per cent was too much of a good thing". Jim saved Isaac from being killed, but clearly relished his being beaten up.[8]

The hatred of Germans in the 1920s is so obviously a consequence of the First World War that it needs no further analysis. Norma Lorimer's *The White Sanctuary* has the merit of putting it, along with antisemitism, into the context of the general racism of the period. The heroine, Eunice, who has no living family, is the paid companion to an Englishwoman, and part of the British community in Dubrovnik (Ragusa in the novel). Although she was brought up in England and speaks perfect English, she is in fact German, a terrible secret which she hides from everyone, as she has her living to earn. "If she was to be treated like a *white woman* she must hold her tongue and continue the deception". Nathaniel Marks of Birmingham, a rich manufacturer of cheap jewellery, discovers the truth, but proposes to Eunice. Her violent reaction is a reminder of how bad antisemitism was in Germany. "She was to mingle her blood with his. Mingle Prussian blood with the blood of a Jew". She had been brought up "to despise his race, to consider marriages between Jews and Germans as bad as marriages between coloured and white races". Her employer thinks that Eunice should have accepted the offer – "He's so rich that his being a Jew won't matter a bit – socially", but she would not have suggested marriage to a *German* Jew. However, Eunice remarks later that "In England, if you are only rich enough, your unclean blood is washed pure in the river of gold".

Eunice is provoked into telling her employer that she is a German, and is sacked on the spot, so, when Marks suggests that they take a holiday together in a platonic relationship, she accepts. He is "a kindly, generous soul, who need never have looked so vulgar, or have appeared to others so thick-skinned, if the world had not for all the Christian centuries despised the race which gave the world its

Redeemer". He is also strictly honourable, and Eunice knows that he will keep his promise not to take advantage of her. He just wants her to get to know him better and change her mind about marriage. "I come of a race that has had to wait and wait". By this time Eunice has fallen in love with Philip Madden, who reciprocates her passion, but has done his best not to show it. She is convinced that, in any case, he would never marry a German, or, as she puts it, "He would not risk the horror of a mixed marriage". Marks' strategy works to the extent that Eunice becomes ashamed of her antisemitism, and grows fond of him. The problem is that he lacks Philip Madden's sexual magnetism. However, having set up this interesting situation, Lorimer ruins it by having Marks conveniently fall over a cliff. He dies instantly, leaving Eunice and Philip to mourn his great qualities which are no longer in their way. The last barrier to their union is removed when Philip reveals his own terrible secret – he is German too. Despite the feeble ending, the core of the book, with Eunice both guilty of racial prejudice and its victim, provides a perceptive commentary on the clouds of racism swirling around Europe during the 1920s. Russian and French hatred of the Germans and the antipathy between Italians and Slavs are also touched upon.[9]

A slightly later novel, *Props* by Naomi Jacob, also deals with the triangular relationship of Jews, English and Germans. Hermann Frank is sent from Dresden to Victorian England, although his uncle Hans says, "He will never be an Englishman, because he is a Jew, and a Jew is fundamentally a Jew, whatever ticket he may tie round his neck". However Hermann marries an Englishwoman, although she will not meet his Jewish friends – "I suppose they were Cohens and Lewis and Jacobs…. Awful names they have, these people". Not surprisingly the marriage ends in divorce, and Hermann falls in love with Leah, whose husband offers her everything, except passion. She says, "Meyer is a great Jew, he has all the greatest attributes of the Jews, and he has the greatest failing of his race. He loves to possess his wife! I believe that Meyer could face anything if it was for my happiness. He could even face my taking a lover, but he could never face my appearing in public shabby or badly dressed". It looks as though he will face Leah taking Hermann as a lover, but before this could happen Leah dies. Hermann is now in limbo, especially as his love of both England and Germany has left him devastated by the First World War and the hatred between the two countries. "He heard his countrymen stigmatized as murderers, thieves, liars, and cowards, and as he listened he thought of his own father, narrow but kindly, a model of integrity". In this context his father is seen as German rather than Jewish, and Hermann is more hurt by anti-German feeling than by antisemitism. If he cannot be an Englishman it is because of his German rather than his Jewish background. He returns to Dresden, hoping to make the Germans think better of the English. England is for him a "kind, wise, a great nation. Individuals may have hurt me, but the country is not judged by its worst, but by its best – and your best is very, very good".[10]

During the interwar years, detective stories were as popular as thrillers. It has often been noticed that many, not least some by still famous authors, reveal questionable attitudes to Jews. Those of Dorothy L Sayers are a case in point. Once a character has been established as Jewish, we are never allowed to forget it. In *Whose Body* a man, perhaps a missing Jewish financier, is found murdered. It was, we are told, stupid to arrest a frail-looking girl who is "quite unequal to downing a tall and sturdy Semite with a poker". It is relevant that the man was "tall and sturdy", but surely not that he was a Semite. The same book contains a meandering speech from a duchess, the mother of Lord Peter Wimsey, the detective. She knew the Jewish financier's late wife, a Gentile. "I remember so well the dreadful trouble there was about her marrying a Jew. That was before he made his money of course…. Of course we're all Jews nowadays, and they wouldn't have minded half so much if he'd pretended to be something else, like that Mr Simons we met at Mrs Porchester's, who always tells everybody that he got his nose in Italy at the Renaissance… and I'm sure some Jews are very good people, and personally I'd much rather they believed something, though of course it must be very inconvenient, what with not working on Saturdays and circumcising the poor little babies and everything depending on the new moon and that funny kind of meat they have with such a slang-sounding name, and never being able to have bacon for breakfast".[11] The Duchess is being satirised, of course, and the speech is an amusing compendium of the vague ideas attached to Jews by not very intelligent aristocratic circles in 1935. It is reprehensible, but reflects the disquiet which Jews inspired in such people, rather than intense animosity. However Sayers does not convince us that her attitude is very different from the Duchess's, especially as her regular readers would have found doubtful passages elsewhere. In *Five Red Herrings*, a witness to a crime is Jewish, "a stout little gentleman with a pronounced facial angle"; he lisps throughout the only three pages on which he appears, and is very agitated about "the interrupthon to my bithneth".[12] In her biography of Sayers, Janet Hitchman points out that the books were published by a Jew, Victor Gollancz, who does not seem to have objected, and that Sayers was equally insufferable towards black and working class people. She may well have been reflecting the society around her, but Hitchman is surely right to say that her prejudices are particularly deplorable in a woman of talent and intelligence.[13]

R Austin Freeman's questionable attitudes to Jews in his popular detective stories has been analysed by Norman Donaldson in his *In Search of Dr Thorndyke*. He points out that Freeman was the son of a tailor, who perhaps suffered from Jewish competition, and that he had a keen interest in eugenics and theories of race. Donaldson pays particular attention to *The Missing Mortgage*, which first appeared in *Pearson's Magazine* in 1914, but has been republished many times since. In this book, Elton is in the hands of Gordon, a Jewish money lender, whose tastes were "money, first for its own sake, and then those coarser and more primitive gratifications that it was capable of purchasing". His dishonest clerk is "a small gentleman of sallow and greasy aspect with heavy eyebrows and a still heavier nose". Elton "looked askance at the vampire by his side, at the plump blue-shaven cheeks, the thick black eyebrows.... Though he was a mild-tempered man he felt that he could have battered that sensual, complacent face out of all human likeness with something uncommonly like enjoyment". Donaldson mentions comparable passages, but points out that Thorndyke, Freeman's detective, never shows racial bias, presumably because it would betray the scientific attitude which he is supposed to represent. In Donaldson's view "Thorndyke had to rise above his class and culture, even if Freeman could not". If it is true that Freeman represented his class and culture, enlightenment had set in by 1940 when his *Mr Polton* treats Jews more sympathetically.[14]

As the most popular writer of detective stories, Agatha Christie's racial attitudes have been examined many times, and will be touched on only briefly here. Under the pseudonym she used for her non-detective works, she wrote *Giant's Bread* in which anti-Jewish prejudice is deplored, and the main Jewish character is depicted as a good and generous friend. This is a sign that the sins she commits elsewhere stem from insensitivity rather than malice.[15] *Bread* was published the same year as *The Mysterious Mr Quin*, a collection of short stories, one of which traces the decline of a countess at Monte Carlo. She had descended from a Grand Duke to an Austrian Baron, then, "on successive years her friends had been of Hebraic extraction, sallow men with hooked noses, wearing rather flamboyant jewellery. For the last year or two she was much seen with very young men, almost boys". Another story describes "Lady Roscheimer who was a fat Jewess with a *penchant* for young men of the artistic persuasion. And he knew all about Sir Leopold Roscheimer who liked his wife to be happy, and, most rare among husbands, did not mind her being happy in her own way".[16] Two years later in *Peril at End House*, one of Poirot's suspects is a Jewish art dealer. Readers upset at his being described as "a Jew, of course, but a frightfully nice one", have the satisfaction of discovering that the speaker turns out to be the murderer. After the Second World War Christie's American publishers received complaints, and took care that she should not offend again.[17]

Christie's prejudices are only interesting because her books have sold so many copies. For the same reason, it is worth observing that in P C Wren's *Beau Geste*, a Jewish pawnbroker gives John Geste only a small fraction of the value of his goods: "I entered and found a young gentleman of markedly Hebraic appearance behind the counter. I expected to hear him say, 'Vat d'ye vant Mishter?' and waggle his hands, palms upwards, near his shoulders.... A very large watch-chain adorned his fancy waistcoat that was certainly worn by him at meal times also, and his diamond tie-pin bore testimony to his financial solidity and good taste".[18] However, in a sequel *Beau Ideal* Jacob is "famous among the brave for his courage, brilliantly clever, bitterly cynical, and endowed with a twofold portion of the mental, moral and physical endurance of his enduring race". John Geste tells him, "There are good and bad in all religions, Jacob.... I have the highest admiration for your great people – but I have met rotten specimens, Bad as some of my own".[19] There are enough examples of authors creating a positive Jewish character, after being offensive in an earlier book, for one to wonder how many were following Dickens' example when he tried to atone for Fagin by creating the virtuous Riah in *Our Mutual Friend*.

Elinor Glyn became a famous author before P C Wren, but *Love's Blindness* was published two years after *Beau Geste*. Hubert, Earl of St Austell, applies to Benjamin Levy "the straightest and most highly respected money-lender in London", for half a million pounds, which he is offered, provided he agrees to marry Levy's daughter, Vanessa. The Earl "was too modern to have bombastic pride about his old name and race – but, underneath, the notion of marrying the child of a Jewish money-lender was simply revolting to him". Vanessa is very beautiful, but "he detested dark Jewesses". His friends think that, "when they see you with some half-effulgent Jewess no one will believe you weren't cornered". Nevertheless, the marriage goes ahead, with the Earl planning the earliest possible separation and divorce. He is so blinded by prejudice that only later does he notice

Vanessa's beauty. The preposterous plot involves a number of unlikely misunderstandings. Vanessa thought that Hubert was in love with her when they married, and he wrongly believed that she was party to her father's blackmail. However, with a child on the way, love blossoms and the misunderstandings are cleared up. "She was not the Jewish minx who had schemed to be a countess, then". As in Farjeon's *The Pride of Race*, the pride of the aristocrat has been broken down by the decency of the Jews. The happy ending is credited to the money-lender. "Hubert knew his father-in-law for what he was – a wise and honest gentleman, and Benjamin Levy had pierced through the curse of ten hundred years of inherited pride, and found his son-in-law a human man". They are both paid too much honour, as the Earl is a racist snob for most of the novel, and forcing a man to marry your daughter is an unlikely way to ensure her happiness. However, the book has the merit of deploring racial prejudice, a merit all the more welcome in default of literary ones.[20]

Daphne Du Maurier's popularity has lasted longer than Elinor Glyn's, so making *The Progress of Julius* with its Jewish protagonist particularly interesting, although it has never been one of her best loved works. Here again we have a Jew whose mother is not Jewish; she is a French peasant who treats his father with contempt because of his Jewishness, and is strangled by him when little Julius proves that she is unfaithful. His sympathy for his father leads him to feel Jewish, and his boyhood experiences make him hard and ruthless. When he comes to England in the 1870s, it is through no love of the English. "He hated them from the beginning, but he would make his money out of them, and they could laugh and jibe at him as they pleased". He becomes a social success as well as immensely rich. "Privately they gossiped about him in their fear and called him vulgar, an upstart, a foreigner, a Jew. He knew all this and he laughed, and he invited them to his house so that he could despise them". He treats his Jewish wife brutally, and drives his father-in-law to suicide by refusing him the loan he desperately needs. When his daughter grows into a beauty, he is obsessed by her, and spends money extravagantly on indulging her every whim. "It's my money isn't it? I've worked for it, God knows. Worked a damned sight harder than any thick-headed Englishman". He gives out that his wife died of cancer, although, desperately hurt at his ill-treatment, she has killed herself. He makes another fortune in the First World War, and is knighted for his patri-otism, although he has merely been cynical in advertising his wares with patriotic slogans. His feelings for his daughter become more and more unhealthy, and when she at last finds a young man to love, he strangles her, as his father strangled his mother.[21] The inspiration for the story seems to have been Du Maurier's relationship with her own father, whose love for her she found oppressive. It seems likely, therefore, that she made her protagonist a Jew in order to distance herself from him. It is nowhere stated that he is nasty because he is Jewish, but there is nothing in the book to prevent readers from drawing this conclusion. *The Progress of Julius* is very much a book of the 1930s, a period of transition for the Jews in Britain. Popular fiction was kinder to the Jews then than in the 1920s, but the real break-through did not come until the 1940s.

CHAPTER 9:

Jews on Jews

"Of course nobody nowadays said 'Smoggy van Jew!' at Rabbi
Shulman or any member of his family… people did not feel that way
so much in the post-war years in England".[1]*

Among Jewish novelists of the interwar period, who wrote specifically about the life of Jews, Louis Golding was Israel Zangwill's heir.
His subject was immigrant families, although they emerge from
the ghetto. In *Day of Atonement*, Eli and Leah leave Russia for
Doomington, Golding's version of Manchester. He is a religious
scholar; she has become a religious fanatic after convincing herself
that she is responsible for her father's death. Despite their poverty, she
will not accept money from a Christian philanthropist to pay for the
Sabbath meal. "What a taste would the Sabbath dinner have if
bought with Gentile money – an unholiness!". When Eli converts
to Christianity, her love for him turns to hate. "'Do not touch me,
meschummed', she shrieked. 'Apostate, lay no finger upon me, a daughter
of Israel'". She casts him out, as does the rest of the community. He is
equally fanatical. Even when their only child Reuben warns him that
a mob of young Jews intend to attack him at the street corner where
he proposes to preach, he goes ahead regardless. When the mob pur-
sues him to Leah's home, she will not let him in. His pain comes from
the fact that although Christ has conquered the Jew in his soul, the
Jew in his marrow remains – "the Jew of the exile in Babylon, the
burnings in Spain, the massacres in Russia … the pudding made out
of raisins and stewed carrots, the spinning top to play with on the
Feast of the Maccabees". The unfortunate Reuben moves backwards
and forwards between mother and father; Judaism and Christianity.
Nothing changes in his dreary life "excepting this meaningless hateful
battle between God and Christ…. It meant nothing to him; it
seemed to be about nothing at all. Who were they? What did they
want? They had broken everything, destroyed everything, and they
were not even as real as the white, sooty, nameless cat or Miranda the
hen". Eventually when Eli, crucifix in hand, tries to preach Christianity
on Yom Kippur in front of the Ark of the Covenant, Leah kills him.
Revolted by both religions, Reuben turns to the classical world, and
becomes a shepherd in Sicily.[2] Despite Golding's affection for his
Jewish heritage, his attack on religious fanaticism is harsher than
Zangwill's.

His best known Doomington novel is *Magnolia Street*, which is set
between 1910 and 1930. Jews live on one side of the street, and

---

* "Post-war" here of course means post First World War.

Gentiles on the other. Crossing it involves a long journey "all the way from the ghettoes of Russia, the walled towns of Judaea, the black camel-hair tents of the wilderness beyond Jordan, for the dwellings of the Jewish pavement have something of the quality of all those". The other side of the street is the North of England. Unlike the Gentiles, the Jews are ambitious. They want more money and look to America, except for some of the younger ones, who are becoming like the youngsters on the other side of the street. "They played football and cricket and studied the team-scores with, if anything, more passion". Rose Berman is characteristic of this society in flux. She works in a classical music shop, the first Jew to do so. Nobody asks if she is Jewish, and when she did not turn up on Jewish feast days, "the understanding was that she had a cold". She loves a Gentile sailor, but is terrified of their being seen together, particularly by her mother. Her inhibitions delay the marriage until the end of a very long novel, although her mother knows what is going on, and is sympathetic.

It takes a dramatic event to bring the two sides of the street together, but after Bennie Edelmann saves little Tommy Wright from drowning, "the Gentiles found that the Jews were not so outlandish after all. You certainly couldn't say about them, as you had always been taught to believe, that they counted each penny as they spent it. They were just simple folk like themselves, some more pleasant, some less". However, the big party in Benny's honour is a disaster because he and Tommy's mother do not turn up; they have run away together. After their marriage, she bullies Benny and is unfaithful. "She hated Jews. She hated them all the more violently when her Jew crushed her in his arms till she was breathless with ecstasy". Lust for this one Jew coexists with Jew-hatred.

The two sides of the street drift apart again. Racial antagonisms begin to resurface with the outbreak of the First World War. Benny's mother attributes it to Jews taking trams on the Sabbath and mixing milk with meat, but some Gentiles think Jewish financiers started it. In fact, as in Naomi Jacobs' *Props*, hatred of Germans proves stronger than hatred of Jews. The Gentiles decide that it was the Germans who crucified Christ, "or, more specifically, Elsa Stanley [a German woman] rather than Rabbi Shulman".

One character, Bella Winberg really does get from Magnolia Street to America. Her husband is a Jew from Sweden – almost a Gentile. "For, who had ever heard of a Swedish Jew? It was the last word in chic, and as though that were not enough he was also an American citizen". Even more impressively, a Jewish boy from Magnolia Street has become world light heavyweight boxing champion. For the Gentiles he is just an Englishman now, his Jewishness forgotten, like Christ's. Back from America, he and Bella throw a party for both sides of Magnolia Street. It is more successful than the first, although problems remain. It would have been embarrassing to have had Rose Berman and her Gentile husband there, as some people are more embarrassed by their successful marriage than by the Edelmann's failure. Benny has lost a leg in the war but his mother still rejects him for marrying out. Nevertheless, by 1930, after the Jew–Gentile relationship has gone through many vicissitudes, cautious optimism seems justified.[3]

Naomi Jacob was one of the most prolific chroniclers of Jewish life. Her first novel *Jacob Ussher*, published in 1920, was an adaptation of a West End play. The title character's salient quality was pride "not only pride of race which lives in every Jew", but also pride in his power, wealth, and achievement. This ruins his marriage to an earl's daughter, who deserts him, as "she was only another possession and not a woman at all". His daughter Leah, despite her Gentile mother, is also "full of the pride of race". However, she falls in love with Rupert, an impoverished aristocrat working as her father's secretary, although she knows that he is intimidated by Ussher, and, it seems, Jews in general. "Nothing stops them, nothing frightens them, they know what they want, they know whom they love – and they have the Christian beaten to a frazzle every time". Ussher knows that he does not want Rupert to marry Leah, and he seems to have him beaten to a frazzle because he can blackmail Leah over a forged cheque. However, he relents when, to buy the cheque back, Rupert sells a ring, which has been in his family for generations. Jacob realises that Rupert has inspired his daughter's love, which he himself has failed to do. He also knows that the young couple are already lovers, although perhaps not that a child is on the way. He has had to conquer his aversion to the marriage, premarital sex and possibly illegitimacy in the name of love. In this *Merchant of Venice*, Jessica has reformed Shylock. The novel improves on the play, in which Leah was called Constance, and Rupert bought back the cheque with money from a win at the races. In selling a family ring instead, he, like Ussher, is sacrificing his pride of race.[4]

Naomi Jacob's most sustained account of Jewish life is her popular trilogy on the Gollantz family. In the first book, *That Wild Lie*, handsome young Emmanuel Gollantz arrives in London from Vienna in 1865 and makes a fortune as an antique dealer. Despite his success, he is blackballed from a club on racial grounds. "'What they know of Jews', he said, 'they know from Jews. I am paying for the mistakes of men like Bernstein. He has changed his name to Burns, and the men who know him call him – The Sheenie'". Emmanuel's wife dies young, but he has two sons, Max, who is loyal to his father's traditions, and Algy a Jewish Jew-hater. At school, Algy has "mixed with boys who had no pride of race in particular, but heartily despised Jews". He thinks his father dresses too opulently, that his voice is too rich. He eventually leaves home, saying, "I'm sick of living in the Ghetto. I'm going to live with decent people, to marry a decent girl, a Christian". In fact, he abandons the decent girl, Julie, and their son. Julie seduces Max, but Emmanuel persuades him to give her up, as the liaison would put Jews in a bad light. "Down in their hearts Englishmen despise us…. They all say at some time or another. 'The dirty Jew, the scheming low Yid!'" Max marries Angela, another Gentile girl, but far from this being a problem she develops a touchingly affectionate relationship with her still elegant and charming father-in-law.

In the First World War, it is feared that the missing Algy might be in the German army. As Max says, "Of course, he may not be fighting, but it's rather a nightmare to think that I might have to kill my own brother or Frank his father". Frank is Algy's son, whom Emmanuel has brought up and who in fact dies for Britain. It was the fate of some Jewish families to have relations fighting on both sides. Max is sent to Switzerland to deal with an enemy agent, who by a melodramatic coincidence turns out to be Algy. He has become a spy purely for mercenary reasons. The Jewish Jew-hater is a bad lot in every way. He dies before the end of the novel, when Max reflects that "more than fifty years ago his father had come to England, unknown, poor, and a nobody; now, because of his integrity, his wisdom, and his personality, he was known, sought, and honoured".[5] It surely says something for the host country too.

Readers seem to have liked Emmanuel. The blurb for the sequel to *That Wild Lie* announced, "we meet again old Emmanuel, that romantic figure which age has not faded, and who still retains his fascination". This is also a story of two contrasting brothers, the sons of Max and Angela, the *Young Emmanuel* of the title and his brother Julian. The latter becomes a Member of Parliament and, when caught in a raid on a louche nightclub, gives his brother's name. He pulls a similar trick when he is blackmailed for a youthful homosexual indiscretion and makes it seem that his brother committed it. As with Algernon before him, it is part of Julian's dishonourable character that he dislikes Jewishness, although he is cynical enough to say, "I'm the one person in the family who has reverted to the type of Jew who makes a success of life. The rest of you are sentimentalists; you believe in uprightness, truth and integrity, because you think that by those things you will make men confess that your race is altogether admirable".[6] This turns against the older Emmanuel a remark he made in the earlier novel, "I am so proud of my race that for nearly sixty years I have tried to make my English friends t'ink not only well of me, but of Jews because of me".[7]

The patriarch dies, a graceful symbol of the rise of the Jew in twentieth century England, and his young namesake has many emotional upheavals before the end of the novel, but Angela and Max continue their happy marriage. She says, "My people – the earth, the soil, old houses, fields, and things that go to make up old England. Your side – your people – the best that the Jews can produce, and one side shall never forget what it owes to the other".[8] Naomi Jacob herself was a product of this synthesis. In her own words, she was "half-Jewess, half-Broad Acres", and wrote novels about Yorkshire folk as well as about Jews.[9]

Max's Englishness is stressed in the third novel of the series *Four Generations*. "He was sound as the English oak which he had made so popular". His son, the young Emmanuel buys a Reynolds on his behalf to keep it in England. He does so, dressed as his grandfather – an indication that the old patriarch lives beyond the grave. His portrait in the dining room pervades the whole house. Max's daughter-in-law asks, "Do you know one of the things which hurts Max most? The younger generation of rich Jews, and their attitude to life in general. I never realized how proud Max was of his race until I saw how it pained him to see the post-war Jews. You see, they always do everything a little more than anyone else … they're finer or more base". Jew-lovers and Jew-haters were both prone to this generalisation. Max's third son, Bill, speaks to young Emmanuel about the Jewishness of his brother Julian: "I should hate to think he was typical, but I do believe he's a type. One of the types that has made us hated and feared by other nations, and I don't blame 'em either!"

A Gentile friend of the family doubts if any Englishmen are "so typical as the Anglicized Jews who admire and love the country of their adoption". It was Max's father who adopted England but the remark is otherwise accurate about Max. Emmanuel, though is different, and father and son clash over Max's wish that Emmanuel join the antiques business, which is part of a family inheritance remarkably like that of an ancient family of aristocrats – "this damned business, that damned great house, the park, the furniture, the pictures…". This is something, which Jews can now attain, but they do not all want it. Emmanuel has turned his back on family tradition by establishing himself in Italy. When his wife dies, he comes back and offers to join the firm, but wants too much freedom for Max to accept his terms. The head of the family must rule.[10]

Jacob's family saga makes an interesting contrast with that of G B Stern, written over much the same interwar period. Whereas Jacob is mainly concerned with the Gollantz men, Stern's *The Rakonitz Chronicles* is about a family remarkable for its dominating and domineering women. The first book, which, appeared in 1924, was called *The Tents of Israel*, although it was later republished under its American title *The Matriarch*. The family tree was so complicated that it had to be printed with each volume. "Even if one of them cleared a temporary space by dying, it was quickly crowded up again by at least three new babies, and the arrival of an entire family which had been forgotten somewhere in Central Europe until now, but who were cousins by marriage two generations removed". Gentiles marry into the family, but the Jewish element swallows them up. The Rakonitz have blue eyes and short noses, and when an exception appears, there is mock horror: "She's worse than Jewish, she's Yiddish". One such exception is "fat and oily with a long black moustache and a nose that really was Jewish – a nose that disgraced the entire clan". Val, an artist with a sense of irony liked to introduce him to her Gentile friends, "because he was the kind of Jew they could easily understand". This is all fun; there are no Jew-hating Jews here, but a lot of self-confidence.

The Matriarch herself is Anastasia, an old lady born in 1835. She is a domineering monster, brilliant at getting her way, always working for the family, sure that she knows what is good for her hapless relations better than they do, always helping them, whether or not they want help. She might have been unbearable in the hands of an unsympathetic author, but her monstrous qualities are tempered by her warm heart, and Stern's affection. The comparison with Zangwill's warmth towards his narrow-minded "children of the ghetto comes to mind", although the Rakonitz never think twice about the ghetto. Also important in the first volume are Anastasia's granddaughter, Toni – it does not count that her father was a Gentile – and Danny who loves her, but will not marry her because belonging to the family is "like travelling with an awful lot of baggage when you could do with none". He is relieved when he finds that he is not Jewish and not a Rakonitz after all.

The Rakonitz are nomads who "settled and moved on again, and were legally granted other nationalities and bought other people's houses and gardens and left them again, and they spread and spread without rooting, and scattered and scattered without rooting; but invincibly the face survived". The English Rakonitz never thinks of themselves as either English or anything else. They include all sorts of Jews, including Richard, who is stolid, unemotional and keen on games. Proud of his English birthright, he is amazed and hurt to be classed as an enemy alien during the First World War because he happened to be born in Germany. He resists the Matriarch's pressure by calling off marriage to a Jewish girl, and marrying his Gentile sweetheart. He wants an English son, "a kid that got some pluck, and won't show when he grazes his knees; and a kid that speaks my language without a foreign accent". His son will be English, and his son's son. "By that time, if there's another war, it wouldn't have mattered that his grandfather had been an alien. He could fight on the English side". At the end, Toni, who is starting up in the fashion business, is emerging as the Matriarch of the younger generation, as Danny had predicted, and Richard crosses out Danny's name on the all-important family tree.[11] A dramatised version of the book ran for nearly 250 performances, with a Gentile actress, Mrs Patrick Campbell, the star of *Bella Donna* as the matriarch.

The first sequel, *A Deputy was King*, begins in 1921, a mere five years before the book was published. Times have changed; "this younger generation of Rakonitz met only spasmodically, not with the solid regularity of their elders; nor, when they had a plan, did they bother to lay it before a tribal council". With Anastasia dead, Toni is now the main character; she is of the first entirely irreligious generation. She makes a success of her dress shop, and when she marries Giles, a Gentile, she wants a child soon. "The racial instinct was soon resilient in her; so that she looked upon the next generation as the generation that counted.... Only half an Israelite herself, and she had married a Christian, there would not be much of a Jew in Toni's child. Still...".

Toni is not really a monster, certainly less so than Aunt Elsa or Loraine who suddenly arrives from nowhere, and proclaims herself a family member, although the only connection she can offer is "some great-uncle or other". Loraine is a fanatic for the family, but runs off with Giles. However, Toni gets him back. She sells her business and buys a 17-bedroom house in Italy. "Her secret longings... were to have rooms for any members of the Rakonitzes tribe who might at any time need to be sheltered and fed". "The remnants of the family, one by one obliged to give up their big houses, had since had unwelcome experiences of what was second-rate and dingy; they had scattered and rebelled, intermarried with aliens, broken the rules and forgotten the glory". They needed a big house again, where they could meet, hear news, recuperate after bad luck, be ill, and grow old. Toni wants Loraine to live there, as "it really is the deepest passion of her life, this desire to be near her own people; to settle down with them, and be counted in". Giles, ashamed of his fling with Loraine, will not have it, and uses his illness to get his way, so destroying Toni's illusion of prep school Englishmen who do not hit below the belt. He says she is "more of a decent Englishman than I am". Toni, Giles, and Richard illustrate the complications of the relationship between Jewishness and Englishness. Like the relationship of the various characters to their own Jewishness, this is more important than the plot.[12]

Toni and other old friends reappear in *Mosaic*, the third volume of the series, but the main characters are the sisters Berthe and Letti, who live together in Paris after the death of their husbands. Berthe is another female monster. Her feud with Aunt Elsa is comic until one of the latter's daughters arrives at the Paris flat and Berthe lets her in, even though Letti has scarlet fever. Letti survives, but the girl dies. When Letti's son Etienne marries, his wife cannot stand living with Berthe, and the young couple decamp to Italy. Berthe convinces herself that Letti was the problem. She makes a second attempt to take over a young man's life when Rudi arrives from Vienna for the Paris production of a musical he has written. Berthe wants him to send for his wife and live with her and Letti. When it looks as though she will get her way, Val says, "In the same building – God, these Rakonitzes! Aunt Anastasia was the same... nearly killed poor Susie until Toni came to the rescue of her mother. They're complete tyrants and on a sublime scale".[13] Sensing disaster, Letti makes sure that Rudi returns home. This leads to a blazing row between the two sisters, and Berthe makes for Vienna, expecting to install herself with Rudi. It had been said of Toni in the previous novel that "She had never been to Vienna or Budapest, but she knew them through legend, through snatches of song... and she knew them racially because they were in her blood".[14] Berthe goes further, thinking she is an honorary Viennese, but she learns differently from Rudi's steely English wife who remorselessly takes her on tourist trips until she returns to Paris. The sisters are reconciled, and a letter arrives from Aunt Elsa making it up with Berthe, but the Rakonitz reconciliations are less convincing than their quarrels.

It is extraordinary that no antisemitism is recorded in these books, even *Mosaic*, which takes place in Paris and Vienna as well as London.

The characters are preoccupied with their relationships with other family members; those with the Gentile world show no signs of strain. *The Rakonitz Chronicles* are a monument to the confidence of well-off cosmopolitan Jews before the storm broke. Admittedly, the Nazi horror could not be avoided in the last volume, *The Young Matriarch*, as it was published in 1942. Much of the plot is about getting family members out of Hitler's Europe, but their plight is conveyed less vividly than the family power struggles over who shall take in each batch of new arrivals. Babs, an eighteen-year-old, is in the strongest position when she inherits a house. Even when the house is bombed, she continues to show signs of becoming the latest in the long line of matriarchs.[15]

The Rakonitz scarcely noticed the rise of the Nazis, but Simon Blumenfeld's *Jew Boy* begins in 1933 with a protest march. "What an example of solidarity! What a lesson for the whole world! These bloody Jews, these murderers, these misers, these money grabbers were sacrificing the best day of the week. Throwing away trade worth tens, perhaps hundreds of thousands of pounds to march to Hyde Park, because other Jews were being ill-treated in Germany". Navvies repairing the tramway urge them on, and give them mugs of tea, but other working people react with tight-lipped whispers and vicious glances. "Alec could guess what *they* were saying. 'Serves 'em bloody well right! We ought to do the same thing here'". He reflects that it would be hard to rid them of the lies hammered into them from the cradle. "The priests and parsons and Imperialists had done their work well". He does not mention the novelists.

Alec's girlfriend's sister has married a Gentile, who is glad that Alec does not look very Jewish. "She didn't want her sister to fetch along any snotty Vitechapel Jews. She didn't want the whole neighbourhood to know she was Jewish". This makes it difficult for a friend of hers. "Of course she knew that Mrs Saunders was a Jewess, but she never liked to mention it... It was tacitly understood that Jews were non-existent as far as Mrs Saunders was concerned. She really would have liked to know more about that peculiar people, but her friend was so secretive on the subject. She always turned red, and shut up like a clam whenever Jews were mentioned". Alec realises that in marrying out Mrs Saunders had to be brave: "leaving her home and her people for the man she loved, marrying a Gentile in spite of bitter parental opposition ... but to throw overboard one set of hidebound prejudices, and take up a whole set of new ones. To masquerade as a hundred per cent Aryan! Why, they only had to look at her nose!"

Alec has a one night stand with Elspeth, a wealthy young woman, but her attitudes make a longer relationship impossible. "My father is a landowner, our money comes from the earth, the English earth, my country. 'Stolen from us!' Why, you should be the last to speak. You and your people are only guests here". It is clear from this conversation that Alec has left-wing views, and class is almost as big an issue in the novel as race. When he argues that England is more his country than Elspeth's as he works and creates wealth, she answers, "Now you are talking like a Jew.... One who has no country".

This remark burns into him. He remembers how, after he and his Jewish friends had played cricket in the park with other schoolboys, "they had to go home in batches because there would always be a mob of youngsters from Bethnal Green waiting for them at the cinder path. The cry would go up 'Here come the Jew boys!' and they'd be pelted with stones, gravel and other rubbish". In the end Alec's left-wing views would have taken him to the Soviet Union, had the authorities there let him in. He has to carry on the international struggle from home.[16]

Alec's employer in the rag trade could not have been depicted more harshly by an antisemitic novelist, and the theme of class is continued in Blumenfeld's *Phineas Kahn, Portrait of an Immigrant*. In 1900, Phineas and his wife are sent from Russia to London, to the care of his Uncle Samuel, an East End sweater, who owns a cap factory, where he puts Phineas to work. "Every one pound rise was dragged out of Uncle Samuel like meat from the paws of a hungry tiger". The other workers did not complain, because, although pay and conditions were terrible, they were far better than what they had known in Russia and Poland. Moreover England meant a degree of freedom after the despotism of the Czar. At another firm, Orthodox Jews accept low wages because their employer shares their religious beliefs. Phineas is a talented musician, but he is never in a position to be a professional. He has too many children ever to drag himself out of poverty, and much of the story is about what happens to them. In the end he at least succeeds where Alec failed in the earlier novel by leaving for the Soviet Union of the 1930s. As the journey begins, he passes the Tower of London. "It represented a culture in which he had no part. The Tower he left for his children; its history belonged to them; they might be able to learn its lessons".[17] They have prospered, as he has not, although they have not reached the safe world, portrayed by Naomi Jacob and G B Stern, in which the struggle for acceptance is over.

Whichever class of Jews they were dealing with, Jewish novelists of between the wars could be relied upon to offer all the criticisms, which their detractors levelled against them. Zangwill's remark that "Jews are very fond of telling stories against themselves" held true then and still holds true today. Jewish novelists could see when a nose or diamond ring was too big, but they knew their wearers were not irredeemable. They could recognise greed and cruelty, but knew that a greedy or cruel Jew did not represent millions of others. More self-confident than B.L Farjeon, they did not need to idealise their Jewish characters. No progress is constant, but read carefully these books suggest that Jews were not only better off materially in 1940 than in 1890, even if the facts of the Holocaust had to become known for casual antisemitism in Britain to become totally disreputable.

The Blacks

Why the story is so painful; sex and the colour bar; colonial attitudes for the British reader; black people and the novelist's world view; the travails of the black man in Britain.

CHAPTER 10:

Coping with Africa

"What is a gentleman? I don't quite know, and yet I have had to do with niggers – no I'll scratch that word 'nigger out', for I don't like it".[1]

This is the most distressing section of the book. During the period we are discussing, it was not really disreputable to consider black people inferior and treat them accordingly. The white British may have seen blacks on stage or exhibited in some show or other, but few ever met any. Nearly all who did, did so under colonial conditions, where they themselves were the rulers and the blacks the ruled, where their own level of material and technological progress was so advanced that it was usual to describe blacks as primitive. It is hardly surprising that these circumstances engendered a feeling of superiority in the whites. In technology and material well-being they were superior, but this led them to assume the same degree of superiority in essential human qualities, and, worse still, often to deny or ignore the common humanity which black people shared with them. Some African customs, like West African ju-ju, admittedly encouraged such attitudes, but human sacrifice, and cannibalism were wrongly assumed to be everyday practices. Brian Street has defined the problem in his book *The Savage in Literature*, where he says that "any custom 'discovered' among a 'primitive people' is assumed to dominate their whole lives". Characteristics could be attributed to a whole people, who might be blithely gullible, faithful, brave, childlike, savage, bloodthirsty, noble etc. This was the result of heredity, so they were incapable of change.[2] One conclusion drawn from this, time and again in popular novels was that black people, who tried to adopt Western customs, were doomed to failure. As the vast majority of Britons never visited the colonies, their views of blacks were largely formed by what they read, and fiction was therefore crucial in opinion forming.

The story does not begin too badly in that, from the 1880s on, the most popular author to write about blacks was Rider Haggard. His black characters were mainly Zulus or based on the Zulu he had admired in South Africa. His novels began to appear shortly after the Zulus burst upon the British consciousness by inflicting, at Isandhlwana in 1879, greatest defeat the British army ever suffered at the hands of a non-European power. Whereas awareness of the Chinese and Arabs was dominated by an image of the enemy hordes besieging European civilization in the sieges of Peking and Khartoum, the Zulus became known for winning an open battle fair and square. Britain's eventual victory in the war removed the bitterness which might have followed, and made it possible to admire the Zulus' martial qualities unreservedly. Shortly after the war, Zulus were brought to Britain to give displays of their customs or merely to be stared at. This was deplorable, but confirmed that men of this warrior nation were physically imposing. Victorian women were particularly impressed. Any naked men they had seen, their husbands for example, were unlikely to have been such fine physical specimens.

Haggard's blacks were often seen through the eyes of the author's alter ego, the big game hunter, Allan Quartermaine, who is the source of the quotation heading this chapter. In *King Solomon's Mines*, Quartermaine says he has known "natives" who are gentlemen, and whites who are not. Sometimes they are also heroes. The people of the imaginary kingdom, which Quartermaine and his companions discover, are much like Zulus, although the women, "for a native race, exceedingly handsome", are "as well-bred in their way as the habituees of a fashionable drawing-room, and in this respect differ from Zulu women and their cousins the Masai". Haggard did not like the Masai. It is a Zulu boy who gives his life to save Quartermaine's friend, Sir Henry Good, and, during the battle between rival forces of the imaginary tribe, one section of the victorious army defend a narrow pass, knowing that in doing so they will ensure victory but will all die in the process. Haggard's educated readers would have spotted the implicit comparison with the Greek heroes of Thermopylae. Another admirable figure is the beautiful young tribeswoman, who is in love with Sir Henry, and is stabbed to death by a wicked female witchdoctor as she tries to save him and Quartermaine. Her death, however, reveals the limitations of Haggard's benign attitude to even his favourite black people. Quartermaine considers it fortunate, "Otherwise complications would have been sure to ensue.... No amount of beauty or refinement could have made an entanglement between Good and herself a desirable occurrence; for as she herself puts it, 'Can the sun mate with the darkness, or the white with the black?"[3] This is not a matter of cultural differences making for a difficult marriage; it stems from the revulsion against sex between black and white partners which remained strong, well into the twentieth century. It is the most difficult aspect of the fiction of the period for the modern reader to stomach.

In the novel named after him, Allan Quartermaine dreams "of the sight of Zulu impis breaking on their foes like surf upon the rocks" and his heart leaps "in rebellion against the strict limit of civilised life". The Zulu was the noble savage. This is the book which sees the death of Quartermaine's faithful Zulu follower, Umslopagaas, who has killed more than a 100 men in combat, only counting the ones he has ripped open according to custom. He holds a palace gate single-handed, just as, in the Roman legend, Horatius held the bridge. However, when, in a later novel, Quartermaine sees that the Zulus are about to attack the Boers, "'I won't leave the other white men', I said; 'it would be the act of a coward'".[4] Haggard's admiration for the Zulus is unquestionable; he liked to compare them with the warrior heroes of Greece and Rome; he was exceptional for his time in disliking the N-word; his work is a far cry from the crudeness of a William Le Queux, who refers in *The Eye of Istar* to cannibal warriors leaping forward, "grinning from ear to ear and rubbing their paunches with their hands with lively anticipation".[5] On the other hand, Haggard's very real decency did not transcend the prejudices of his time.

He had his followers. Charles Montague's *The Vigil* must stand for many Zulu tales, all bloody, as Haggard's were, although his Zulu narrator untypically fights for the British at Isandhlwana. He has lived for years under the British flag, and found that "wherever it waves, man's right as man is recognised and justice is not sold". The battle was lost, in his view, because "the English lords, being themselves brave as the cubs of a lion, did not sufficiently regard the courage and discipline of the Zulu country". He tells his story to an Englishman, who records that "there was a singular quiet manner and dignity in his speech", and that the Zulu is often homely but not vulgar; and does not breach the canons of good taste. When the Zulu narrator, over six feet and beautifully proportioned, wins his girl, his close friend, who is also in love with her, gives way graciously. Hero and villain fight a duel at the end. The Zulus in this story are less classical warriors than medieval knights.[6]

For most British readers, Zululand was scarcely more real than the imaginary black kingdom of *King Solomon's Mines*. Cutcliffe Hyne's tales of Captain Kettle, however, purport to describe how an Englishman really engages with foreigners in various parts of the world. Historians make much of antisemitic pamphlets of our period which, unpleasant though they are, had tiny readerships. Less attention has been paid to the virulent racism of these stories which, from the late 1890s on, appeared in best-selling magazines and books. There was also a West End play. Kettle is a brave, opinionated, peppery sea captain always in financial difficulties because of his integrity and refusal to bow the knee to ship owners or anyone else. Hyne distances himself from his hero to some extent, showing how often his short temper gets him into scrapes, and stressing the contrast between his chapel-going piety at home and his engagement in skulduggery when he sails round the world. However, Hyne does not distance himself from Kettle's loathing and contempt for foreigners; his autobiography confirms that he shared them.[7] Kettle "was one of those aggressive Islanders who would as soon fight as shake hands with a foreigner",[8] and, given his popularity, it would seem that his many readers cheered him on. Because he rarely gets good ships, his crews are made up of many nationalities, and he regularly hurls racist abuse at them, preventing mutinies only by his pistol and the force of his will. He finds East Europeans and Jews, loathsome and contemptible, and we are repeatedly told how much he dislikes Dagoes, meaning South Europeans, particularly Portuguese. He features in this chapter, though, because of his attitude to blacks. It is particularly marked in *The Further Adventures of Kettle*, which mostly take place in Africa: "We're going to have no foolery about the nigger being as good as the white man. He isn't, and no man that ever saw him where he grows ever thought so". To which his doctor friend replies that "speaking scientifically", he is "an animal placed by the scheme of creation somewhere between a monkey and a white man. You might bracket him, say, with a Portuguese". Kettle is of course more than a match for such people, "one slight, slim, white-clad white man against that reeking, shining mob, and they struggled away before him in grotesque tumblings and jostlings, like a flock of sheep". He makes short shrift of a black stowaway, who, having refused to leave the ship, "was lowered ignominiously in a bowline, and then, as he still objected loudly that he came from Sierra Leone, and was a free British subject, some one crammed a bucket over his head, amidst the uproarious laughter of the onlookers". Kettle sets him to work. "High-minded theories as to the rights of man" were not appreciated here, and "under the sledge-hammer blows of whoever happened to be next to him, the unfortunate coloured gentleman descended to the grade of nigger again". This is a practical application of Kettle's view that "When the black man gets too pampered, he has to be brought low again with a rush, just to make him understand his place".

Hyne tells us that "from long acclimatisation, the Portuguese might almost count as African", a hint that there has been too much interbreeding for his taste. Kettle also despises their treatment of blacks – "there's a limit to everything and this snuff-coloured Dago goes too far". When a Portuguese captain throws sick black seamen overboard to prevent the authorities knowing that there is smallpox on his ship, it makes Kettle ill "to see how those poor beasts of niggers are left to die". The cruelty of the Belgians in the Congo is also too much for him. In a row with a Belgian Commandant, Kettle says, "Understand once and for all, that I will not have England abused". To which, Hyne tells us, "the man of the weaker nation subsided".[9] A reviewer in *The Times Literary Supplement* commented that "It is pleasant to keep company with this breezy, buoyant little captain", and pointed out, no doubt correctly, that the stories were successful not because of their plots but because of the character of Kettle himself.[10]

Hyne was still offering these stories to an eager public in the mid-1920s. By this time the Africans answer back a little more, but Kettle treats them the same and maintains his ascendancy over them. He has only a walk-on part in *Kate Meredith, Financier*, a novel in which the colour question is the main theme. The male protagonist, Carter, who is new to Africa, arrives on a boat which is having difficulties coming ashore, but "whatever a white man may feel, he always assumes coolness and indifference before the black". The anxious Carter wants to shout at the black sailors, but "almost to his astonishment, pride of race kept him grimly silent. He had never felt before the whole debt that is owing to a white skin". Carter falls in love with Laura Slade, and when she tells him that she is one-eighth African, he professes indifference. Hyne comments: "A man who had been longer in Africa would have had the wisdom of one who had lived in the Southern States, and have picked out the African blood at a glance, and, as is the way of men who have eaten of the tree of that wisdom, would have ordered his civilities accordingly". Moreover, Carter's father has told him before he left for Africa, "Remember always you're a white man, and don't get mixed up with any woman who owns a single drop of blood darker than your own. If you do, you can never come back here, and you'll hate yourself for the rest of your life". His father, a clergyman, offered his experience of India as evidence that he knew what he was talking about. He is later described as "a splendid old man". Laura is beautiful, and loves Carter, but there is wide agreement that the one-eighth of her will cause trouble. A naval captain remarks, "How that little girl's shot up! It's a dashed pity she's a nigger". And even her own father says, "If I were a man that ever looked so much as half a day ahead I believe I should go mad at the thought of what will become of Laura in the future". Laura herself knows that even if Carter makes her his wife, he will never take her to England, and she marries a Portuguese, leaving Carter free for Kate Meredith, who is wholly white. This is particularly unconvincing as the Portuguese are treated with the same contempt as in the Kettle stories, and the man in question has tried to kill

Carter and suffered a whipping by him. However Hyne is determined that his hero will marry a white woman.[11]

Only a decade after Kettle's first appearance in print, Edgar Wallace invented Commissioner Sanders, whose popularity was even greater and lasted until well after the Second World War. His territory in West Central Africa is inhabited, most improbably, by "some quarter of a million cannibal folk", over whom he has the power of life and death. He "knew the native mind better than any man living". According to Wallace, "there is one type of man that can rule native provinces wisely, and that type is best represented by Sanders".[12]

In 1940, Jack Maclaren published *Gentlemen of the Empire* in praise of District Commissioners and other officials of the Colonial Service, "that fine flower of the genius for colonisation which has made the British Empire the greatest ever known" and which has "carried the light of Western civilization, shouldered the White Man's burden" and achieved more than the officials of any other nation. One of the officers praised by Maclaren, with the help of only 12 African policeman, prevented war after a chief had ordered the murder of a member of another tribe. Then "all that remained for the officer to do was to burn the town to the ground as a warning to the people to behave themselves in future". After long service in Africa, such men are not quite at home in London, where the sight "of white men doing coolie labour" jars on them.[13] It is against the background of such thinking that the Sanders stories were eagerly read for so long. Maclaren is right that many colonial officers were fine people, of whom their country could justifiably be proud, but they were not like Sanders.

When blacks do not do what he wants, they are beaten up. One is kicked "scientifically in the stomach, which is the native's weak spot". When a suspect confesses because Sanders is threatening to set fire to him, Wallace comments, "If you ask me whether Sanders would have employed his lighted stick, I answer truthfully that I think it possible". Although God-fearing, Sanders dislikes missionaries. They represent a rival source of power. He will accept them if they are white, but "black missionaries I will not endure". Wallace endorses this attitude through his portrayal of a missionary, whose behaviour "will be incomprehensible to any who do not know how thumbnail deep is the cultivation of the cultured savage". Sanders keeps his assistants well away from black women – "monkey tricks of that kind are good enough for the Belgian Congo, or for Togoland, but they aren't good enough for this little strip of wilderness".[14] He himself is resolutely chaste – like Captain Kettle, although the latter has a wife back home.

He despises his superiors and visiting do-gooders, but admires Joseph Chamberlain, the great imperialist Colonial Secretary.[15]

Missionaries are not the only educated black men Sanders dislikes: "the civilised native, the native of the frock coat and top hat – was Mr Commissioner Sander's pet abomination. He also loathed all native men who spoke English – however badly they spoke it", assuming, one supposes, that by speaking English to him the black man was claiming an equal status.[16] The one exception, his ally Bosambo, an escaped convict from Liberia, knows only about fifty English words. Bosambo helps Sanders keep order, while feathering his own nest at every opportunity. He is a thief and a liar, like all Monrovians in Wallace's view. He is a brave man who puts heart into the tribe which Sanders gives him to rule over, but his love of incongruous finery and his low cunning make him a figure of fun. He claims to have white blood, and on one occasion, to be related to the British Prime Minister.[17]

Film-goers who had not read the Sanders books would have been unaware of Bosambo's original character, because in the famous 1935 film, he was played as a much more dignified and admirable figure by Paul Robeson. The characters of both Bosambo and Sanders himself were sanitised for the screen. Even later, when Robeson came to believe that he was wrong to have taken the part, his regrets were over the film's general endorsement of colonialism rather than his own role. Although it was called *Sanders of the River*, the title of the first collection of short stories, its plot was loosely based on *Sandi the Kingmaker* of 1922, the only full length Sanders novel. There are more stories featuring the silly ass Lieutenant Bones, in which Sanders is only a supporting character, but their ethos is much the same.

Bosambo is in some ways like Sexton Blake's great friend, Lobangu, the chief of the imaginary Etbaia tribe. Lobangu is described at various times as wholly or partly a Zulu, but he is a cruel parody of Rider Haggard's dignified heroes. He is far more like Bosambo in his sly cunning, huge appetite and taste for inappropriate finery, and sweet champagne. Sixpence, "one-time cook boy in South Africa, and now Prime minister of the Etbaia nation" is even more absurd in his bowler hat and baggy frock coat. Lobangu is supposed to represent "all that was best in unspoilt native life ... eagled-eyed with the fierce, strong face of the born ruler of men" but he repeatedly makes a fool of himself, especially when he comes to England. When taught to play billiards, he makes a huge hole in the table and smashes three cues; when taught to drive he smashes up the car. He is bitterly disappointed when told to remove a "magnificent fur coat, in which he looked rather like a huge bear with a funny-shaped head" because of his alleged resemblance to "the manager of a coloured jazz band". He will travel any distance and brave any danger to help Blake or his other white friend, Sir Richard Losley on their many adventures in Africa, but, fond of him as they are, their condescension is insufferable today. They bear with his black man's attempt to appear civilised only because they find it comic. The "savage" is always breaking through the surface. In a fight with a baboon man, he "had forgotten his veneer of civilisation" and his distorted face was "almost as bestial as that of his opponent, the sounds that issued from his mouth were entirely animal".[18]

* * *

> "A White woman and a black man, the thought brought its little neces-sary shiver of disgust. 'It would have been better to have killed herself, wouldn't it?' he said presently".[19]

As a common feature of life in the colonies, interracial sex was a recurrent theme of novels with a colonial setting. The horror it evoked among authors and novel readers may even have increased its appeal. In practice, lonely white officials and traders did not often stay celibate. Particularly in West Africa, where the climate was considered unsuitable for white women, it was hard to find any but a black partner. At least the people back home did not know about it.

In *Wilton's Silence* by Paul Trent, Taynton, a newcomer to colonial administration, is taught the local language by Addah, a young "half-caste" woman with a white skin. "She's a beauty. It's a pity there's black blood. Some white men have a good deal to answer for". Taynton loves her, but will not offer marriage. "He sprang from good blood, and the idea of offspring made him shudder". Seeing half-caste children on the coast, he "could not doubt that, behind each of them, lay tragedy". Addah herself has been led to think the same, saying "It is a terrible thing to have black blood. We are not the equals of the white people". Her white father, who has lost sight of her for years, says that she is "glorious in every way, and yet no decent man would take her for his wife. She'd be better dead". When she sickens, and the doctor says that half-castes have little resistance to disease, it becomes clear what will happen. She duly dies, and her father's view is endorsed: "In many ways the ending is the happiest possible for Addah". It needs emphasising that her problem was not skin colour but blood. She could not marry an

Englishman because some of her blood was deemed to be black; a white skin was not enough.[20]

The view expressed by Addah's father seems particularly unfair because her mother had saved him from alcoholism years ago. This is a theme which recurs in Trent's *A Wife by Purchase* in which Claude Drummond, who is drinking himself to death in West Africa, is told by his friend, Jack Alston, "A native wife does help to avoid the liquor". He duly buys Akole from her grandmother for five ounces of gold. Trent remarks that, despite all the efforts of the authorities, "from the first settling of white man on West African shore it has been his custom to take to wife, one or as many native girls as his purse will allow". Akole's skin is white but her speech and outlook African. She saves Claude from drink and is devoted to him. However, when he takes long leave in England, he inherits an earldom and has no need to return to the terrible West African climate. This leads to an all-too common tragedy. The "wife" of the white man has gone through no marriage ceremony; when he returns home and no longer needs her, she is abandoned. Claude becomes engaged to Jack Alston's cousin, Olive, and Alston takes his revenge for being ousted in her affections by getting Akole to England. Claude tries to reject her, but her sexual allure proves too strong, and he sets her up in a villa as his mistress. This leads to an embarrassing situation when he and Olive return from their wedding to be confronted by a pregnant Akole. She becomes desperately ill, and is nursed by Olive. The latter's father is an old Africa hand, and has taken his pleasure in the usual way. Akole and Olive are half sisters. The melodramatic coincidence is outrageous, but it serves to underline the hypocrisy of colonial West Africa. Claude says, "What blackguards we Coasters are. We buy our 'mammies' and when we have done with them, we leave; never giving a thought to the possibility that brats of our own blood may be naked little savages". His father-in-law replies, "I have come to the conclusion that the climate of West Africa warps one's morals". Heroically, the dying Akole, who notices that her presence has cooled relations between Claude and Olive, urges them to love one another. As Olive has reproached Claude with seducing her half-sister, he is not confident that things will work out, but once again the death of the African woman is very convenient.[21]

In 1924, one of the great hits of the London stage, Leon Gordon's *White Cargo* addressed the same theme. Allen Langford takes over his firm's trade in a remote outpost of West Africa where there are only three other white men, one an alcoholic doctor. He is told that the loneliness and the absence of white women mean that sooner or later he will resort to "mammy-palaver" or sex with a black girl. His answer is "I've heard of it as one hears of plagues and other unpleasant things. I am white and I am going to stay white". However, he is seduced, by Tondeleyo, whose father was French, but inherits her personality from her African mother. The doctor repeats received wisdom with his comment, "That's the trouble with mixed blood. The colour always predominates. Of course they can't help that, but it deprives them of all delicacy". Langford is determined to buck the trend by marrying Tondeleyo. His companions are appalled at this is crime against the white man's tropical code. "It's something you can never repair. Something you will regret till the last breath you draw. Something that is unwholesome". Nevertheless the marriage goes ahead, but Tondeleyo tires of Langford. When the doctor tells her that she has contracted to stay with him until death do them part, she draws the conclusion that the way out of her predicament is to poison him. The murder is prevented, and the poison is forced down Tondeleyo's throat.[22]

The assumptions of all the white characters, particularly that the African woman is fit only for sex, makes the play particularly repugnant today, but *The Play Pictorial*, described it as "a wonderful picture of the life and environment of those who build up the Empire and the Empire's trade".[23] *The Times* praised the leading actress for her portrayal of "the coarseness of the she-animal".[24] On the other hand, in one of the few novels of the 1930s written by a black author, the protagonist acts in a production of *White Cargo*, and comments "I prefer not to think of those days or how humiliating to our race I found that play to be". The black girl is played by a cockney actress, and he complains that no black woman would behave or look like her. His point is granted, but, he is told, it would be unthinkable for a black woman to play opposite a white actor.[25] This was unfortunately true. Even the immensely popular entertainer, Hutch, was not allowed to appear on stage with white women. Paul Robeson in *Othello* was a famous exception.

Langford's initial comparison of "mammy-palaver" with "plagues and other unpleasant things was echoed in the title story of William Plomer's collection, *The Child of Queen Victoria*. Plomer, a literary writer, describes how young Frant works in West Africa for the MacGavins, a racist Scottish trader and his wife. Frant has always given MacGavin the impression "of being a bit too fond of the niggers, and treating them a bit too much as if they were human beings". So when the trader asks Frant if he ever feels in need of a woman, he is surprised to be subjected to a tirade: "He said he would rather do anything than touch a black woman; he said that they were dirty, that they stank, that they were no better than animals; he said that the blacks and whites were in his opinion races apart, and that on no account should they mix in any way; he said that white men ought to be respected by black ones, and that that could only be possible if they treated them as inferiors, absolute inferiors". The fact is that Frant is lusting after a young black girl, and he is trying to deceive both MacGavin and himself. Plomer has cleverly highlighted the guilt and fear behind much of the abhorrence of interracial sex.[26]

As early as 1904, Stuart Young tried to show in *Merely A Negress*, which is set in Liberia, that an Englishman *can* enjoy a happy marriage with a black woman. The dice are loaded because Frank Benson's Liberian wife is another of the strangely numerous fictional women of this period whose white skin belies their "black blood", and she is unusually well versed in English culture. When he returns to England, Frank leaves her behind and neglects her badly, but in the end the marriage is a happy one. In contrast, a repulsive man called Clayton has already made an African girl pregnant in Sierra Leone and then abandoned her. Although he intends to marry a girl back in England, he behaves equally shabbily to a young Liberian woman, who kills herself and her child when she too is abandoned. Young has Clayton murdered by the woman's brother, and writes that the black man "displays noble human traits under proper circumstances and a congenial environment". However, the novel is quoted only as an exception. It did not sell.[27]

Marriages between white women and black men aroused most opposition. The dislike of educated blacks is linked to this theme because they often acquired their education as law, medical or theological students in England, where they met Englishwomen. In A J Dawson's short story *The Treatment of Brierly*, Daryll is a black lawyer who has married 17-year-old Daisy. She is a "poor little bundle of schoolgirl vanity" fresh from finishing school. He is "full-blooded, you understand – very intensely a negro". When the story opens in Lagos, she "has reached the shuddering stage. Perhaps you have not seen that. It is too unpleasant to write or think about – much. Ask any woman who has seen a white girl married to a native". The other white women will have nothing to do with her. Reports have reached the club that she has been heard screaming. Brierly falls in love with Daisy and catastrophe is only avoided by transferring him to Calabar. He is not out of harm's way, however, as he falls in love with the daughter of a chief and marries her. "He was absolutely and thoroughly socially damned. Of course he cannot go home. Yet a man who saw him last year said he seemed very happy. The man may, to be sure, have spoken ironically. Anyway a white man cannot live very long at a stretch in the Oil Rivers". Of the two marriages offered in the story the one involving a black man and a white woman is a complete disaster; in the other, the white husband is socially dead and, in the opinion of his peers, might as well be physically dead too.[28] The same collection of 1900, offers another story, also set in Nigeria, involving a ship's purser who falls in love with a black girl, only to see her killed in a ju-ju sacrifice. He dies throwing himself into the river after her.

A few years later Harold Bindloss published *Beneath Her Station*, in which working class Addy is out of work and penniless, which is why she agrees to marry King Konnoto and go to Africa with him. Millicent, the heroine is in favour of imperial unity and, so far as she understands it, the brotherhood of man, but feels queasy seeing him bending over a white girl. The hero, whom Millicent eventually marries, tells her, "I scarcely think the woman who would marry Konnoto would be one you would care to make a friend of, and one cannot afford to ignore the prejudices of one's countrymen". Konnoto confirms the worst fears about him by falling under the influence of the ju-ju men. As one of them spoke softly in his ear, "there was a portentous glitter in his eyes; his face was animal-like and brutal with its suggestion of sensuality and cruelty, while he clenched a big dusty hand on the table".

Along with the climate, whites in West Africa found ju-ju particularly hard to take, and it made it harder for them to treat the Africans as normal human beings. Addy is frightened of what the ju-ju men may make her husband do, and asks him to get out to the Canaries with her. To his credit, he is tempted but has advanced too far in a rebellion against the British to go back. Bindloss comments that "While the untaught African is not infrequently brave and, when he has the blood of the Arab in him, makes the grimmest kind of soldier, the civilised one is seldom remarkable for his temerity". Addy learns that the mission station is going to be attacked and braves great danger to sound the alarm. "I couldn't stay there and do nothing while they killed white people. Nobody at home ever thought much of me – and Konnoto was as kind as he dared to be until lately – but I'm white". Reduced to poverty in England and snubbed by the other white women in Africa, Addy proves herself a heroine of Empire, and is rewarded when Konnoto is killed in the uprising.[29] However, hers has been another disastrous mixed-race marriage.

In Arthur Weigall's *Madeline of the Desert* the heroine has been driven into such a marriage, not by poverty, but worse, by lust.

She tells the hero about her husband. "'My daddy gave him a sum of money to go away'. 'Why?' 'Well, you see, he wasn't English'. 'Jones', replied Robin; 'he was Welsh then?' 'No' she replied. She braced herself, and forced a smile. 'He was a negro', she said. 'Good Lord!' exclaimed Robin, looking at her with horror. 'Wasn't it awful of me?' she whispered, trying to laugh. 'What on earth did you do it for?' he asked. 'He was a magnificent creature', she replied, 'and I was only a girl, a naughty girl'".[30]

Ignoring the black man's sexuality could also cause problems. In *A White Man's Burden* by Charles Beadle, a white woman in a state of undress thoughtlessly asks a black servant to help her on with her dressing gown, and he assaults her. He must suffer the death penalty because the blacks would treat mercy "only as evidence of weakness in their rulers and as a direct incentive to crime". In his heart the husband, a government official, feels that "he and all Europeans who persisted in treating a native as a thing of wood or brass, an automaton, anything but a human being, were really to blame". This is humane and perceptive, but he goes on, "a savage, nearer to the animal, has stronger passions and control weaker than the civilised races, yet the fact was ignored – because they were natives, a conquered people". The "savage" has been in domestic service for ten years.[31] A decade and a half later, in *Kenya Calling*, Nora K Strange also addressed the danger of allowing a black male servant too near his white mistress. Strange's novels advance the cause of the white settlers in Kenya, but they have to be the right kind of settlers. Those with nicknames like Pixie and Tubby are; Lucille, an ex-waitress, is not. Dressed in a frayed and stained kimono, she shows too much nightdress, and Sheila, the heroine, asks her, "Don't you mind the native servants seeing you like this?" Lucille answers, "Oh savages, don't notice what you wear … why should they when they wear so precious little themselves". Sheila thinks they all notice how whites behave. She tells Lucille, "You are lowering the prestige of the white woman in a city populated mainly by natives who only a short time ago were savages". Lucille's houseboy is "good-looking if not actually handsome for an African native", his mother's African features being refined, we are told, by his father's Arab blood. He is "undoubtedly a fine animal". It seems that the "fine animal" is disappointed in Lucille, because, "maddened by drink or jealousy or both", he shoots her dead, so demonstrating that it is a mistake to let blacks become too familiar.[32]

In Louise Gerard's unpleasant novel, *The Hyenea of Kallu*, sex is an important but secondary issue. Molly Seaton weds a black man who takes her back to West Africa. She writes to her best friend

Leslie Graham: "I think I must have died and gone to hell, a hell full of negroes. They are all around me; I can't get away from them. And so hideously real. So real that it makes me scream. The one, my husband, the most constant and most vivid of them all, comes to me and kisses me and asks me what the matter is, holds me close against him when I say that Africa frightens me. It is not Africa and I think he knows". However, the main protagonists are Leslie and Lebrassa, whose father was white and whose mother was African. He has brought about Molly's marriage by a trick and is anxious to help Leslie join her in Africa as Molly has begged her to do. Lebrassa can be very charming, and Leslie is all the more sympathetic to him because when she first meets him in Yorkshire, he is the victim of racist remarks: "'There's a crowd of buck niggers for you', the speaker went on in the same loud, offensive manner. 'It's bad enough to have to deal with them in the land set apart for their sort, but to have to rub shoulders with them in England is beyond all bearing'". Leslie allows Lebrassa to escort her to Africa. She finds Molly seriously ill in bed, and immediately shoos away the black people crowding the bedroom. "It was only one little girl, but of a dominant race, and the room cleared".

It emerges that Lebrassa, the charming, westernised man of the world, is also the fearsome *Hyena of Kallu*, "a savage African sultan with a price on his head, who is always ready to take a hand in any and every rising against the whites, to raid and burn and do murder for no reason that can be discovered". Before his identity is revealed, Leslie has a theory that the Hyena must be "some unfortunate wretch suffering from a loathsome disease that is a constant torture to him, and which he knows neither time, patience, repentance, nor any earthly remedy can cure". This is prophetic, but the loathsome disease, or what he considers to be one, is the genetic inheritance from his black mother. The man is in torment: "My friends! I never had any. Those I would have, despise me. Those who would have me, I despise. I am nothing, neither black nor white, above the one, below the other. An outcast and a pariah". His white father had told him "I must grow up to be an Englishman, and not let my savage instincts conquer me. I must learn to control myself, to master all the wild black blood in me". His father, one of the many earls crowding popular fiction in this period, died in Africa after siring Lebrassa, but not before sending the boy to England to be educated, and bequeathing him his wealth and title. However, Lebrassa was cheated of both, by his father's brother; hence his return to Africa and revenge on the whites.

Leslie is aghast to learn that it was her own late father who usurped the earldom at Lebrassa's expense, and later murdered the high priestess of the tribe. Lebrassa, her cousin, has lured her to Africa to wreak his revenge, but fallen in love with her instead. She agrees to marry him, but only to obtain the release of Captain Fletcher, whom she loves and Lebrassa has kidnapped. Fletcher is the man who made the racist remarks in Yorkshire, but they no longer count against him. The marriage is prevented by Lebrassa's savage followers. He had promised them that Leslie would be killed, and when they learn that she is to become their queen instead, they depose him. He suffers a long lingering death rather than betray Leslie's hiding place. His belated heroism continues when he tries to save her feelings by pretending that he lied to her about her father's guilt. When he says, "A life in hell makes one oblivious of pain, cousin", "the depth of love and suffering in the voice was more than Leslie could bear". Lebrassa is a man of great qualities, urbane and cultured in England, a leader of men in Africa and in the end he earns Leslie's platonic love. He turned against the whites because he was robbed and reviled, and led a constant battle against the worse side of his nature.

The problem is that all the good in him is supposed to come from his white ancestry and all the bad from his so-called "negro taint". This alternative to the theory that people of mixed blood inherit only the worst qualities of both sides is equally pernicious, particularly as the man himself believes it: "I am the son of an English nobleman, an upright and honourable man who would have had me the same; but he reckoned without my mother and the race of savage rulers she sprang from". The author does not seem to notice that her only irredeemable character is Leslie's father, a white man.[33]

The Hyena of Kallu appeared in 1910, the same year as John Buchan's *Prester John*, and the comparison is instructive. Buchan's protagonist is the Reverend John Laputa, who inspires this tribute from Captain Arcoll, the master spy intent on thwarting his plans, "I tell you, in my opinion, he is a great genius. If he had been white he might have been a second Napoleon. He is a born leader of men, and brave as a lion…. There is a fineness and nobility in him. He would be a terrible enemy, but a just one. He has the heart of a poet and a king". Buchan's portrayal of Laputa bears this out and makes nonsense of Arcoll's claim that black men "can see the first stage of a thing, and maybe the second, but no more". Arcoll gets into this tangle because, for all his great qualities, Laputa cannot be allowed, in 1910, to give Africa back to the Africans by launching a rebellion against the British.

The narrator, David Crawford, was still a boy when he first saw Laputa, who had come to Scotland to preach. Buchan is merely being realistic in showing that the message that "a black man was as good as a white man in the sight of God", and that one day "Negroes would have something to teach the British in the way of civilization", did not go down well with late Victorian Scots. David observes that "the man's face was as commanding as his figure, and his voice was the most wonderful thing that ever came out of human mouth.... He had none of the squat and preposterous Negro lineaments, but a hawk nose like an Arab, dark flashing eyes, and a cruel and resolute mouth".

As a 19-year-old, David finds work in the Transvaal, where he gets to know Laputa and stays with him to the end. "I had seen Laputa as the Christian minister, as the priest and king in the cave, and as the leader of an army at Dupree's Drift, and at the kraal we had left as the savage with all self-control flung to the winds. I was to see this amazing man in a further part. For he now became a friendly and rational companion". Laputa, the modern version of the legendary African prince, Prester John, is also a classical scholar, with a profound knowledge of Western culture. David comes to admire him enormously – "he was an open enemy playing a fair game. But my fingers itched to get at the Portugoose – that double-dyed traitor to his race". As so often, it is the Portuguese who have the most reason to complain of racism.

Laputa's fall is compared to Lucifer's, and, unlike Lebrassa, he is convincing as a tragic figure. Arcoll's nonsense about the native mind is soon forgotten. Whereas Louise Gerard tries to show that a man who is half black must be half a savage, Buchan shows a black man whose extraordinary qualities inspire commensurate admiration. Of course Buchan was brought up under Queen Victoria. Looking back on his adventures, David reflects that they taught him "the meaning of the white man's duty. He has to take all risks, recking nothing of his life or his fortunes, and well content to find his reward in the fulfilment of his task. That is the difference between white and black, the gift of responsibility, the power of being in a little way a king; and so long as we know this and practise it, we will rule not in Africa alone, but wherever there are dark men who live only for the day and their own bellies". We do not think like that now, but it is not reasonable to expect a novel to be a century ahead of its time. If *Prester John* is flawed, it is because, to modern eyes, the age in which it was written is flawed. There are certainly phrases that jar, and *Prester John* certainly confirms that in 1910 almost everyone had racial prejudices. Nevertheless, with all its limitations, it is one of the few books in this survey which can be commended to the modern reader.[34]

Most of the novelists being discussed here had lived in Africa; some settled there, but their expertise was mainly in how the expatriates lived. The most distinguished of these writers, Haggard and Buchan, used what they knew of Africans as a spur to their imagination rather than as material for a realistic portrayal of African life. Perhaps the author who made the greatest effort at realism was Sir H. Hesketh Bell, a colonial administrator, who used his knowledge of the country we now call Ghana to write the short stories collected in *Love in Black*. Although the book was published in 1911, they are set in the 1890s, when Bell was in the Gold Coast, "when Ashanti was an independent kingdom, and before we started to 'protect' the country against its will and inclination". This is an example of the cynical detachment with which Bell writes about blacks and whites alike. He is critical of the Africans, of their practice of human sacrifice, of their belief in ju-ju and fetishes, and particularly of the treatment of women. However, although he portrays vain, foolish, and even cruel African characters, he does not treat them as inferiors to whites. "It is very generally believed that African tribes possess but a scanty amount of respect for the usual forms of morality. This is a mistake. A comparison between the average moral behaviour of a central African tribe with that of the inhabitants of civilised lands would be, I think, to the credit of the savages. Wives are bought, it is true, but probably the very idea of property causes the marriage tie to be less frequently abused than among more civilised races". Far from sharing the common distaste for educated Africans, Bell refers to doctors, clergymen, responsible officials and lawyers; in ability "they compare favourably with their white competitors". In one story, an African con man succeeds in England because "the ignorance of people 'at home' about the geography and condition of British possessions in West Africa is so astonishing". The con man abandons his white wife, but Bell points out that his is not a typical case. "The extraordinary aptitude shown by the West African for the adoption of European manners and customs sometimes leads him to undesirable and incongruous channels, but the marvellous progress often made by the natives of the Coast in a single generation is a happy augury for the future of the race". Bell is innocent of the dangerous assumption that one bad man of a particular race or colour must be typical of the rest. His progressive outlook does not make his stories great literature, but it does make them worth taking seriously. They contain an unusual feature. In one story, the narrator, travelling by canoe, "could not help admiring the fine proportions of the stalwart native" in the stern. Another refers to "as fine a type of West African male as you could wish to see. The features of his face were perhaps a long way behind those of a Greek god, but the form of body was divine. He had the lissom grace of a black panther, and the firm muscular throat, the broad chest, the small waist, the lean flank and the velvety black skin would have filled with delight the eye of a sculptor". They seem to have filled Bell with delight; perhaps it was not only African women whose relationships with white men were better not known about back home.[35]

W H Adams also served in the Colonial Service in the Gold Coast. Like the stories in *Love in Black*, the action of his novel *The Dominant Race* is supposed to take place before the Ashanti war of 1895. It will be remembered that in *The Hyena of Kallu*, Leslie was able to eject a crowd of black people from her friend's bedroom because she was of "the dominant race". The chief character in this case is James Brown who arrives on the Gold Coast for his first posting, having, in his father's opinion, shown no sign of belonging "to a dominant race". The phrase recurs when, in a shameful incident, James and the District Commissioner, "both men of the dominant race" leave their black sergeant to face danger without them. James's inexperience shows in his arrogance and overestimation of his own abilities, but also in his desire to be popular with the blacks under his rule. "It would have been far better to have treated the people like dirt.... The chief weapon which enables the white man in such circumstances to rule savage peoples was the colour of his skin. If he degrades that the people despise him". James earns his spurs by saving a little girl from being sacrificed in a tribal ceremony, but in most other respects he makes a mess of things. However, it is enough to show his father that he is worthy of belonging to the "dominant race" after all. The most interesting character is in fact the District Commissioner, John Hillary, a safe hand in preventing trouble, but without the showier qualities which gain promotion. While on leave in England, he lies to James's fiancée in an attempt to gain her affections, but his experience and tenacity are the stuff of which the Colonial Service is made, and he usually saves the day. He is an astute if brutal judge of the political situation – "It's black or white here. The natives would kick every white out of the country if they could. It's them or us. We are bound to fight the Ashantis soon". On balance Hillary is presented as a sympathetic character, as is his friend the Moslem commander of the Hausa troops.[36]

If it is hard to like a novel in which the title *The Dominant Race* is used without irony, the book of the same title by Florence E Mills Young is less likeable still. Young was based in South Africa. She wrote mainly about the whites there, and familiarised the British public with their attitude to racial questions. In *The Almonds of Life*, published in 1920, Young proved that it was possible to write a novel of more than 200 pages about life in South Africa in which the only reference to a black person is the single sentence "Almost instantly a Kaffir servant came out and went to the cab to fetch the baggage".[37] Admittedly, in Young's *The Dominant Race*, the heroine Penelope has only just arrived from England when "the natives struck her oddly, they appeared rather like animals in human shape with a curious admixture of child-nature in the blending that was not without its attractiveness. She was a little afraid of them. The dark skins and thick lips, the roving, prominent eyeballs repelled her". It could be argued that a newcomer to Africa could well have reacted like that, having never seen a black person before, but she does not learn a lot in the course of the novel. She "wondered whether, when she learnt to know them better, she would lose her fear of them – that instinctive shrinking which some people feel in relation to what they fail to understand. She felt the same repulsion towards snakes, and the large hairy spiders, the bite of which sometimes means death". She gets no help from the hero, Charles, who says, "We despise the coloured races, and they know it. They fear us; in a sense they look up to us as the dominant race, but that sort of feeling does not breed affection". He does concede later that "One has to consider the rights of the individual – even of a nigger". Penelope goes to live in the bush with an Afrikaans couple. The husband puts up with the insolence of his black servant, Jim, because he has sired a child by Jim's wife. Jim murders a black girl, and Charles shoots him dead. If "shooting was too merciful for the brute", this is because he has also attacked Penelope. "The death of a coloured girl … was regarded as a minor offence compared with the attack on a white woman". According to Young, "the pride of these fair-skinned people was great. It was this pride… which was responsible for maintaining the supremacy of the dominant race" in a country where they are so outnumbered.[38]

By "dominant race" she means the whites in general, Afrikaners as well as British. This is a specifically South African point of view, but because in most stories set in Africa the British were the only whites involved, the distinction between nationality and skin colour was seldom made. The British were considered superior on both counts; although there was room for argument about how pale a white skin had to be. Did the Portuguese qualify? In any case, "blood" was the most important factor of all. If blacks featured in popular literature, they were nearly always Africans at an early stage of their material and technological development. The sense of superiority which this fostered in readers was all the greater because the stories reflected the often ferocious attitudes towards black peoples in colonial societies. If South Africa is a notorious example, West Africa, and Kenya were scarcely better. Being so greatly outnumbered, the whites were almost considered heroic by the very fact that they kept the blacks down. The methods by which they did so were, therefore, not subjected to the usual moral standards. Physical courage counted for more than more subtle virtues. In a Sexton Blake story, we are to admire a 16-year-old who shouts at his black workers: "You brutes! You'll do this job as I want it done, or, by gad, I'll kill some of you". One of them raises an axe over his head, but the boy never wavers, and, as soon as the man puts the axe down, hits him on the jaw. In a story of West Africa, Blake talks of kicking a native ruler on the shin – "that's the nigger's sore spot. But I don't want to kick niggers. I mean the worst type who talks in coast 'pidgin' talk. I should want to have my boots cleaned afterwards. Give me a nice decent cannibal…" Even the standards of the American South can be treated uncritically; in another Blake adventure, the Klu Klux Klan is said to be "as fair as it was relentless".[39]

All these attitudes were absorbed by readers who had no experience of black people, and as the Sexton Blake examples show, often absorbed from an early age. Popular literature, of course, reflects the society in which it is written. It did not create the circumstances under which blacks were held in such low esteem, but it certainly reinforced them.

CHAPTER 11:

Blacks in the Caribbean and at Home

"English people are criticised very much in some quarters… if they mix with Jamaicans at all".[1]

The comparatively few black visitors to Britain came from the West Indies as well as Africa, and they inspired some interesting writing on the relationships between blacks and whites there. The case of Haiti is particularly instructive as it was an independent country. Most white people found this incongruous, witness a series of articles by Hesketh Prichard in *The Daily Express* from April 1900, which were republished as a book. The title was *Where Black Rules White*, meaning, as the first article explicitly states, that "there the law of the world is reversed". Prichard notes that in Haitian courts the evidence of a white man was nothing to that of a Haitian, the reverse of the situation in most countries where black people lived. Haiti was not the only black-ruled state, but it was billed as "the greatest Negro Republic the world has ever seen". Moreover, voodoo was practised there. This was West Africa in the Caribbean, but worse, because there was no white authority to suppress blood-curling religious practices and oppose the power of the priests. According to Prichard, "it would seem that the perpetration of a cult so degrading must have its source deep in the character of the race" although "these undoubted cannibals can on occasion be both kind-hearted and hospitable". He attributes the cruelty of voodoo rites to the supposition that "negroes have far duller nerves and are less susceptible to pain". This was a convenient theory for the Captain Kettles and Commissioner Sanders of this world. Prichard's tendency to lump all black people together is reflected in his frequent use of "black" rather than "Haitian". It is hard to argue with his criticisms of Haiti's rulers; its more recent governments and many post-independence African regimes have been no better. The point is, however, that the attention given to Haiti gave ammunition, as the Amins and Bokassas in Africa have done since, to white people with a low opinion of blacks in general. By their vices Haitian governments confirmed the necessity of British rule in the West Indies; by their very existence, they were in danger of giving blacks living under that rule dangerous ideas.[2]

It is not surprising that, despite his onerous world-wide responsibilities, Sexton Blake found time to visit an island with such opportunities for melodrama. Melodrama, as we have seen, lends itself to racial stereotyping, and a story called *The Full Moon* is one of the most racist in the Blake canon. The "bestial savagery" in the Haitian faces is lacking in those of "the harmless Jamaicans". The Haitian has degenerated into "a bunch of animalism and superstition" while the

Jamaican has reached "as near the ways of the white man as the limited capacity of his brainbox would permit". The Haitians would murder every white man if they dared, but need the leadership of someone with white blood. This is provided by Mavis Galante, whose father is white, but who has been under the hypnotic influence of her mulatto mother, "a devil in human form" since she was a baby. She is set free only by the latter's death at the end of the story, when the attempt to sweep the whites from the Caribbean is thwarted. In a later story Mavis tries again. When Blake is offered another chance to take her on, Tinker says "Let's take it, guvnor... I wouldn't mind having a shot at some of those niggers".[3]

Eleanor Mordaunt's *The Cost of It* of 1912, is mostly set on an imaginary British-ruled sugar island, so that Jamaica comes to mind. The story begins in England, where the protagonist, Henry Mostyn, gets into a fight at school because someone tells him that his mother was black. When he confronts his father, he learns that this is true. As was the case with so many relationships entered into in Africa, his father had left his mother behind when he returned to England. He would not have had a *"liaison* with an ordinary negress – let alone marry her", but this one was fair and beautiful. Henry calls him "an unspeakable cad", and sets off for the sugar island to join his mother. It was highly unusual for a man of mixed parentage to reject the white and identify with the black. It lands him in a lot of difficulties, which start on board ship when he has to listen to the rant of a ship's engineer about "half and halves" having "the stinking vices of both sides of the family and none of the virtues of either". It was a pity the Lord "didn't make 'em like mules, so that they couldn't breed no more". Nor do things improve on arrival. He finds his family appallingly coarse, and their sugar estate is being mismanaged and robbed by an uncle. We are told that his mother's small figure "was too fragile to show any hint of the revolting animalism of the other women". Because of his mother, Henry is blackballed from the island's main club, and vows never to reapply. Ten years later he is still suffering discrimination. Although he sits on the island's Riot Commission, he is ignored in favour of ignorant men who happen to be entirely white. Clare, a young Englishwoman new to the island, is told that Henry's relations look as if they are straight out of a comic opera, but she marries him nevertheless. All is well until she becomes pregnant, and is seriously alarmed by a magazine article on the perils of interbreeding. A single drop of black blood is deemed indestructible like an atom of radium. A female cousin and her mother arrive and upset Clare by saying respectively "Thank Heaven he's got a wholesome English girl for his wife.

I had expected to hear of him with a harem and a tribe of piebald piccaninnies", and "Fancy interbreeding from that stock". The baby is born with a white skin but dead. The novel shows what torments even a loving couple can undergo by swallowing then conventional theories about mixed-race children.[4]

The popular novelist Eden Phillpotts was best known for his romances of Devon life, but he set a collection of short stories in the West Indies. In one of them, Peter Paul, perhaps descended from "the yellow Caribs of old", falls in love with the daughter of a sea captain, who is white, and does not want him for a son-in-law. However, the captain's mysterious voyages turn out to involve slave trading, and it looks as though he will be captured by the United States navy until Peter Paul finds him an ingenious escape route. The story is supposed to have a happy ending because this persuades the captain to agree to the marriage, but it can only be accepted as such by ignoring the fate of the slaves. In *Carnival*, set on Martinique, a black man kills a white-skinned octoroon girl for spurning his advances. He then murders a deaf and dumb man, also black, who is a well known figure at carnival time, and by wearing his costume and carnival mask, avoids capture for a while. White naval officers debate which is the worse murder. One says, "If it had only been for killing another nigger, I could have forgiven the devil, but not, of course, for killing that unfortunate girl".[5] Another disagrees, arguing that a crime of passion is not as bad as the murder of someone who is deaf and dumb. The girl is not entirely white, and it is not clear whether, according to the first officer, killing her is worse because she is a girl, or because she has the lighter skin, or both. He rates the death of a black as less serious, and it may be that the second officer would have done so, had it not been for the man's disabilities. The arguments are not enlightened, but a little less brutal than in F E Mills Young's South African story, where injuring a white woman was assumed to be worse than killing a black man. The Caribbean lent itself to such arguments because of the many variations in skin colour and mixed ancestry. One novelist referred to "the prejudices that pervaded the whole social structure of Jamaica, from white through the multiplicity of shades of yellow and brown, down to black".[6] It was much the same elsewhere in the Caribbean. These prejudices mattered when people were judged, and were not held only by whites. Phillpotts found them useful tools in the telling of a good story. His own approach was one of detachment, and one character talks of civilisation coming "with a lie on her lips and a smile on her face, and a scourge behind her back – which is the way she generally do come to the savage".[7]

Although they did not have wide readership, novels by black authors did reach print. An advertisement for *I Rise. The Life Story of a Negro* describes its author, Rollo Ahmed, as "of partly West Indian origin", and as "having spent his early days among these people". It adds: "it is generally accepted that White and Black can never understand each other, but any reader of this book will obtain a deep insight into and sympathy with the outlook and mentality of the darker brethren".[8] The first part of the book is set in Georgetown, British Guyana about 1914, where Caleb Buller's father, a big, well-muscled seaman, is looked up to for not being the descendant of slaves. A caustic critic of whites, he does not take sides in the First World War, but thinks it better, on balance, for the British to win, although "Britain always expects coloured men to die for them". They can be trusted to look after you the best, as long as they are boss. They look after their animals the same way. He speaks better of the French, who take the black man's country but treat him like a Frenchman. The Englishman will not treat him like himself "unless yo' got a bank full o' gold, or can sing, act, anything to amuse him, or youse... can make a spectacle fo' him to watch fightin' ". This man, who has spent his life travelling the world, eventually chooses to go to Haiti to die, and he offers a view of the island which will have been news to white readers: "A good place for men of our race – one of the few places in the world where we are free and equal, and de President of de Republic is a coloured man".

The Lovegrove family treat black people well, but when Caleb is taken to their house, their little girl says, "Why! He's a real live nigger boy". "Instantly I felt as if she had slapped me". Her mother tells her off for being rude. Then they play at being her doll's parents, or rather "ladies don't have black husbands but I'll pretend that they do".

When his mother dies in a road accident, Caleb is taken in by the Lovegroves as a servant. His father tells him "Don't forget yose a nigger an' de white folk owe you all you can take". Caleb goes to school where he finds the teachers connive in the bullying. "Those whose skin was only a shade lighter considered themselves 'white' and made life as unbearable as possible for the minority they called 'niggers'". His father's view of the War is confirmed by a man who comes home minus a leg, and declares that if the black man is good enough to fight for the white man, he is good enough to be equal. "Christianity's just another ruddy sham; point of de organisation's to keep folks under. Ah've seen enough Christianity in Europe to give me mah belly-full fo' life". Nor are things better at home. Caleb observes of the sugar workers that "young men, stalwart negroes, already bowing beneath the weight of hours toiling in scorching sunshine, would curse the Empire for which they laboured". But they had yet to learn that "the white man also sweated his own people, packed and swarming like vermin in smoking cities".

Caleb is not only critical of whites. He notices that the black professionals do not care about the poor, and that flashy girls and idle young men are impossible to help. He is impatient with his fellow countrymen who only want a fair wage and have no "racial ambition". On the other hand he has no sympathy with political agitators who "preached race hatred and warfare, which I felt instinctively was the last hope of achieving progress". He has always felt a black man rather than a Guyanan until he leaves for England, at which point he longs to see Guyana as a country of freedom and equality.[9]

This account of life in Guyana has the stamp of autobiography, and is convincing for that reason. Caleb's criticisms of white attitudes are all the more effective for their moderation, and his father is a vividly drawn character, whose remarks have to be taken seriously. In particular this part of the book is interesting for a view of Empire, as experienced in a black urban society rather than in tribal villages or remote outposts. The Lovegroves are kind, if condescending, but, like that of the good slave owner in *Uncle Tom's Cabin*, their kindness cannot justify an unfair social system.

Claude McKay was another talented black Caribbean writer, and his *Banana Bottom* can be recommended as a convincing account of a black Jamaican girl. It was reprinted quite recently as a 'Black Classic' and deservedly so. The heroine Bita – short for Tabitha – returns to Jamaica from her education in England, where she had a good time. Her schoolmates' worst sin was ignorance, which led them to suppose that if she married in Jamaica, her husband would be a cannibal. Although published in 1928, the story is set at the beginning of the century. Bita was sent to England by a missionary couple, the Craigs, after being raped at the age of 12 by a crazy young man of mixed race, the descendant of a Scot known as the Liberator because he sold off parcels of his huge estate to blacks. Although the Craigs have been good to Bita, they are depressingly narrow-minded. Brought up in the tradition of Greece and Rome they can see no merit in African art. When needles disappear from a sewing group, Mrs Craig discounts the possibility of kleptomania – "How can such a crime of high society exist among such backward people?" The Craigs have lined up a black trainee preacher as their successor and as a husband for Bita. However, because he apes his white patrons in pursuit of advancement, she rightly considers him unsuitable, even before he disgraces himself with a goat, and flees the island. He provokes her into saying, "I take pride in being coloured and different, just as an intelligent white person does in being white. I can't imagine anything more tragic than people torturing themselves to be different from their natural selves. I think all the white friends I ever made liked me precisely because I was myself. I hope I shall never hear any more of that nauseating white and black talk from you". Bita eventually shows her independent spirit by marrying a worker on her late father's estate, a sign that although she has benefited from her British education, she values her Jamaican roots most. Her husband "accepted with natural grace the fact that she should excel in things to which she had been educated as he should in the work to which he had been trained". Bita, like her creator, is an astute observer of white racism, and "marvelled at the imbecilities of a sepulchre-white world that has used every barrier imaginable to dam the universal flow of human feeling by suppressing and denying to another branch of humanity the highest gifts of nature, simply because its epidermis was coloured dark". For once McKay lapses into overwriting here, but his anti-racism is heartfelt. He is free of the vice which he condemns in others.

In fact the most admirable character in the book is an Englishman, albeit an unconventional one, whose life's work is spent researching black folklore and folk songs. He has no interest in class, and, being of no religion himself, wants the same respect shown towards traditional Jamaican beliefs as towards the Gods of Greek, Roman, and Norse mythology. He is a good friend to Bita, and bequeaths her his house and land. He seems to be McKay's ideal Englishman. Other whites "had come to conquer and explore, govern, preach and educate to their liking, exploit men and material. But this man was the first to enter into the simple life of the island negroes and proclaim significance and beauty in their transplanted African folk tales, and in the words and music of their native dialect songs". He had found artistry where others saw nothing "because he believed that wherever the imprints of nature and humanity were found, there also were the seeds of creative life".[10]

Esther Hayman's *Study in Bronze* is another portrait of a Jamaican girl, although she is of mixed race, as the title's reference to the colour of her skin indicates. Lucea is the product of her single, white father's "moment of lust" with, it is implied, a black prostitute. This coupling took place despite "his innate objection to the taint of negroid blood, his very strong distaste for the primitive and ugly type of woman who had become, by virtue of circumstances, the mother of his child". He brings up his daughter himself, but fears for her future. There was not the outspoken prejudice in England that there was in America, but "socially, what chance had she?" His black servants share "the usual contempt of nearly all races for the individual who belongs to two races and to neither". She knew that they felt for her father "the respect due to a higher race – for in their hearts they admitted inferiority, even if their speech frequently denied it". When her father is killed in the First World War, he leaves Lucea well off, and she longs to go to England. She has made friends at school with Cynthia, a white English girl. This friendship is put to the test when Lucea, Cynthia, and Cynthia's mother meet Lucea's black governess. The latter is accompanied by some of her relations, who recall Henry Mostyn's in *The Cost of It* by their lack of refinement. Cynthia's mother warns Lucea that her social position is "too precarious" for her safely to know them. Hayman seems a little muddled at this point. "There were still people in Jamaica who scarcely distinguished between animals and natives", but English snobbery and colour prejudice are said to have been nothing to that of the Jamaicans. The statement that "the islands, though becoming more and more democratic, had not yet reached the almost complete outward merging which later years foreshadowed", seems an optimistic assessment of the period leading up to 1928, when the book was published.

Lucea arrives in England, where apparently the ignorant still believe that Jamaicans are cannibals. She lives for two years in bohemian circles where there is little colour prejudice, but "eyes were never incurious when she went into a restaurant. Especially – especially with a white man". She eventually realises that she is even more of an outsider to good society than she thought when she finds that many of her friends are high class tarts. She is invited to share their way of life, but refuses. She thinks of marrying an elderly white man who has befriended her since they met on the boat, but he does not have marriage in mind. She lives with another Englishman, who does want to marry her, but she breaks with him, when his all too common prejudices become clear. He does not want any of his friends or colleagues to see him with her, and he does not want to have children with a dark-skinned woman. Lucea returns to Jamaica, feeling that she is not "part and parcel of any race or set of people", and that her mixed blood gives her independence from both black and white. She has come to the conclusion that "there was justice in the fact that experienced and educated races should, for what it was worth, govern the world"; any other system would be worse, but "that the individual, the essential person was superior or inferior intrinsically was ludicrous".[11]

* * *

"He was already beginning to know that look. All coloured men do".[12]

Those few white people who met black people in Britain had at least a chance of moderating their prejudices, hard though they might find it. In Henry Nevinson's short story of 1894, *Sissero's Return*, Ginger, a working class woman is referred to as "Mrs Kentucky, or Tennessee, or Timbuctoo… for the thing as made 'er famous was she'd married a nigger and she couldn't never get over it". Her neighbours, who liked Sissero, her husband, well enough before the marriage, could not get over it either. According to the cockney narrator's mother, the men were upset "through none on 'em likin' a nigger to get the pull of 'em" and the women didn't want him but liked him unmarried – "you never know". Sissero "'ad a mug almost as good as a white 'un to look at, only for its bein' black and shiny like a top 'at". He was also extremely well built, like many black men in real life, and a markedly higher percentage in fiction. There is the usual prejudice when the children arrive – "Would yer like to see the Tower 'Amlets wake up one mornin' chock full o' little niggers?" Ginger is proud of her two children, however, especially the one she thinks the lighter of the two, although no one else can see the difference. She leaves the elder boy with a neighbour when she goes to work, but is told that he scares the other children away through being black. As a result, she gives up her job, and Sissero, a ship's stoker, sails longer distances for better pay. Their marriage continues happily until he fails to return from one voyage, and Ginger sinks into poverty. To keep herself and her children alive, she gives herself to the Jewish rent collector, but she remains convinced that Sissero will come back. Her neighbours are sure that he will not, and has probably found a black woman. However, one day he does return, explaining that he missed his ship in China and lived with a Chinese girl until he was in a position to start for home. The neighbours make sure that he never hears about his wife's relationship with the rent collector, which she only entered into under duress. Apart from the fact that the children start crying because a black man is suddenly living with them, all ends reasonably happily. Sissero is a genial, pleasant character and the relationship with Ginger is touching. Even the narrator's mother, the most hostile of the characters, softens her stance. The story shows both the existence of deep prejudice, and that personal qualities can make a difference.[13]

* * *

" 'Pete is not our servant', said Jack. 'He is our friend' ".[14]

Perhaps the most popular black character in England, among the characters of early twentieth century fiction, was created for children. Of the three "comrades" Jack, Sam, and Pete whose adventures ran for 20 years in *The Marvel* boys' magazine, (and also in *The Boy's Friend*), the first was an English lad, the second American, and Pete was black (and apparently American too). Pete soon became the dominant character, and it was he who sold the magazine, witness the frequency with which he was pictured on the cover. "There were few men, women or children who had spoken to Pete who did not like him, and his dauntless bravery naturally appealed to his comrades' hearts". Like Sissero, and the majority of fictional black men of the period, he is exceptionally strong. He is also very brave, wins the fights he is always getting into, and, when he throws an opponent through a window, always checks first that they are on the ground floor. He is passionately fond of animals, particularly the Airedale, Rory, who accompanies the three comrades on their adventures, after Pete has rescued him from starvation. It is true that Jack and Sam tease Pete about the colour of his skin – "you beautiful chunk of ebony", "you black chunk of mischief" – but, unlike Lobangu in the Sexton Blake stories, he gives as good as he gets, and is not condescended to. Pete was once a circus and fairground entertainer so he is good at lifting pianos with his teeth as well as acrobatics and sports. He makes linguistic mistakes, but some are genuinely funny – "an infant in waddling clothes". He gets into silly scrapes, many resulting from his brilliance as a ventriloquist, and his delight in putting inappropriate words into the mouths of authority figures, but it is all caused by his anarchic streak, such as children love. Pete certainly suffers colour prejudice, from hotel keepers who will not give him a bed, and people who will not eat with him or shake his hand, but they all get their come-uppance.

These stories are such a refreshing antidote to prejudice against blacks that incidents involving Jews make all the sadder reading. A Jewish trader rubs his hands "which looked as though washing them would have done more good". Another with an enormous hooked nose tries to throw Pete out of his shop. When Pete humiliates him, "'I vish you may die', hooted the Jew in his impotent fury". In another instance, Pete suggests that the Jew's dreadful second-hand clothes offer should include himself. "'We could sell him for rag and bones, or dey will gib us a bit at the hospitals or sausage shops for him'…. 'Don't be nasty, Pete' laughed Jack, 'they don't make sausages of Jews'".[15]

A clever short story in *Pearson's Magazine* also shows sympathy for black people. Carter, the journalist narrator, is involved in an accident and wakes up to find that his skin has turned black. He goes to his office where a colleague suggests that his presence there is inappropriate, as the paper has always opposed colour equality, and some of the strongest articles have been written by Carter himself. This puts Carter on the spot, and he becomes incoherent as he protests that factors other than colour are involved. His colleague disagrees. What if a white race emerged in South Africa just like the blacks there, in everything except skin colour? "Are you sure … that you would have written of their descendants in the same strain, holding that mere education and culture could never put them on an equal footing? When has the paper ever condemned the lowest white immigrant because of his political ambition or desire for social progress?" On the other hand, hasn't the paper repeatedly criticised the public appointment of some educated and talented man "because he was of the black race?" There is no answer to this, and the story bears out the argument because Carter is evicted from his lodgings and finds that his girlfriend cannot bear to touch him, although only the colour of his skin has changed. In the final paragraph he waits for an operation to turn him white again, and hopes that if it fails, he will never wake up. *Pearson's* had a lot of readers, but whether the story changed many minds is another matter. Certainly its author remains obscure.[16]

It has to be said that novels about the problems of black people living in England were not best sellers. If tackled at all, the subject mainly attracted literary writers, eventually a few of them black, who were interested in the outsider. The first half of Leonard Merrick's *The Quaint Companions* is about Elisha Lee, whose parents had come to Britain as music-hall performers from the American South. Elisha is a star tenor who earns big money at the Albert Hall and elsewhere. His colour is forgotten, but only when he sings. "He was vain, he was prodigal, his failings were the failings of the average negro, intensified by the musical temperament and a dazzling success…. He could buy gay companions, but he could never gain affection". He meets a white widow called Ownie, and his money gradually overcomes her aversion from his looks. "She had noticed niggers with much wider nostrils than those that had looked so wide to her a week ago; and his lips didn't seem to protrude so much as they had done at first". His ears would have been lovely if white. Elisha knows why Ownie tolerates him, and his pain is touching: "Doesn't it strike you that inside here I may feel all a white man feels, though no white woman will ever feel the same for me". They get married, but Ownie does not respect her husband, and flirts with other men. There are constant scenes in which he loses his temper and then begs forgiveness. They have a son together, but "it was her contempt for their baby that showed him how he himself was despised". Because his wife treats him so badly, Elisha takes to drink. This affects his voice, and he gradually declines.

The book then takes up the story of David their son, who also suffers from colour prejudice. "At school they prayed God to pardon the Jews and the infidels – Take from them all hardness of heart – and came out from the service and beat the nigger". However, his second collection of poems, *A Celibate's Love Song* is a great success. They have a special admirer in a young woman with curvature of the spine. She does not know that the poet is black, and he does not know of her affliction, because, in her embarrassment, she has sent him a photograph of her sister. When they meet and the misunderstandings are sorted out, the author envisages them coming together, but only in a world where skin colour and physical handicap do not count. This is hardly an optimistic ending. H G Wells envisaged a future for them in which David is a literary success and they get married, but, significantly, with no children. Wells admired the book, and rightly. Despite its faults, it tells a touching story of a father and son, whose yearning for affection is thwarted by their skin colour.[17]

In a rare autobiographical account of a black man's experience of late Victorian and Edwardian Britain, A B C Merriman-Labor is more concerned about lack of respect. *Britain Through Negro Spectacles*, is the story of an educated man whose education counts for little because he is black. "Even the sewage-man, whose English is as bad as his job, will consider himself better spoken than you, although you have graduated at a British university with honours in English". Merriman-Labor suffered from the assumption, met with in so much fiction, that a black man's civilization can be only a veneer. He is particularly scathing about the popular press. "It likes to report, and that often, anything wrong or exaggerated about the Blacks as would throw discredit on the race as a whole". Most interesting, because most modern, is his comparison between the plight of blacks and that of women. He argues that historically both have been used as the playthings of white men; both were enslaved until the Church and public opinion ended their slavery; and education is bringing progress to both, despite false claims that they are intellectually and morally inferior. This is an interesting comment to have been published in 1909.[18]

A year later, Cullen Gouldsbury published his novel *The Tree of Bitter Fruit*, which reflects precisely the attitudes which Merriman-Labor resented. It transfers to Britain the values of Rhodesia, where the novel begins and others by Gouldsbury are entirely set. George Callaster, a colonial official returns home because of ill health. He believes, "despite the jeers of men who ranked the Kaffir as an animal", in the equality of blacks and whites. He is encouraged by a newspaper article which proclaims that the day has dawned when "colour may be washed away in universal friendship", that, especially in Central and Southern Africa, "schools should be thrown open to the native-born" and that "the sense of fair play that is the Englishman's birthright must eventually triumph". Despite being advised by an African chief not to meddle with the will of the gods, he decides to show that a black boy can benefit from education as much as a white by bringing one called Mkonto, back to England. (Mkonto's mother is Arab, but this is never made relevant, unless to hint that he would otherwise have been less intelligent.)

"Although to the average Londoner, there is nothing extraordinary in the sight of a well-dressed man escorting a little black boy", a crowd collects when Mkonto is left alone for a moment in the Strand. He is insulted by a man who turns out to be the author of the article just mentioned. This is Carson Carnegie, a self-serving hypocrite, who only writes in support of black people to make his name as a journalist. Mkonto is sent to a public school, where "colour is hardly more of a disadvantage to its possessor than red hair or a squint". He gets into more fights than most boys, but generally prospers. This does not impress a friend of Callaster's, who thinks that "in growing from boyhood to youth, the savage intellect usually reaches its zenith and thereafter declines into stout boorishness". Nevertheless, Mkonto is sent to France for his further education, and is taught Hegel, Kant, Rousseau, Tolstoy, and Mill. By this time he is enamoured of Callaster's ward Averil. He tells her, "If I had you out in my country, I'd beat you till you couldn't stand! That's the way we win our women – yes and the way we keep them too", but she neither rejects nor accepts him. Mkonto is then sent to Africa to rule his people, but, still thinking of Averil, he refuses to marry the late chief's wife. This does him no good with his subjects or with Mitchell, Callaster's successor. Mitchell tells him "White women do not mate with niggers". The author agrees, saying Mitchell's attitude may seem brutal to anyone who has "never faced the question of colour", but to one who has lived "face to face with this question in all its nakedness, the mere ideas of a white woman condescending in any way towards a lover of an inferior race is enough to make the blood run cold". In other words, you have no right to a view on racial questions unless you have lived in the colonies.

Mkonto needs Mitchell to bolster his authority, but has to endure remarks like "You mustn't think that a few years in England entitles you to consider yourself a White Man ... you are dirt under my feet if I choose". Mkonto fails as an African ruler, as he is too Europeanised to be accepted by his people. Back in England, Carnegie employs him to lecture about Africa. When his secretary sees Mkonto for the first time, she screams in horror, never having seen a black man before. Matters come to a head when Mkonto proposes marriage to Averil. She accepts him, because that is what she thinks her beloved guardian wants, even though "there was still, at her heart, that horrible shrinking feeling which realised that there would be something wrong about this mating of theirs, something monstrous and unclean". Callaster's approval of interracial sex does not survive the news that his beloved ward is to marry a black man. He collapses and never walks again. Understanding his remorse, Averil offers to spend the rest of his life with him, as either wife or daughter. When Callaster tells Mkonto that the marriage is off, "All the unreasoning hatred of the Black Man against one of the dominant white race surged up anew within him", although he surely has reason enough to be angry. He describes himself as "not flesh nor fowl – neither black nor white, neither here nor there". This is how Lebrassa in *The Hyena of Kallu* thought about himself because of his mixed parentage, but Mkonto is black, and blames Callaster for educating him into a false position in life, "because in your gross conceit you dreamed that you could revolutionise the world". The interview is so stormy that it kills Callaster. Carnegie sacks Mkonto and offers his lecturing job to Mitchell. He knows his racist views, but has decided that "the nigger's as dry as a squeezed orange now, so I'm going on the opposite track". Mitchell turns down the job, but marries the lovely Averil. To scrape a living, Mkonto performs a war dance in native costume on the music-halls, where Kant and Hegel are of little use to him. He dreams of revenge and of leading a revolt back home.[19]

The novel accepts all the worst racist assumptions of its day about the black man, and assumes that any white believing in racial equality is a fool or a hypocrite. *The Times Literary Supplement* concluded that it proved nothing, as Mkonto never has a fair chance. Although one Englishman tries to raise him, two deliberately set him back. This is true, but the reviewer thought the book "well worth reading". Yet again it is the lack of outrage which strikes us most forcibly today.

A quarter of a century later, Keate Weston, in *London Fog*, also chronicled the failure of a black man who has come to England for his education. The story begins in Tanganyika where there is general agreement among the whites that "the black man always has been, and always will be, intellectually and morally inferior at every point to the white man". However, this author clearly sides with the opposite point of view expressed by Carmine, an American, who befriends the protagonist, Mubia. Mubia wins a scholarship to come to England to learn to be a teacher, although it is hinted that he won because he told the board what it wanted to hear.

Mubia lodges at a boarding house where colour prejudice is rife. The landlady only takes him in after consultation with the other lodgers, one of whom, fortunately, is Carmine. The widow of an Indian army officer refuses to use the same bathroom, and threatens to leave. The others are careful not to be unkind, but do not accept black men as equals. One of them tries to atone for a racist remark by taking Mubia to a pub, but is careful to choose one where he is not known. Mubia is unused to alcohol and gets drunk, so confirming his companion's prejudices. He gives to a beggar in the street, but, not having much change, refuses another, who curses him as a "bloody nigger". This is only less bad than an incident recorded by Merriman-Labor in which several black men club together to give sixpence to a beggar, who then shouts racial abuse at them.

As a teacher-training student from Tanganyika, Mubia is even invited to a Buckingham Palace garden party, but his problems continue, partly because he has had to leave his young wife at home. Fanny, a waitress who cannot get another boyfriend, goes out with him, but will not let him have his way with her, and, when accosted by a prostitute, he has no money, and so gets another blast of racial abuse. When Carmine invites him to a cottage in the Essex countryside, he is only prevented from molesting a young girl when a dog attacks him. However, Weston attributes this not to the savage breaking through the civilised veneer, but to the loneliness of a young man not used to sexual abstinence.

Mubia derives solace from membership of the African Freedom League, although, as a steward at one of its meetings, he is injured when Fascists start a brawl. He increasingly neglects his studies for politics, and becomes the League's treasurer at a pound a week. This means giving up his studies and his student grant, but he becomes an artist's model, and is taken up by a society girl, and does tribal dancing at her parties. Tempted into a life style which he cannot afford, he starts taking money from the League, and is eventually dismissed. The girl's flirtatious attentions and her opinion that modern Englishmen are over-civilised give him the wrong idea. He tries to force himself on her, and she will have nothing more to do with him.

Mubia has now made Fanny pregnant and offers to marry her. She turns him down, but they live together to save expenses and get on well enough until he is killed in a road accident. The crude ending suggests that Weston sees no possible future for his protagonist except further decline. The novel certainly has its faults, but it portrays the difficulties of a black man in England, without the racial venom of a Gouldsbury. In a single lapse, Weston uses the phrase "every vestige of civilisation had slipped from him", when Mubia assaults the society girl. Nevertheless, it is not argued that the failings which bring him down are the particular inheritance of black men. He is a fallible human being, and the odds against him are too great. In another contrast with *The Tree of Bitter Fruit*, although Mubia meets a society full of racial prejudice, nobody is out to destroy him.[20]

This also applies to the protagonist of *Black* by Humphrey Gilkes. We first meet Michael Black as a small boy who is employed as a page in a brothel to add exotic colour to the entertainment. He is taken to the country in an outing for slum children. They are under the care of a woman who "had a peculiar shuddery feeling when she talked to black people", although she finds Michael better mannered than the white children. She is particularly upset by the contrast of pink palms with an otherwise black skin. At first there is difficulty finding Michael a place to stay. The vicar says that he cannot be put up with the others. The rector is more sympathetic – "nice type of lad, though black" – and invites him to sing and dance at a party, but the guests are upset by his suggestive movements, and do not know that they were learnt in the brothel rather than from tribal dancing. After a short spell as a page boy at a hotel, Michael earns his living as a performer. His black American mentor tells him that, once you have a name, being black is an advantage. "A black face, white teeth, and red lime-lights. It makes 'em laugh". He is told that the friendship of white people always stops short of being intimate, and that "You won't get any black girls here and you won't get any decent white girls because of your colour". A policeman describes his position equally brutally: "Your colour'll stop you getting work in most places. Cabaret or the docks, that's the place for you blokes". On one occasion, he does manage to take a white girl to a film, but unfortunately it was about Africa. There were a lot of naked black bodies, and the audience laughed a lot. "It was almost as if the producer had only allowed these naked Africans to appear when they looked comic or ridiculous". Michael eventually decides to leave for South Africa when he gets a letter from a black girl there, whom he met years ago on the village outing. He has concluded that "a black man should not try to live in England. His proper place was a black man's country". Nevertheless, his last experience is more positive. On the voyage out, a South African passenger complains at having to travel with a black man, but the captain tells him, "Both of you are British subjects on a British ship. Both of you have paid for your passage". Michael's adventures in South Africa do not concern us. The account of his stay in England has a great deal of documentary value. It confirms that despite prejudice, black people had more opportunities in show business than elsewhere, and that their least unsympathetic reception was on the fringes of society.[21]

In *I Rise, the Story of a Negro*, Caleb, having arrived in England from Georgetown, meets a Jamaican who also finds that the stage offers him the most opportunities. The range of small parts is limited, but at Christmas there is always *Peter Pan*. This man is not too unhappy at his welcome in small touring companies and chapel communities, but it is a precarious existence. Caleb himself gets a job as a singer in a cafe, but is sacked for associating with the customers. He sues, against the advice of a lawyer, but winning his case does not help, as he becomes known as a trouble-maker. He gets a job at the docks, but the white dockers go on strike to get rid of him. When they tell him he is not British, he replies, "Wasn't there room for us in the firing line? Don't we provide cheap labour?" When asked why a "nigger" should be wanted, when white men are starving, Caleb replies, "Do you eat sugar? Do you drink tea? Do you wear cotton? Drink rum? Smoke tobacco?" One or two of the dockers see his point of view, but he is sacked with a day's pay.

Caleb is an attractive man, and white women are always available. He gets angry at a fellow black who talks of being picked up from parks by well off ladies in their cars, and tells him "You make it bad for every other coloured man". The man is unabashed: "If you want to get on in this country, you'll do so by the favour of the women alone. Leave it to the average Englishman and he would sweep every one of us out of the country tomorrow". Nevertheless Caleb is against interracial marriage on social grounds. He is critical of Indian and black seamen who marry white women, and then return home, abandoning them and their children, the colonial situation in reverse. For these white women, "The first step was lodgers, usually coloured again, next the streets". When he is ill, Caleb is looked after by a white, half-French, prostitute, who is angry when he shies away from her: "There are hundreds of girls in Liverpool married to black men, and they're happy enough". Eventually she kills herself for love of him.

In his uphill fight to earn a living, Caleb comes to understand how easy it is for black men to drift into the underworld. Some live on vice. He does not think that the black man is as oversexed as he is made out to be, "but his sex impulses are periodic and impulsive in comparison with the white man". Even this kind of generalisation of course would be considered racist today, if expressed by a white writer, as would Caleb's opinion that Indians are "completely sex-ridden". He believes that "life in the cities of the white man is conducive to constant sex stimulation", which many blacks are not strong-willed enough to resist. One wonders what he would think 70 years later. Caleb accepts that hundreds of coloured men in London live on vice, but often whites initiate them. Many who are tempted with money and luxury are little more than boys. "It takes very little time to ruin these boys, who nearly all ultimately swell the criminal roll of the country, while their original seducers go unscathed. They spend their comparatively short lives in a false atmosphere of extravagance and debauchery, until disease or the drug habit claims them". Black people are also accused of overstepping the mark, even when they do not. Caleb meets a pharmacist from Barbados who has been accused of carrying out an abortion. He was acquitted, but gave up the pharmacy, because men would come in and say, "Congratulations, Mr Oldfield, of course we all know you dark fellows carry on the trade, but you wriggled out of that all right. Now my wife…".

Like Mubia in *London Fog*, Caleb becomes an artist's model. He likes an artist who asks "What does it matter if a few niggers – pardon me – marry a few Englishwomen? It's probably their misfortune. What does it matter if a few half castes are running round our streets. It would take an invasion of negroes, a mass marriage to create a problem. Just as if there weren't enough real ones what with unemployment and whiskey at the price it is". In fact, Caleb is generally contemptuous of the arty crowd, but all that no longer matters when he falls in love with a white woman, and marries her, his reservations about mixed marriages swept away. The marriage is a happy one, although "she was told I should ill treat her – that I probably already had a wife of my own race … she would find that I had a swarm of dreadful relatives little better than coolies, … our children would inherit the vices of both races and the virtues of neither". The "swarm of dreadful relatives" in particular evokes the world of Eleanor Mordaunt's *The Cost of It* of a quarter of a century earlier. In fact, the two sons become a musical comedy star and a medical student, but when the daughter falls in love, her boyfriend is threatened with being disinherited by his father, a Harley Street surgeon, if the marriage goes ahead. The young man leaves the decision to the girl, who breaks off the engagement, and then hangs herself. Caleb attributes the blame to "racial hatred, racial superiority, man's inhumanity to man". It will be clear that by this time he has prospered in England, but the author has loaded the dice by having him inherit £10,000.

The novel ends with Caleb returning to Guyana, although, as in *Black*, there are potential difficulties aboard ship. The booking has to be arranged carefully to make sure that his wife is not ostracised. Nevertheless, optimism reigns on the last page: "Intelligent and reasonable men and women are awakening to the fact that spiritually the earth is for all her sons in equality, and that man himself cannot afford to raise artificial barriers". There were hardly enough "intelligent and reasonable men" in 1937. Nevertheless, the account of Caleb's years of struggle is as convincing as the record of his early life in Guyana.[22]

Caleb's optimism seems particularly misplaced now, because we know that, after the Second World War, when West Indian immigrants arrived in Britain for the first time in large numbers, they experienced painful discrimination. Immigrants always have a problem when they compete for jobs and housing, but the constant denigration of black people in previous decades contributed to the post-war climate of ignorance and fear. This denigration was based on casual and often false beliefs about heredity and racial purity, all the more dangerous for being taken for granted. By the 1930s a few black authors, and white liberals were using the novel to put a different case, but this was not the fiction which most people read.

AFTERWORD

All racism is bad, but some manifestations are worse than others. The Jews were different from the Chinese, the Arabs and the Blacks, because they mixed with the rest of the community in ever increasing numbers. A novel in which Jews were insulted or belittled did direct harm because Jews were likely to read it. However, if it is accepted that prejudice is largely based on ignorance, the possibility that a racial bigot might actually meet a few Jews left open the possibility of his being converted, hard though that might be. What is more, the Jews were the only group who contributed to popular literature, and, in so doing, might contribute to greater understanding. The few black novelists who published before 1940 were not widely read.

The works of Sax Rohmer and his followers did little direct harm, because only a very few educated Chinese were in danger of reading them. Similarly, novels about Arabs were scarcely read by the people likely to be offended. The same could be said about the blacks, but in their case, direct damage was done after the Second World War, when large numbers of black people arrived in Britain. Readers of the last two chapters of this book can scarcely be surprised at the ignorance and fear which led to the immigrants receiving such a harsh welcome. These emotions were being hatched in the preceding decades when popular fiction not only reflected society's worst prejudices, but confirmed and reinforced them. Again, it has to be emphasised that fear of sexual relations was at the heart of the problem.

Readers will have noticed the number of unfavourable allusions to the personal appearance of people of other races. A different skin colour alone made people look strange, but there were also the slant eyes of the Chinese, the hook nose of the Jew, the thick lips of the black. The words "strange", "stranger" and "foreigner" are closely allied, and these strange or foreign looks were constantly stressed. By definition, people with such looks did not conform to Western ideals of beauty. Sexual, and even physical, contact was felt to be repulsive by any white who accepted the prevailing ideas about race, but this feeling was all the stronger because of the perceived ugliness of the people concerned. On the other hand, they could also exercise a dangerous attraction. The lure of the young Eurasian woman is a recurrent theme of thrillers. If ugly faces are often ascribed to black people in fiction, their bodies were equally often assumed to be beautiful. To be attracted by someone who should have been found repulsive was highly alarming, and the ensuing self-disgust often increased the hostile reaction to the object of the white person's desire. *The Sheikh's* huge sales were based on the heroine's sexual relationship with an attractive man who was taboo, or seemed to be.

In colonial situations sex between ruler and ruled was particularly dangerous. Quite apart from the ideological considerations and the appalling prospect of children, it made the ruler potentially vulnerable to the ruled. Such a danger did not exist at home, but the influence of colonial values, often transmitted in fiction, was so strong that attitudes were scarcely different. It is worth remembering too that colonial situations existed outside the formal boundaries of the British Empire, for example, in the Concession areas of certain Chinese ports and parts of Africa where the British traded but did not administer.

The demise of the British Empire is one of two major factors which make the period 1890–1940 different from the present. The second is the growth of our multiracial society. The former means that white people no longer have an interest in believing in the old racial hierarchy; the latter that they have an interest in rejecting it. Quite apart from the immorality of fellow citizens being treated as inferior, society needs everyone to be able to contribute to the best of their ability. Many of the quotations in the foregoing chapters show by their very offensiveness how far things have changed. Readers will know that this is not a matter of political correctness. They do not need any guardian of public morality to tell them what is unacceptable. If they also find some wry amusement at the pretensions behind some of the remarks quoted, this is a sign of change too.

Much of what seems so offensive now was the norm within the lifetime of today's older generation. There is still racism in our society, of which it is right to be ashamed, but surely the progress made bodes well for the future. This is admittedly the judgement of a white man with no personal experience of racism. He readily concedes that those whose experience is different may well have other views.

NOTES

INTRODUCTION

1. Sapper, *The Black Gang*, quoted in Richard Usborne, *Clubland Heroes*, 1953, revised edition 1974, p. 144.
2. Cyril J Silverston, *The Dominion of Race*, 1906, p. 296.
3. Kathlyn Rhodes, *Desert Justice*, 1923, p. 7 and Kathlyn Rhodes *The Relentless Desert* p. 8.
4. Athur Weigall, *Madeline of the Desert*, 1920, pp. 38, 68–69.
5. W S Gilbert, *H. M. S. Pinafore*, 1878.
6. Norma Lorimer, *The Shadow of Egypt*, 1923, pp. 25 and 227.
7. Brian Street, *The Savage in Literature*, p. 7.
8. Notably in Colin Watson, *Snobbery with Violence*, 1971 and Richard Usborne, *Clubland Heroes*.
9. Usborne, *Clubland Heroes*, revised edition 1974, p. 5.
10. P C Wren, *Beau Ideal*, 1928, p. 215.
11. Burton J Hendrick, *The Life and Letters of Walter H. Page*, 1925, vol. 1, p. 151.
12. Arthur Weigall, *The Way of the East*, 1924, pp. 39 and 40.
13. Douglas Sladen, *The Tragedy of the Pyramids*, 1909, pp. 157 and 418.
14. *The Bookman*, April 1919, p. 18.
15. "At the Full Moon" in *Union Jack*, 19 May 1917.
16. M P Shiel, *The Yellow Danger*, 1898, p. 218.
17. Rollo Ahmed, *I Rise. The Story of a Negro*, 1937, p. 308.
18. E M Hull, *The Desert Healer*, pp. 51 and 161.
19. Wren, *Beau Ideal*, p. 34.
20. Guy Thorne, *Not in Israel*, p. 214.
21. A J Dawson, *Bismillah*, 1898, p. 77.
22. A Conan Doyle, 'The Tragedy of the Korosko', in *The Strand Magazine*, 1897, vol. 13, p. 490.
23. P C. Wren, *Sowing Glory*, 1931, p. 240.
24. Steve Nicholson, *The Censorship of British Drama*, 1900–1968, 2003, p. 284.

1: THE YELLOW PERIL AND THE BACKGROUND TO VILLAINY

1. Admiral Sir Edward H Seymour, *My Naval Career and Travels*, 1911, p. 342.
2. *Daily Mail*, 24 July 1900.
3. *The Times* 5 May 1898. According to *The Spectator* of 11 December 1897, Kaiser Wilhelm II was the first statesman to refer to the "Yellow Peril" in a public speech.
4. *Daily Express*, 6 July 1900.
5. *Daily Mail*, 3 July 1900
6. *Daily Mail*, 6 July 1900.
7. *Daily Mail*, 16 July 1900.
8. *The Mystery of Dr Fu Manchu*, p. 139 and 143.
9. Cay Van Ash and Elizabeth Sax Rohmer, *Master of Villainy*, 1972, p. 75 and 60.
10. M P Shiel, *The Yellow Danger*, 1898, p. 12 and 184.
11. *China*, compiled by A Cunningham, 1912, pp. 5 and 23.
12. *The Times*, 25 May 1912.
13. Percy F Westerman, *When East Meets West, a Story of the Yellow Peril*, 1913, p. 39, 148–49, 151, 40 and 174.
14. *Daily Mail*, 30 June 1900.
15. *The Times*, 16 November 1908.
16. Quoted in *The Review of Reviews*, January 1909, p. 43.
17. *Daily Mail*, 21 June 1900.
18. 'The Yellow Cord A Tale of Life Among the Chinese' in *Union Jack* XII, 310, 1909.
19. 'The Ruse of the Dowager Empress' by A V in *Pearson's Magazine*, XVII, 1904, p. 50.
20. Lousie Gerard, *It Happened in Peking*, p. 176.
21. Mrs Archibald Little, *Li Hung Chang*, 1903, p. 1.
22. *The Times*, 24 June 1896.
23. Published in *Union Jack* 757, 19 April 1918.
24. *Evening News*, 4 October 1920.
25. *The Sphere*, 8 May 1926.
26. *East London Observer*, 24 February 1934. The press quotations on Limehouse are from a file in the Bancroft Library in Mile End. My thanks to the staff there.
27. *East London Observer*, 11 January 1890.
28. Sax Rohmer, 'Emperor Fu Manchu' , 1959, in *The Fu Manchu Omnibus*, vol. 4, 1999, p. 367.
29. George A Wade, 'The Cockney John Chinaman' in *The English Illustrated Magazine*, vol. 23, no. 202, July 1900.
30. *East London Observer*, 25 December 1920.
31. P J Waller, 'Racial Phobia and the Chinese Scare 1906–14' in *Essays Presented to C. M. Bowra*, 1970, p. 91–2.

32. J P May, 'The Chinese in Britain' in *Immigrants and Minorities in British Society*, ed. Colin Holmes, 1978, p. 119.

33. *Evening News*, 5 October 1920.

34. *Evening News*, 5 and 6 October 1920.

35. *Evening News*, 5 October 1920.

36. *Daily Graphic*, 7 October 1920.

37. Sax Rohmer, *The Yellow Claw*, 1915, pp. 148–9 and 175.

38. Sax Rohmer, *The Si-Fan Mysteries*, 1917, 14th edition, 1934, p. 38.

39. *The Collected Plays of W. Somerset Maugham*, 1961, vol. 3.

40. *East London Observer*, 15 July 1916.

41. *Daily Telegraph*, 3 October 1916.

42. *East London Observer*, 10 April 1909.

43. Rohmer, *The Devil Doctor or the Return of Dr Fu-Manchu*, 1916, p. 96, 97.

44. Rohmer, *Dope*, 1919, p. 75, 110, 120 and 280.

45. Sax Rohmer, 'The Trail of Fu Manchu', 1934 in *The Fu Manchu Omnibus*, vol. 3, 1998, p. 54.

46. Thomas Burke, *Out and About, A Note-book of London in War-time*, 1919, p. 40.

47. Cay Van Ash and Elizabeth Sax Rohmer, p. 73.

48. Thomas Burke, *Son of London*, p. 219.

49. Thomas Burke, *Dark Nights*, publisher's advertisement.

50. Thomas Burke, 'The Knight Errant' in *Limehouse Nights*, 1916, p. 238.

51. Thomas Burke, 'White Wings' in *East of Mansion House*, 1928, p. 94.

52. *Daily Express*, 6 June 1900.

53. Thomas Burke, 'The Chink and the Child' in *Limehouse Nights*, p. 30 and 159.

54. *Limehouse Nights*, p. 157, 159 and 66.

55. Thomas Burke, 'The Cue', ibid., p. 102.

56. Thomas Burke, *East of Mansion House*, 1928, p. 12.

57. 'The Message of Chan-Hsu-Tsianah' in *Dark Nights*, 1944.

58. *Daily Express* quotations from Mark Kohn, '*Dope Girls, The Birth of the British Drug Underground*', 2001, which is particularly good on Chang.

59. Oscar Asche, 'Chu Chin Chow', (music F Norton), produced 1916, published 1931.

60. Raymond Mander and Joe Mitcehnson, 'Theatrical Companion to Somerset Maugham', 1955, pp. 168 and 190.

61. *Limehouse Nights*, p. 53.

62. Will Dexter, *The Riddle of Chung Ling Soo*, 1955, p. 56.

63. Text from the Lord Chamberlain's copy in the British Library.

64. Quoted in J P May, 'The Chinese in Britain' in Colin Holmes ed., *Immigration and Minorities in British Society*, 1978, p. 117.

65. Cay van Ash and Elizabeth Sax Rohmer, p. 157.

66. Sax Rohmer, *Yellow Shadows*, 1925, 1928 edition, p. 197.

67. Sax Rohmer, *The Bride of Fu Manchu*, 1933, 1977 edition, p. 27.

68. 'The Moon of the East' in *Union Jack* 795, 4 January 1919.

69. G H Teed, 'Gambler's Gold' in *Detective Weekly* 16, 10 June 1933.

70. Robert Murray, 'Behind the Fog' in *Union Jack* 1526, 14 January 1933.

71. Marion Ormond and J Corbet, *The Chinese Bungalow*, 1929. The quotation is from Act I and taken from the copy in the Lord Chamberlain's Collection, British Library. The play was a dramatisation of Ormond's novel.

72. Marion Bower and Leon M. Lion, *The Chinese Puzzle*, 1918. Text from the copy in the Lord Chamberlain's Collection, British Library.

73. Leon M Lion, *The Time of My Life*, n.d., p. 24.

74. *The Times*, 28 October 1913.

75. Matheson Lang, *Mr Wu Looks Back*, 1940, p. 112.

76. E A Baughan, 'The Drama of the Year' in *The Stage Year Book 1914*, p. 1.

77. Quotations from the copy of the play in the Lord Chamberlain's Collection, British Library.

78. Quotations from copy in Lord Chamberlain's collection.

2: CHINESE VILLAINS AND MASTERMINDS

1. Sax Rohmer, *The Mystery of Dr Fu Manchu*, 1913, 16th edition, 1929, p. 21.

2. The American titles were respectively *The Insidious Dr Fu-Manchu*, *The Return of Dr Fu-Manchu* and *The Hand of Fu-Manchu*. Note that the name was hyphenated in these books only, and, for consistency, I have dropped the hyphen throughout. *The Golden Scorpion* of 1919, is sometimes considered, but not by me, as part of this first series because it features a Fu Manchu type character, along with other similarities.

3. *The Mystery of Dr Fu Manchu*, p. 43, 119, 84, 154 and 228.

4. Quoted in Roger Pelissier, *The Awakening of China*, 1967, p. 241.

5. *Times Literary Supplement*, 17 May 1917, p. 238.

6. Rohmer, *The Si-Fan Mysteries*, 1917, 14th edition, 1934, p. 77.

7. Rohmer, *The Si-Fan Mysteries*, 1917, 14th edition, 1934, p. 109.

8. Rohmer, *The Golden Scorpion*, 1919, 13th edition, 1936, p. 202.

9. 'The Brotherhood of the Yellow Beetle' in *Union Jack* 507, 28 June 1913.

10. 'The Black Abbot of Cheung-tu' in *Union Jack*.1236, 28 June 1927.

11. *Union Jack* 505, 14 June 1913.

12. *Union Jack* 510 and 511, 19 and 26 July 1913.

13. 'The Idol's Spell' in *Union Jack* 510, 19 July 1913.

14. 'The White Mandarin' in *Union Jack* 519, 20 September 1913.

15. 'The Moon of the East' in *Union Jack* 795, 4 January 1919.

16. See note 14.

17. E S Turner, *Boys Will Be Boys*, 1948, p. 118.

18. The Treasure of Kao Hang in *Union Jack* 933, 27 August 1921.

19. 'The Clue of the Cracked Footprint' in *Union Jack* 1172, 27 March 1926.

20. G H Teed, 'Sexton Blake in Manchuria', in *Union Jack* 1494, 4 June 1932.

21. 'The Case of the Poisoned Telephones' in *Union Jack* 596, 13 March 1915.

22. 'The Pearls of Silence" in *Union Jack* 727, 15 September 1917.

23. 'The Tabu of Confucius' in *Union Jack* 1023, 19 May 1923.

24. Sexton Blake in Manchuria.

25. G H Teed, 'Arms to Wu Ling' in *Union Jack,* 11 June 1932.

26. Ibid.

27. 'The House of the Wooden Lanterns' and 'The Case of the Living Head' in *Union Jack,* 1120, 28 March 1925.

28. 'The White Mandarin' in *Union Jack* 519, 20 September 1913.

29. 'The House of the Wooden Lanterns' in *Union Jack,* 23 April 1927.

30. 'The Opium Smugglers' in *Union Jack* 707, 28 April 1917.

31. 'The Black Abbot of Cheung-tu' in *Union Jack* 1238, 9 July 1927.

32. G H Teed, 'The Twilight Feather Case' in *Union Jack* 1368, 2 January 1930.

33. 'The Street of Many Lanterns' in *Union Jack* 1064, 1 March 1924.

34. G H Teed, 'The Blood Brothers of Nan-Hu' in *Union Jack* 1497, 25 June 1932.

35. 'The Case of the Captive Emperor' in *Union Jack* 1315, 29 December 1928.

36. Geoffrey Ellinger, *The Rickshaw Clue*, 1931, pp. 135, 223, 309.

37. Frank Richards, 'The Begger of Shantung' in *Schoolboy's Own Library* no. 275, pp. 50, 60 and

38. John G Brandon, *Yellow Gods*, 1940, p. 22.

39. Introduction to John G Brandon, 'The Trail of the Yellow Ant' in *Detective Weekly* 135, 21 September.

40. John G Brandon, 'The Silent House' in *Union Jack* 1269, 11 February 1928.

41. G H Teed, 'Sexton Blake in Manchuria' in *Union Jack* 1494, 4 June 1932.

42. *Detective Weekly* 139, 19 October 1935.

43. See 'The Trail of the Yellow Ant' and John G Brandon, 'The Secret Cargo of Chi Lee' in *Union Jack* 151, 11 January 1936.

44. John G Brandon, *The Mark of the Tong*, 1938, p. 44.

45. Brandon, *Yellow Gods*, 1940 p. 58.

46. *The Mark of the Tong*, p. 68.

47. Rodney Gilbert, *What's Wrong with China*, 1926, p. 34.

48. *Master of Villainy*, p. 74.

49. David Hume, 'Meet the Dragon' in *Detective Weekly* 151, 11 January 1936.

50. *The Mark of the Tong*, pp. 245 ff.

51. Roland Daniel, *The Society of the Spider*, 1928, pp. 245 and 259.

52. Roland Daniel, *The Son of Wu Fang*, 1935, pp. 49, 250, and 110–1.

53. Roland Daniel, *The Green Jade God*, 1932, pp. 48, 253, and 53–4.

54. Roland Daniel, *Wu Fang's Revenge*, 1934, p. 36.

55. 'The Marley Farm Mystery' in *Union Jack* 866, 15 May 1920.

56. 'The Clue of the Cracked Footprint' in *Union Jack* 1172, 27 March 1926.

57. Rohmer, *Daughter of Fu Manchu*, 1931, p. 278.
58. *The Mask of Fu Manchu*, 1932, p. 114.
59. Ibid., p. 81.
60. Ibid., p. 280.
61. *The Bride of Fu Manchu*, p. 37.
62. *Master of Villainy*, p. 73 and 119.
63. Rohmer, 'The Drums of Fu Manchu' , 1939, in *The Fu Manchu Omnibus*, vol. 4, 1999, pp. 172 and 156.
64. Rohmer, 'The Island of Fu Manchu' , 1941, in *The Fu Manchu Omnibus*, vol. 5, p. 73.
65. Rohmer, 'Re-enter Fu Manchu', 1957 in *The Fu Manchu Omnibus*, vol. 3, 1999, p. 643.
66. Rohmer, 'Shadow of Fu Manchu' , New York 1948, London 1949, in *The Fu Manchu Omnibus* vol. 4, p. 534.
67. Rohmer, 'Emperor Fu Manchu' in *The Fu Manchu Omnibus*, vol. 4, p. 421.

3: GORDAN AND ARAB NATIONALISM

1. N G Travers, 'Too Late', In Memoriam. General Gordon 'The Hero of Khartoum', 1885.
2. William Le Queux, *The Eye of Istar*, 5th edition, 1913, p. 13.
3. A E W Mason, *The Four Feathers*, pp. 215, 267, 392.
4. Gilbert Parker, *Donovan Pasha and Some People of Egypt*, 1902, pp. 179, 17, 232, 109.
5. Gilbert Parker, *The Weavers. A Tale of England and Egypt of Fifty Years Ago*, 1907, pp. 78, 102, 216, 452.
6. Hall Caine, *The White Prophet*, 2 volumes, 1909, vol. 1, pp. 77, 145, 293; vol. 2, pp. 167, 241, 243.
7. See Vivien Allen, *Hall Caine, Portrait of a Victorian Romantic*, Sheffield, 1997.
8. Caine, *The White Prophet*, vol. 1, p. 16.
9. Douglas Sladen, *The Tragedy of the Pyramids*, 1909, p. 190.
10. Marcus Maclaren, *Khartoum Tragedy*, 1935, pp. 18, 13, 2, 194 and 53.
11. Agatha Christie, *Cards on the Table*, 1936, pp. 11 and 65.
12. Percy White, *Cairo*, 1919 edition, pp. 44, 131, 173, 122, 153, 68, 125, 7, 258, 335 and 336.
13. *T L S*, 1 October 1908 in a review of Pickthall's *The Children of the Nile*.
14. Marmaduke Pickthall, *Said the Fisherman*, 1903, pp. 40, 64, 71, 105, 131, 231, 285.
15. Pickthall, *The Children of the Nile*, 1908, pp. 299, 206, 23, 103, 177, 219.
16. Pickthall, *The Valley of the Kings*, 1909, pp. 297, 264, 175.
17. Pickthall, 'Between Ourselves' in *As Others See Us*, 1922, pp. 52–68.
18. Forward to *As Others See Us*.

19. Norma Lorimer, *A Wife Out of Egypt*, 1913, pp. 26, 284, 53, 313, 218–9.
20. Lorimer, *The Shadow of Egypt*, 1923, pp. 32, 204, 243, 131.

4: FRENCH NORTH AFRICA AND THE LURE
OF THE DESERT

1. Ouida, *Under Two Flags*, undated edition, chapter XXXVI.
2. William Le Queux, *Zoraida, A Romance of the Harem and the Great Sahara*, 1895, pp. 17, 218, 207, 159.
3. Quotes taken from the back of Edgar Jepson, *Sybil Falcon*, published the same year as *Zoraida*, for which the blurb claims that the "fifth edition" is "'is now ready".
4. William Le Queux, *The Hand of Allah*, 1914, pp. 99, 101, 89, 265, 322, 273.
5. Robert Hichens, *The Garden of Allah*, 1904, pp. 29, 66, 6.
6. Kathlyn Rhodes, *The Desert Dreamers*, 1909, pp. 17, 44, 220, 294, 335. Less than 25 years later the publishers claimed a sale of 216, 000.
7. Arthur Weigall, *Madeline of the Desert*, 1920, pp. 75 and 409.
8. *The Garden of Allah*, pp. 163–5.
9. A Conan Doyle, 'The Tragedy of the Korosko' in *The Strand Magazine*, vol. 14, p. 145.
10. *The White Prophet*, vol. l, p. 117.
11. Alice M Williamson, *Sheikh Bill*, 1927, pp. 16 and 46.
12. *The Bookman* September 1920.
13. Hichens, *Barbary Sheep*, 1909, pp. 192, 180, 226, 36, 150, 232, 233, 130.
14. Hichens, *Bella Donna*, 1909, vol. 1, p. 185. vol. 2. p. 103, vol. 1, p. 212.
15. Quoted in Margot Peters, *Mrs Pat, The Life of Mrs Patrick Campbell*, 1985, p. 306.
16. Caine, *The Scapegoat*, 1891, opening words.
17. A E W Mason, *The Winding Stair*, 1924, p. 243.
18. A J Dawson, *Bismillah*, 1898, pp. 17, 163, 283.
19. *Bismillah*, p. 74.
20. *Bismillah*, p. 205; Dawson, *African Nights Entertainment*, which contains this story, p. 118.
21. Dawson, *Hidden Manna*, 1902, pp. 77, 92, 305.
22. Edger Wallace, *The Man from Morocco* 3rd edition, 1929, pp. 255, 270, 278.
23. Amy Gilmour, *The Lure of Islam*, 1933, pp. 136, 150, 161, 274, 301, 316.

5: THE SHEIKH AND HIS IMITATORS

1. E M Hull, *The Sheikh*, 1919, p. 62.
2. *The Sheikh*, pp. 58, 80–2.
3. According to Rachel Anderson in *Twentieth Century Romance & Gothic Writers*, ed. James Vinson, 1982.
4. Hull, *The Sheikh*, pp. 108, 95, 132, 211–2, 220–1, 239.

5. *The Sheikh* p. 246; E M Hull, *Sons of the Sheikh*, 1926, pp. 210, 42, 203, 255.
6. Nora K Strange, *Kenya Calling*, 1928, p. 74.
7. P C Wren, *Beau Sabreur*, 1926, 19th impression 1957, pp. 84 and 85.
8. H M Clamp, *Desert Sand*, 1925, 2nd edition 1926, p. 240.
9. Bob Valentine, *The Bloke that Wrote 'The Sheikh'*, music J A Tunbridge, 1923.
10. Alice M Williamson, *Sheikh Bill*, 1927, pp. 15 and 22.
11. Barbara Correand, introduction to *The Sheikh*, 1977 edition.
12. *With Lawrence in Arabia* was first published in 1924. The newspaper reference to Thomas is from *The Daily Mail*, 5 November 1919.
13. E M Hull, *The Shadow of the East*, 1921, 11th impression 1923, p. 228.
14. Hull, *The Desert Healer*, pp. 9, 83, 140.
15. Rhodes, *The Lure of the Desert*, 5th edition 1916, pp. 77, 73, 149, 212, 267, 308, 350.
16. Rhodes, *The Desert Lovers*, 1922, pp. 159, 166, 246, 177, 251, 284.
17. Rhodes, *The City of Palms*, 1919, p. 140.
18. Rhodes, *The Relentless Desert*, 1920, first published as *The Flower of Grass*, 1911, p. 169.
19. Rhodes, *A Daughter in the Desert*, 1940, p. 165.
20. Joan Conquest, *Desert Love*, 1920, pp. 21, 160, 188, 192, 211, 280.
21. Rollo Ahmed, *I Rise. The Life Story of a Negro*, 1937, p. 361.
22. Conquest, *The Passionate Lover or The Hawk of Egypt*, 1933 edition, pp. 16, 27, 145, 218, 220.
23. Margaret Pedler, "Desert Sand", 1932, pp. 18, 226–7, 232, 239–40, 3, 15, 250, 249, 303, 258, 212–3.
24. Mrs. Frances Everard, *A Daughter of the Sand*, 1922, pp. 72, 79, 95, 107, 113, 128, 129, 238.
25. Thora Stowell, *Strange Wheat*, 1925, pp. 94, 34, 45, 99, 93, 147, 271, 177, 259, 264, 318, 319.
26. P C Wren, *Beau Geste*, 1924, cheaper edition reprinted 1939, p. 91.
27. Wren, *Sowing Glory*, 1931, pp. 144–5, 82–3.
28. Rhodes, *A Daughter in the Desert*, 1940, pp. 218, 83, 56–8, 165.

6: GHETTOES AND STEREOTYPES

1. Horace Thorogood, *East of Aldgate*, 1935, p. 83. *East of Aldgate* is a work of non-fiction about the East End of London. Despite its late date, the passage from which the quotation is taken is alarmingly virulent.
2. *Svengali*, the first Completed and Unexpurgated Edition of George Du Maurier's *Trilby*, 1982, pp. 44, 41, 74, 117, 104, 264.
3. Quoted in Hesketh Pearson, *Beerbohm Tree, His Life and Laughter*, 1956, p. 89.
4. Quoted in Daniel Pick, *Svengali's Web*, 2000, p. 12. Pick has far more to say about Svengali than is possible here.
5. *The Times*, 11 July 1905 and 6 April 1908.

6. Israel Zangwill, *Children of the Ghetto*, 1892, 3rd edition 1893, pp. 57 and 291.

7. Joseph Pennell, *The Jews at Home*, 1892, pp. 103, xi, 124.

8. *Children of the Ghetto*, p. 16.

9. 'London At Prayer. The Great Synagogue in Jewry' in *The Pall Mall Magazine*, February 1905.

10. Zangwill, *Children of the Ghetto*, pp. 363, 11.

11. Joseph Hatton, *By Order of the Czar*, 6th edition 1891, pp. 3, 62, 217, 12.

12. Baroness Orczy, *Children of the People*, 1906, pp. 22, 23, 27, 203–4.

13. George Griffith, 'I. D. B.' in *Pearson's Magazine*, vol. 4, July to December 1897, pp. 66–7.

14. F E Mills Young, *A Mistaken Marriage*, 1908, pp. 71 and 105.

15. Freeman Wills Croft, *The Grote Park Murder*, 1924, 1967 edition, p. 64.

16. A J Dawson, *Hidden Manna*, 1902, p. 3.

17. Dawson, 'A Moorish Hero and Juanita' in *African Nights Entertainment*, 1900, pp. 120–1.

18. Dawson, 'The Adventure of Prince Djalmak and the Barbary Jew' in *African Nights Entertainment*, pp. 245 and 253.

19. John A. Stuart, *The Hebrew*, pp. 81, 153, 383, 244, 473.

20. *The Times Literary Supplement*, 8 May 1903.

21. C J Cutcliffe Hyne, *Further Adventures of Captain Kettle*, 1899, pp. 300, 311.

22. M P Shiel, *The Lord of the Seas*, 1901, pp. 15, 17, 53, 421, 492, 493, 491.

23. Violet Guttenberg, *A Modern Exodus*, 1904, pp. 137, 18, 142.

24. William Le Queux, *The Unknown Tomorrow*, 1910, pp. 12, 149, 153, 159.

25. Guy Thorne, *When it was Dark*, 1903, 97th thousand 1905 edition, pp. 7, 8, 25, 347, 64, 307, 321.

26. *The Times Literary Supplement*, 16 October 1903, *When it was Dark* p. 233.

27. *The Bookman* April 1904 and October 1905.

28. *When it was Dark*, pp. 222, 161, 181, 21.

29. Guy Thorne, *Not in Israel*, 1913, pp. 280, 190, 52, 23, 188–9, 272.

30. Sax Rohmer, *The Sins of Severac Bablon*, 1914, pp. 66, 126, 156.

31. Reginald Glossop, *The Jewess of Hull, A Romance of the Antiques Trade*, 1923, p. 285.

32. Osbert Sitwell, *Miracle on Sinai*, 1933, pp. 68, 69, 71, 111. *The Times Literary Supplement*, 26 October 1933.

33. Carlten Dawe, *The Yellow Man*, 1900, p. 154.

34. *The Woman with the Fan*, 1904, pp. 25, 29, 45, 46.

35. Robert Hichens, *Bella Donna*, vol. 1, pp. 94, 4, 48, 3; vol. 2, p. 175; vol. 1 p. 2; vol. 2, p. 84.

36. Sydney A Moseley, *A Singular People*, 1921, p. 138.

37. Robert Hichens, *The God Within Him*, 1926, pp. 54, 452, 347, 384, 519, 172.

38. Hichens, *The Paradine Case*, 1933, pp. 17, 20, 21, 192, 84.

39. Belloc, *Mr Clutterbuck's Election*", 1908, pp. 237, 215.

40. Belloc, *Pongo and the Bull*, 1910, pp. 73, 94, 305. *The Times Literary Supplement*. 30 October 1910.
41. Belloc, *The Jews*, 1922, pp. 3, 34, 50.
42. Gisela C Lebzelter, *Political Antisemitism in England* 1918–39, 1978, p. 29.

7: JEWISH "PRIDE OF RACE"

1. B L Farjeon, *Aaron the Jew*, 1895, p. 278.
2. *Aaron the Jew*, 1895, pp. 265, 324.
3. Farjeon, *The Pride of Race*, 1900, pp. 20, 62, 210, 338.
4. Cyril J Silverston, *The Dominion of Race*, 1906, pp. 136, 157, 211, 296.
5. Violet Guttenberg, *Neither Jew Nor Greek*, 1902.
6. Mary Grace Ashton, *Race*, 1927, pp. 57, 101, 354.
7. Leonard Merrick, *Violet Moses*, 1891, vol. 2, pp. 139, 193.
8. *Neither Jew Nor Greek*, pp. 62, 117, 119, 120–1.
9. Winifred Graham, *The Zionists*, 1902, pp. 171, 163, 4, 6, 7, 179.
10. Sydney A Moseley, *A Singular People*, 1921, p. 184.
11. W J Passingham, *Angels in Aldgate*, 1933.
12. *A Singular People*, pp. 58–9, 88, 124, 137, 167, 191, 250, 254.
13. *The Bookman*, August 1922.
14. *The Much Chosen Race*, 1922, pp. 160–1, 94, 115–6, 12, 66, 75, 17, 45, 68.
15. John G Brandon, *Young Love*, 1925, pp. 81, 102–3, 107, 179, 222, 230.
16. Steni, *Prelude to a Rope for Meyr*, 1928, p. 181.

8: THE JEWS AND SOME FAMOUS AUTHORS

1. Sapper, *The Black Gang*, 2001 edition, p. 4.
2. John Buchan, *The Thirty-nine Steps*, 1915, in *Four Tales by John Buchan*, 1936, pp. 7, 84, 35.
3. Buchan, *Greenmantle*, 1916, 1999 edition, p. 11, *Mr Standfast*, 1919, p. 45 and *The Three Hostages*, 1924, 1955 edition, p. 17.
4. Janet Adam-Smith, *John Buchan and His World*, 1979, p. 80.
5. Richard Usborne, *Clubland Heroes*, 1953, revised edition 1974, p. 21.
6. Fergus Hume, *The Jew's House*, 1911, 1912 edition, pp. 19, 98, 18, 15, 41.
7. 'The Treasure of Sonora' in *Union Jack*, 696, 10 February 1917.
8. Sapper, *The Island of Terror*, 1931, pp. 63–4.
9. Norma Lorimer, *The White Sanctuary*, 1925, pp. 118, 283, 123, 145, 237, 248.
10. Naomi Jacob, *Props*, 1932, pp. 26, 164, 190, 245, 273.
11. Dorothy L Sayers, *Whose Body?*, 1935, pp. 46 and 70.
12. Sayers, *Five Red Herrings*, 1935, pp. 250–2.
13. Janet Hitchman, *Such a Strange Lady*, 1975, pp. 124–5.
14. Norman Donaldson, *In Search of Dr Thorndyke*, 2nd revised edition 1998, pp. 125–7.

15. Mary Westmacott [Agatha Christie], *Giant's Bread*, 1930.
16. Agatha Christie, *The Mysterious Mr Quin*, 1930, pp. 93, 266.
17. The charges against Christie are discussed by Janet Morgan in *Agatha Christie, a Biography*, 1984, pp. 264–5.
18. P C Wren, *Beau Geste*, 1924, p. 155.
19. Wren, *Beau Ideal*, 1928, pp. 11, 35.
20. Elinor Glyn, *Love's Blindness*, 1926, pp. 17, 33, 37, 195, 248.
21. Daphne Du Maurier, *The Progress of Julius*, 1933, pp. 98, 168, 222.

9: JEWS ON JEWS

1. Louis Golding, *Magnolia Street*, 1932, p. 514.
2. Louis Golding, *Day of Atonement*, 1925, pp. 82, 201, 207, 218, 243.
3. *Magnolia Street*, pp. 45, 68, 33, 123, 264, 321, 382, 531.
4. Naomi Jacob, *Jacob Ussher*, 1925. Adapted from H V Esmond, *Birds of a Feather*, 1920. pp. 130, 236, 308.
5. Jacob, *That Wild Lie*, 1930, 49th thousand, pp. 31, 68, 87, 139.
6. Jacob, *Young Emmanuel*, 1932, p. 238.
7. *That Wild Lie*, p. 139.
8. *Young Emmanuel*, p. 20.
9. Jacob, *Me*, 1938, p. 145.
10. Jacob, *Four Generations*, pp. 33, 147, 176–7.
11. G B Stern, *Tents of Israel* in *The Rakonitz Chronicles*, one vol. edition, pp. 46, 126, 185–6, 109, 167, 258.
12. *A Deputy was King* in *The Rakonitz Chronicles*, one vol. edition, pp. 352, 370–1, 412, 685, 722, 699, 734.
13. Stern, *Mosaic*, 1930, p. 323.
14. *The Rakonitz Chronicles*, p. 715.
15. Stern, *The Young Matriarch*, 1942, p. 536.
16. Simon Blumenfeld, *Jew Boy*, 1935, pp. 40, 49, 131, 139, 143, 254–5, 318.
17. Blumenfeld, *Phineas Kahn, Portrait of an Immigrant*, 1937, pp. 140, 378.

10: COPING WITH AFRICA

1. H Rider Haggard, *King Solomon's Mines*, 1885, p. 9.
2. Brian Street, *The Savage in Literature*, 1975, pp. 6–7.
3. *King Solomon's Mines*, pp. 129 and 300.
4. Haggard, *Allan Quartermaine*, 1887, p. 4, and *Allan's Wife*, 1889, p. 66.
5. William Le Queux, *The Eye of Istar*, 1895, p. 151.
6. Charles Montague, *The Vigil*, 1896, pp. 4, 248, 250.
7. C J Cutcliffe Hyne, *My Joyful Life*, 1935.
8. Hyne, *Captain Kettle K. C. B.*, 1903, 9th printing 1940, p. 113.
9. Hyne, *Further Adventures of Captain Kettle*, 1899, pp. 82, 126–7, 160, 165, 176, 18, 21, 16, 57.

10. *The Times Literary Supplement*, 17 April 1903.
11. Hyne, *Kate Meredith, Financier*, 1909, pp. 9, 10, 31, 42, 333, 119, 164.
12. Edgar Wallace, *Sanders of the River*, 1911. Magazine publication was in 1909. The references here are taken to an undated edition, presumably of 1935 as it is presented as the book of the film, pp. 5, 141, 62.
13. Jack Maclaren, *Gentlemen of the Empire. The Colourful and Remarkable Experiences of District Commissioners, Patrol Officers and other officials of the British Empire's Tropical Outposts*, 1940, pp. 11, 50, 90.
14. *Sanders of the River*, pp. 227, 228, 133, 134, 179.
15. Wallace, *The People of the River*, 1912, p. 175.
16. Wallace, *Bosambo of the River*, 1914, 17th reprint 1946, p. 92.
17. *Bosambo of the River* p. 170.
18. *Union Jack* 511, 1 October 1932; 960, 4 March 1922; 491, 14 May 1932.
19. Margaret Peterson, *The Scent of the Rose*, 1923, p. 73.
20. Paul Trent, *Wilton's Silence*, pp. 237, 255, 257, 259, 272.
21. Trent, *A Wife by Purchase*, 1909, pp. 2, 23, 303.
22. See the Lord Chamberlain's copy of the play in the British Library.
23. *The Play Pictorial*, vol. 45, no. 270.
24. *The Times*, 16 May 1924.
25. Rollo Ahmed, *I Rise, the Story of a Negro*, 1937, pp. 314–5.
26. William Plomer, *The Child of Queen Victoria*, 1933, pp. 48–9.
27. Stuart Young, *Merely a Negress*, 1904, p. 339.
28. A J Dawson, *The Treatment of Brierly* in *African Nights' Entertainment*, 1900, pp. 177, 178, 189.
29. Harold Bindloss, *Beneath Her Station*, 1906, pp. 54, 195, 201, 235.
30. Arthur Weigall, *Madeline of the Desert*, 1920, p. 190.
31. Charles Beadle, *A White Man's Burden*, 1912, pp. 264–5.
32. Norah K Strange, *Kenya Calling*, 1928, pp. 50, 55–6, 77, 91.
33. Louise Gerard, *The Hyena of Kallu*, 1910, pp. 40, 10, 91, 23, 143, 61, 237, 212–3.
34. John Buchan, *Prester John*, 1910, 1960 paperback edition, pp. 83, 15, 29, 155, 95, 202.
35. Sir H Hesketh Bell, *Love in Black*, 1911, pp. 13, 51, 120, 126, 140, 232.
36. W H Adams, *The Dominant Race*, pp. 7, 50, 146, 272.
37. F E Mills Young, *The Almonds of Life*, 1920, p. 41.
38. Young, *The Dominant Race*, pp. 14, 140, 53, 185, 252, 204.
39. *Union Jack* 912, 2 April 1921; 199, 1907; 1265, 14 January 1928; 19, 984 August 1922.

11: BLACKS IN THE CARIBBEAN AND AT HOME

1. Esther Hayman, *Study in Bronze*, 1928, p. 90.
2. *The Daily Express*, 24 April, 26 April and 4 May 1900.
3. *At the Full Moon* in *Union Jack* 710, 19 May 1917 and *The Voodoo Curse* in *Union Jack* 984, 1922.
4. Eleanor Mordaunt, *The Cost of It*, 1912, pp. 34, 57, 103, 284, 296.

5. Eden Phillpotts, *Black, White and Brindled*, 1923, p. 254.
6. *Study in Bronze*, 1928, p. 123.
7. Phillpotts, p. 125.
8. Advertisement at the back of Ida Hunt, *A Vagabond Typist*, 1937.
9. Rollo Ahmed, *I Rise. The Story of a Negro*, 1937, pp. 45, 215, 323, 48, 168, 174, 185, 222, 223, 224.
10. Claude McKay, *Banana Bottom*, 1928, 1998 edition, pp. 180, 132–3, 249, 211–2, 247.
11. *Study in Bronze*, pp. 64, 10, 7, 94, 101, 242, 306, 216.
12. Keate Weston, *London Fog*, 1934, p. 97.
13. Henry Nevinson, *Sissero's Return* in P J Keating ed., *Working-Class Short Stories of the 1890s*, 1971, pp. 62–79. See also PJ Keating, *The Working Classes in Victorian Fiction*, 1971, pp. 204–5.
14. *Pete's Patrol* by S Clarke Hook in *The Marvel*, 1904, no. 40.
15. I have not read the whole canon. References are to numbers of *The Marvel*, 1904–45, especially 1904, nos. 28, 39, 40; new series no. 22 and 1905, no. 61.
16. Albert Bigelow Paine, *The Black Hands* in *Pearson's Magazine*, vol. 16, 1903, pp. 657–666.
17. Leonard Merrick, *The Quaint Companions*, 1903, 1918 edition with a preface by H G Wells, pp. 8, 26, 30, 293.
18. A C Merriman-Labor, *Britian Through Negro Spectacles*, 1909, p. 127.
19. Cullen Gouldsbury, *The Tree of Bitter Fruit*, 1910, pp. 14, 17, 57, 92, 93, 144, 190, 209, 188, 292–3, 305–8, 324.
20. Keate Weston, *London Fog*, 1934, pp. 41, 281.
21. Humphrey Gilkes, *Black*, 1935, pp. 7, 42, 88, 139, 174, 193, 198, 208.
22. *I Rise. The Story of a Negro*, pp. 265, 266, 276, 282, 286, 287, 318, 290, 307, 344, 380, 384.

INDEX

A Chinese Honeymoon, 'Chinese'
   musical 28
Adams, W. H. 185
   The Dominant Race 185
Ahmed, Rollo 193
   I Rise: The Life Story of a Negro
   193–4, 205–7
Alexandria, bombardment of (1882) 70
Americans 6, 50–1
Americans and the English/British 2–4,
   50–1
Angels in Aldgate, novel 138
Anglo-Saxon = English 1–4
Arabs, the 59–105
Ashton, Mary 136
   Race 136

Beadle, Charles 180
   A White Man's Burden 180
Bell, H. Hesketh 184–5
   Love in Black 184–5
Bella Donna, novel and stage play 81,
   126–7, 160
Belloc, Hilaire, author 15, 128–31,
   140–1
   A Change in the Cabinet 129
   Emmanuel Burden 129
   Mr Clutterbuck's Election 129
   Pongo and the Bull 129
   The Jews 130–1
Bennett, Arnold, author 25
Biggers, Earl Derr 48
   Charlie Chan stories 48
Bindloss, Harold 179
   Beneath her Station 179
black people 165–207
Blake, Sexton *see* Sexton Blake stories

Blumenfeld, Simon 162–3
   Jew Boy 162–3
   Phineas Kahn, Portrait of an
   Immigrant 163
Bookman, The, periodical 4, 123, 140
Boxer Rebellion, the 12–7
Bramah, Ernest, author 15
Brandon, John G. 46–8, 50, 141–2
   Inspector McCarthy stories 48–50
   Jim Hazeldene stories 47–8
   The Mark of the Tong 49
   The Silent House, stage play and
   film 46–7
   Yellow Gods 47, 50
   Young Love 141–2
Broken Blossoms, D. W. Griffiths
   film 26
Buchan, John 3, 144, 182–3
   Greenmantle 144
   Mr Standfast 144
   Prester John 182–3
   The Thirty-Nine Steps 144–5
   The Three Hostages 144
Burke, Thomas 25, 28
   collected stories 25–7
   Limehouse Nights 25
   The Chink and the Child 26

Caine, Hall 64–7, 79, 82–3, 117
   The Scapegoat 117
   The White Prophet 64–6, 79
Caribbean settings 190–207
Cartland, Barbara 92
Charlie Chan stories *see* Biggers,
   Earl Derr
Chesterton, G. K. 130
China event at Crystal Palace 14–5

Chinese, the 11–57
Chinese Bungalow, The, novel and film 32–3, 47
Chinese communities in Britain 19–28
Chinese Puzzle, The, stage play 30
Chinese seamen 22–3
"Chink", "Chinky", epithet 26–7
Christie, Agatha 68f, 149–50
   Cards on the Table 68n
   Giant's Bread 149
   Peril at End House 150
   The Mysterious Mr Quinn 149–50
Chu Chin Chow, stage musical 28–30
Collins, Wilkie 47
   The Moonstone 47, 51
Conan Doyle, Arthur 6, 79
   The Tragedy of the Koroshko 79
Conquest, Joan 96–8
   Desert Love 96–8
   The Passionate Lover 97–8
Cost of It, The see Mordaunt, Eleanor
Croft, Freeman Wills *see* Wills Croft, Freeman

Daniel, Roland 50–2
   Chief Inspector Saville stories 50–2
   The Green Jade God 52
   The Society of the Spider 50
   The Son of Wu Fang 51
   The Yellow Devil 51
   Wu Fang: An Adventure of the Secret Service 50–1
Dawe, Carlton 138
   Leathermouth 138–9
Dawson, A. J. 82–3, 116–7, 178
   Bismillah 82–3
   Hidden Manna 83, 116
   The Treatment of Brierly 178–9
Desert Song, The, musical 93
Desmond, Shaw, political commentator 40
Detective Weekly magazine 39, 46, 48, 57
Dickens, Charles 150
   Fagin 110, 150
   Our Mutual Friend 150
Doyle, Arthur Conan *see* Conan Doyle, Arthur
Dr No, enemy of James Bond 57
Du Maurier, Daphne 151–2
   The Progress of Julius 151–2

Du Maurier, George, cartoonist and author 110
   Trilby 110–1

Ellinger, Geoffrey 45
   The Rickshaw Clue 45
Everard, Mrs Frances 100
   A Daughter of the Sand 100–1

Fagin 110, 150
Farjeon, B. L. 134, 151, 164
   Aaron the Jew 134
   The Pride of Race 134–5, 151
Four Feathers, The see Mason, A. E. W.
Freeman, R. Austin 149
   Dr Thorndyke stories 149
   Mr Polton 149
   The Missing Mortgage 149
Fu Manchu *see* Rohmer, Sax

Garden of Allah, The, novel and film 77, 79
Gerard, Louise 16, 180, 182–3
   It Happened in Peking 16
   The Hyena of Kallu 180–2, 185, 202
Gilbert, W. S. 2
   HMS Pinafore 2
   The Mikado 28
Gilkes, Humphrey 204
   Black 204–5
Gilmour, Amy 84
   The Lure of Islam 84–5
Glossop, Reginald 124
   The Jewess of Hull 124–5
Glyn, Elinor 150
   Love's Blindness 150–1
Golding, Louis 154–5
   Day of Atonement 154
   Magnolia Street 154–6
Gordon, General George "Chinese" 17, 61–2, 67
   death in Khartoum 17, 62, 67
   Taiping rebellion 17
Gordon, Leon 176
   White Cargo, stage play 176–7
Gouldsbury, Cullen 200–1, 204
   The Tree of Bitter Fruit 200–2, 204
Graham, Winifred 137
   The Zionists 137–8

Guttenberg, Violet 119, 121, 135
  A Modern Exodus 119–20
  Neither Jew Nor Greek 135–7

Haggard, H. Rider
  see Rider Haggard, H.
Hatton, Joseph 114
  By Order of the Czar 114–5
Hayman, Esther 195–6
  Study in Bronze 195–6
Hebrew, The, novel *see* Steuart, John A.
Hichens, Robert 77, 79–81, 126–8
  Barbary Sheep 80–1
  Bella Donna 81, 126–7, 160
  The Garden of Allah 77, 79–80
  The God Within Him 127–8
  The Paradine Case 128
  The Woman With the Fan 126, 128
Hull, Mrs E. M. 88, 91–4, 96
  The Desert Healer 93
  The Shadow of the East 92–3
  The Sheikh 88–94
  The Sons of the Sheikh 90
Hume, Fergus 145
  The Jew's House 145
  The Mystery of the Hansom Cab 145
Hutch, popular entertainer 177
Hyena of Kallu, The see Gerard, Louise
Hyne, Cutcliffe 118, 170–3
  Captain Kettle stories 118, 170–2
  Kate Meredith, Financier 172–3
  The Further Adventures of Kettle 171–2

illicit diamond buying (IDB) 116, 124
inter-racial marriage/sex, horror/spectre
  of 7, 20–1, 83–4, 104, 169, 175–81
I Rise see Ahmed, Rollo

Jacob, Naomi 147, 155–6, 158–9, 163
  Four Generations 158–9
  Jacob Ussher 156
  Props 147–8, 155
  That Wild Lie 156–7
  Young Emmanuel 157–8
Japan, attitudes to 12
Jews, the 107–64, 198

Kipling, Rudyard 6, 25
  The White Man's Burden 6
Koran, translation into English 72

Lang, Matheson, actor and author
  31–2
  Mr Wu Looks Back 31
  The Chinese Bungalow 32
Lawrence of Arabia 'legend' 92
Le Queux, William 62, 76–7, 121, 170
  The Eyes of Istar 62, 76, 170
  The Hand of Allah 77
  The Unknown Tomorrow 121, 124
  Zoraida 76
'Levantines' defined 73
Li Hung Chang, mandarin 17–8, 43
Limehouse Chinatown 19–28, 39, 49,
  54, 57
Lorimer, Norma 73–4, 146
  A Wife Out of Egypt 73
  The Shadow of Egypt 73–4
  The White Sanctuary 146–7

Maclaren, Jack 173
  Gentlemen of the Empire 173
Maclaren, Marcus 67
  Khartoum Tragedy 67
Marvel, The, boys' magazine 198
Mason, A. E. W. 62, 82
  The Four Feathers 62–3, 103
Maugham, Somerset 21, 28
  East of Suez 21–2, 28
McKay, Claude 194
  Banana Bottom 194–5
Meet the Dragon, short story 49
Merrick, Leonard 136, 199
  The Quaint Companions 199–200
  Violet Moses 136–7
Merriman-Labor, A. B. C. 200–3
  Britain Through Negro Spectacles 200
Mills Young, F. E. 116, 185–6, 192
  A Mistaken Marriage 116
  The Almonds of Life 186
  The Dominant Race 185–6
Montague, Charles 170
  The Vigil 170
'Moonstone' plot *see* Collins, Wilkie
Mordaunt, Eleanor 191
  The Cost of It 191–2, 196, 206
Morrison, Arthur, author 27
Moseley, Sydney A. 139–41
  A Singular People 139–40
  The Much Chosen Race 140
Mr Wu, stage play 30–1, 33, 47

Nevinson, Henry 197
  Sissero's Return 197
Novello, Ivor 43
  Careless Rapture musical 43

opium-smoking and the Chinese in
    Britain 19–20, 23, 51
Oppenheim, E. Phillips 32–3, 145
  Prince Chan 32–3
Orczy, Baroness 114–5
  Children of the People 115
  The Scarlet Pimpernel 115
Ouida 76, 103
  Under Two Flags 76, 103

Paradine Case, The, novel and movie 128
Parker, Gilbert 63, 66
  Donovan Pasha stories 63
  The Weavers 63–4
  While the Lamp Holds Out 63
Pedler, Margaret 98, 101
  Desert Sand 98–101
Pennell, Joseph 112–3
  The Jews at Home 112
Phillpotts, Eden 192
  Carnival 192
  stories of the West Indies 192
Pickthall, Marmaduke (Mohammed)
    69–73
  Between Ourselves short story 72
  Said the Fisherman 69–70, 73
  The Children of the Nile 70–1
  The Valley of the Kings 71–2
Plomer, William 177
  The Child of Queen Victoria 177–8
Prichard, Hesketh, journalist 190
  Where Black Rules White 190
"pride of race" 1, 115, 133–42, 156
Protocols of the Learned Elders of Zion,
    The 131

"race" and nationality 1
"race hates race" 1, 135
racism, wickedness of 6
Rhodes, Kathlyn 78, 94–6, 104
  A Daughter in the Desert 96, 104
  Desert Lovers 95–7
  The City of Palms 96
  The Desert Dreamers 78–9
  The Lure of the Desert 94–5

The Relentless Desert 96
Richards, Frank 45–6
  Billy Bunter stories 45–6
Rider Haggard, H. 76, 168–70
  Allan Quartermaine 169
  Allan Quartermaine stories 169
  King Solomon's Mines 76, 168–70
Rohmer, Sax 6, 13–4, 21, 25, 29, 37–9,
    49, 53–4, 56–7, 124, 209
  Dope 23–4
  Dr Fu Manchu stories/films 6, 13–4,
    17, 21, 23, 25, 29, 32, 36–40, 49,
    53–7
  Emperor Fu Manchu 56
  President Fu Manchu 55
  The Bride of Fu Manchu 55
  The Daughter of Fu Manchu 53
  The Devil Doctor 36
  The Drums of Fu Manchu 55
  The Golden Scorpion 38–9
  The Island of Fu Manchu 56
  The Mask of Fu Manchu 53–4
  The Mystery of Dr Fu-Manchu 36, 39
  The Si-Fan Mysteries 36
  The Sins of Severac Bablon 124
  The Yellow Claw 21, 23

Sanders of the River movie 174
San Toy, 'Chinese' musical 28
Sapper, cult author 3, 145
  Bulldog Drummond 145–6
  The Black Gang 146
  The Island of Terror 146
Sayers, Dorothy L. 148–9
  Five Red Herrings 148
  Whose Body 148
Sexton Blake stories 39–46, 48–9,
    51–3, 55, 57, 145, 174–5, 187,
    190–1
  Lobangu, chief of the Etbaia 174–5
  The Full Moon 190–1
Shaw, George Bernard 66
Sheikh, The, novel and movie 88–91, 210
Sheikh Bill, parody 79–80, 91–2
Shiel, M. P. 14, 118, 121
  Lord of the Sea 118–9, 121
  The Yellow Danger 14–5
Shylock 110
Silverston, C. J. 135, 140
  The Dominion of Race 135, 140

Sitwell, Osbert 125
　Miracle on Sinai 125
Sladen, Douglas 66–7, 117
　The Curse of the Nile 67
　The Tragedy of the Pyramids 66–7, 117
Stead, W. T. 17–8
　The Splendid Paupers 17–8
Stern, G. B. 159, 163
　A Deputy Was King 160–1
　Mosaic 161
　The Matriarch 159–60
　The Rakonitz Chronicles 159–62
　The Tents of Israel 159
　The Young Matriarch 162–3
Steuart, John A. 117
　The Hebrew 117, 141–2
Stoker, Bram 3
　Dracula 3
Stowell, Thora 101
　Strange Wheat 101–3
Strange, Nora K. 91, 180
　Kenya Calling 91, 180
Street, Brian, literary commentator 2, 168
Svengali 110–2

Thomas, Lowell, American journalist 92
　With Lawrence in Arabia 92
Thomas, Reginald G., author 57
Thorne, Guy 121–2, 124
　Not In Israel 123–4
　When It Was Dark 121–4
torture, and Chinese villains 52–3
Trent, Paul 175–6
　A Wife by Purchase 176
　Wilton's Silence 175–6
Tzu Hsi, Chinese Empress 16, 43

Union Jack, adventure weekly 39, 46
Usborne, Richard, literary commentator 3

Wallace, Edgar 84, 173–4
　Sanders of the River movie 174
　Sanders of the River stories 173–4
　Sandi the Kingmaker 174
　The Man From Morocco 84
Weigall, Arthur 79, 179
　Madeline of the Desert 79, 179–80
Wells, H. G. 25, 200
Westerman, Percy F. 15
　When East Meets West 15
Weston, Keate 202
　London Fog 202–4
White, Percy 67, 69, 72
　Cairo 67–9
Williamson, Alice M. 91
　Sheikh Bill 79–80, 91–2
Wills Croft, Freeman 116
　The Grote Park Murder 116
Wren, P.C. 3, 5, 7, 91, 103–4, 150
　Beau Geste 103–4, 150
　Beau Ideal 3, 5, 150
　Beau Sabreur 104
　Sowing Glory 7

Yates, Dornford, author 3
Yellow Jacket, The, stage play 31
Yellow Peril, the 11–57
　origin of the expression 12
Young, F. E. Mills
　see Mills Young, F. E.
Young, Stuart 178
　Merely A Negress 178

Zangwill, Israel 112–3, 117, 137, 140–1,
　154, 164
　The Children of the Ghetto 112–3
Zion, The Protocols of the Learned
　Elders of 131